W9-ADD-299

Drop That Knowledge

Drop That Knowledge

YOUTH RADIO STORIES

ELISABETH SOEP AND
VIVIAN CHÁVEZ

UNIVERSITY OF CALIFORNIA PRESS
Berkeley Los Angeles London

University of California Press, one of the most distinguished
university presses in the United States, enriches lives around the
world by advancing scholarship in the humanities, social sciences,
and natural sciences. Its activities are supported by the UC Press
Foundation and by philanthropic contributions from individuals
and institutions. For more information, visit www.ucpress.edu.

University of California Press
Berkeley and Los Angeles, California
University of California Press, Ltd.
London, England

Library of Congress Cataloging-in-Publication Data

Soep, Elisabeth–.
   Drop that knowledge : youth radio stories / Elisabeth Soep and
Vivian Chávez.
       p.   cm.
   Includes bibliographical references and index.
   ISBN 978–0-520–25021–5 (cloth : alk. paper)
   ISBN 978–0-520–26087–0 (pbk. : alk. paper)
       1. Youth in mass media—United States.   2. Mass media and youth—
United States.   3. Youth—United States—Social life and customs.
4. Youth—United States—Social conditions.   5. Radio broadcasting—
United States.   6. Mass media and education—United States.   I. Title.

P94.5.Y722 U675   2010
791.44/65235—dc22   2009019424

Manufactured in the United States of America

19   18   17   16   15   14   13   12   11   10
10   9   8   7   6   5   4   3   2   1

This book is printed on Cascades Enviro 100, a 100% post consumer
waste, recycled, de-inked fiber. FSC recycled certified and processed
chlorine free. It is acid free, Ecologo certified, and manufactured by
BioGas energy.

To the young people who created these stories,
to the ones the world hasn't heard from yet,
and to the three living in our hearts:
Roma, Simone, Rolando.

Contents

Illustrations

Acknowledgments

Many big things happened while we wrote this book—babies were born, relationships were made and unmade, buildings were bought, tenure was achieved, crises were averted, websites were launched, a U.S. president was elected—and we are enormously grateful to the funders who helped us keep coming back to tell this story: Corporation for Public Broadcasting, National Science Foundation, Open Society Institute, Robert Bowne Foundation, San Francisco State University's Institute for Civic and Community Engagement, and Surdna Foundation. We also want to thank the scholars in our lives who advocated for the book when it was still just an idea, and then helped shape its contents: Elliot Eisner, Shirley Brice Heath, Glynda Hull, George Lipsitz, Jabari Mahiri, Ray McDermott. Scholar-educator Dawn Williams deserves special thanks as coauthor of the Teach Youth Radio segments we offer in the book's appendix. To Naomi Schneider, our editor at University of California Press: we are so blessed that you chose to believe in this project, saw it through, and thus brought the stories of and by the young people featured in these pages to new audiences. Youth Radio's media partners made that audience connection possible in the first place and helped form the young people's stories from the earliest years: at National Public Radio, Ted Clark, Neva Grant, Anne Gudenkauf, Ellen McDonnell, Christopher Turpin, Sara Sarasohn, and Ellen Weiss; at American Public Media, Deborah Clark; at KCBS, Ed Cavagnaro; at KQED, Joanne Wallace, Raul Ramirez, Mark Trautwein, Louise Lo, and Faith Nee; at the National Federation of Community Broadcasters, Carol Pierson and Ginny Berson; and Pacifica supporters Adi Gevins, Michael Couzens, Jim Bennett, and Michael Yoshida. Finally, Ellin O'Leary, this book can't begin to acknowledge all that you've created and all the lives you've changed. Thank you.

Unbury the Lede

In 2005 eighteen-year-old Quincy Mosby walked into Youth Radio's newsroom and announced, "We all have AIDS." "Okay," I said. "So what does that mean?" Quincy told me that his mom was HIV-positive and that he wanted to write about how her status was affecting him and his sister. We sat down together at the computer and he started describing the conditions of their lives leading up to his mom's diagnosis:

> When I was a little kid, I idolized my mom. Friday and Saturday, those were our days. We didn't have any furniture, but we'd just sit on the floor and watch movies and eat day-old take-out and laugh. I used to think, if I could be a parent, she was the kind of parent I wanted to be.
> But that was before we moved to an apartment out in Georgia, and a lot of things changed. Actually, an apartment is a grandiose term for where we were living. It was more of a one-room shack. When we were

kicked out of that place, we started sleeping on office floors and brush-
ing our teeth in water fountains. It was all bad for a while.

Eventually we moved into a place that was even worse than the
shack. But when my mom went to the owner to complain, I guess she
impressed him, because he hired her on the spot to help manage the
apartments. It was a great job, and she started making a lot of money.
For the first time we had everything we needed and wanted. The crazy
thing is, right when everything was going well, that's when my mom
started smoking and drinking, staying out too late. It was like living
with a different person.

She started getting sick all the time. She was sleeping a whole lot
more, not going to work as often. But she held off on getting tested for
HIV. She's one of those moms who takes care of everyone else before
she takes care of herself.

Reading this draft of Quincy's story, I was struck by the mix of
admiration, respect, disappointment, and anger he expressed about his
mother before and after she discovered that she was HIV-positive. I also
thought about the history he was writing into and against: dehumaniz-
ing accounts of families in poverty and black mothers in particular. What
were Quincy's responsibilities as a son, telling his mom's struggle, and
his own? As a writer? And what were mine, as an educator? An editor?
A colleague to Quincy? A beneficiary of all the protections afforded
white mothers like me? With these questions looming large, there were
also more practical matters to worry about. The standard two-minute
radio commentary runs only six or seven paragraphs total, and Quincy
didn't get to his mom's health status until paragraph five. I told Quincy
that it seemed almost as though he were working on two interconnected
stories, one centered on his family history cycling in and out of poverty,
and the other about his mom's HIV. I couldn't see how he could tell one
without the other, but then again, how was he going to force-fit both into
a short radio piece? Several drafts later, the commentary that aired on
NPR's *All Things Considered* started like this:

For as long as I can remember, every time my sister and I would fight,
my mom would say, "You two have to stick together. I won't always be
here." But I still thought she would.

I've seen my mom broken, bruised, bleeding, even hooked up on machines. But still, even with all that, I believed she couldn't die. I don't believe that anymore. . . .

When I was fourteen years old, my mother called me into her room. I remember the look on her face. There was something in her voice. I knew she was about to tell me she was HIV-positive. I think she cried. I know I didn't.

In this version of his story, Quincy unburied his lede. It's one of the most common challenges young writers face at Youth Radio, just as it has been for us here, as we have repeatedly, maddeningly, haltingly tried to find the right place to begin this book. A lede is the big idea that drives a story, and "burying" it means waiting too long to get to the point. The story of Quincy's mom's HIV status, which advanced to full-blown AIDS while he was writing about it, was inextricably tied up in his family's larger narrative of intimacy, struggle, and migration. If he were composing a memoir, he could tell the whole story and take his time getting to the revelation that made him want to write it in the first place: "We all have AIDS." But he was producing a radio commentary. Quincy had to unbury his lede without flattening his narrative or betraying his mother. That's youth media. You think you're tweaking sentence structure or reorganizing paragraphs or voice-coaching or just making cuts to fit a time slot, but really you're navigating relationships, emotions, and unfinished histories.

When writers bury the lede, we lose readers. When educators bury the lede, we lose our students. In this book we aim to dig out the lede that too often gets buried in discussions of youth culture and education. Somewhere deep below (and also inside) all those tests, bureaucracies, systems of regulation, and economies of disappointment, young people are producing stories together and with adults in ways that have the potential to reorganize our shared social world. That production process, its outcomes and implications, is our lede.

YOUTH RADIO

Drop That Knowledge is composed of stories about young people making media while creating new relationships with adults as colleagues and the public as audience. Our focus is Youth Radio, a youth development organization and independent media production company founded by Ellin O'Leary in 1992 and based in Oakland, California. Young people come to Youth Radio from the nation's economically abandoned, heavily tracked, and resegregating public schools. They spend afternoons at the organization's Oakland headquarters or at its bureaus in Los Angeles, Washington, DC, and Atlanta. Alternatively, young people might experience Youth Radio through partnerships and outreach programs in the Bay Area and with other youth groups around the country: in a coal-mining community in eastern Kentucky, a gentrifying Chicago neighborhood, a Native American reservation in Arizona, a juvenile detention facility just outside Oakland.

Recruited by program graduates, students working at Youth Radio's headquarters begin with introductory multimedia classes and advance through specialized courses and eventually paid positions as media makers, engineers, and peer educators. There are no academic requirements to join, although applicants do need to fill out some basic information and participate in an interview. Placement decisions are guided by efforts to fill a class of twenty, four times per year, which is balanced in terms of gender and geography, diverse in terms of race, and composed primarily of low-income youths and young people of color. All programs are free. Students receive individualized education and career counseling, and in 2007 the organization began offering high school and community college credit and brought onboard a licensed social worker, Tuere Anderson, who offers one-on-one therapy and leads the organization's model health programs.

Youth Radio students deliver content on deadline to commercial, public, and community-supported radio stations, including National Public Radio, as well as outlets including the *San Francisco Chronicle*, Current TV, iTunes, and the Internet's various social media sites. The organization works with more than twelve hundred young people per year. Youth Radio has been honored with George Foster Peabody, Alfred I. DuPont, Edward R. Murrow, and Gracie Allen Awards. It's undoubtedly an unusual organization, but lessons from Youth Radio have relevance for any place where young people find, frame, articulate, and spread stories they feel a pressing need to tell. Implications extend to any site where adults and young people convene to work on high-stakes projects in a collaborative fashion, with some kind of a public effect in mind. Our goal in this book is for readers to experience and apply Youth Radio methods and sense its vibe, a feeling connecting people with technology, knowledge, production, and most of all, with one another.

DROP THAT KNOWLEDGE

The book's title comes from a line in a Youth Radio feature story that aired on National Public Radio's *All Things Considered* (2005). In it, reporter Brandon McFarland interviews friends and family on the subject of "sagging," a style of wearing pants far below the waist. A longtime sagger, Brandon finally gets fed up and decides to resist the trend and tighten his belt. He goes on a mission to convince others to do the same, including his friend and Youth Radio colleague Gerald Ward II, who compares sagging to speaking "Oaklandese."

> GERALD: It's like code switching when you speak. I speak Oaklandese when I'm speaking to other folks that are from the town, and when I'm not, I might switch into a more universal language or lexicon. Same thing with my pants. I might sag in certain areas, and in the other areas I'll pull them up so I can infiltrate the system.

In his script, Brandon follows this clip with the line, "That's my man Gerald, dropping that knowledge." Casually and with an inner smile, Brandon conveys the fact that he's impressed by what his friend is talking about and he wants the world to know it. Gerald has always insisted that he was being somewhat facetious in this statement, but clearly his observations extend the story beyond youth fashion. *Drop that knowledge* can be interpreted as the value and recognition of wisdom that comes from lived experience and analysis. Gerald contextualizes his remarks in Oakland, a city with rich cultural and artistic heritage, internationally known civil rights activism, and local public schools that lose 50 percent of students before graduation: a complicated place governed by a dizzying mix of codes. When Gerald describes Oaklandese, he connects an everyday practice to larger cultural, economic, and political narratives, all without taking himself too seriously; he is, after all, just talking about how he wears his pants.

Drop that knowledge is not a rhetorical call to celebrate "youth voice." On the contrary, it challenges young people to hear and get in touch with what they think, see, and experience in their communities and social worlds. With a sense of urgency, young people can *drop that knowledge* and honor the subjective as legitimate, while exploring, examining, and interrogating other points of view. There is, however, a very specific mandate for adults embedded in the book's title. *Drop that knowledge* is the imperative for adults to drop that expert posture for which we often get rewarded—a stance of distance and authority. The imperative is especially pressing in education. Despite never-ending cycles of innovation in teaching methodology, traditional education tends not to foster collegiality between students and their teachers. "Expert" knowledge unilaterally handed down to learners reproduces existing power relationships through its methods and content. The expression *drop that knowledge* urges adults to work on changing hierarchical relationships and establish a setting that fosters an open and free exchange of ideas. In essence, the double meaning of *drop that knowledge* calls for youth to step up and for adults to let go of assumptions about what passes as truth about youth, education, success and failure, struggles and conditions young people face. Authority and power circulate through every single learning experience; indeed part of what we're always learning *is* power, how we shape it and how it shapes us. Adults are expected to hold institutional power, manifest maturity, possess expertise, and meet goals. In turn, students are expected to shut up, listen, and learn. As a result, many students shut down, appearing to have nothing to contribute. These ingrained patterns limit creative opportunity and critique.

Although this book is definitely not a self-satisfied celebration of always getting it right, *Drop That Knowledge* is a story of what effort looks like and what trying sounds like. Each chapter offers insight into what it takes to build toward a learning community where youths and adults share without fear, an environment where young people are safe to be, to hear, to question, and to tell. The media stories emerging from this process can be read as evidence of what George Lipsitz (2001, p. 29) calls "the other American Studies," not an academic field canonized in university departments, but the practice of theorizing about culture and power by folks who might not "look or sound like the authority figures that run our society," but who are "determined to have a hand in shaping the future they will inherit."

DIALOGIC STORIES

As storyteller-researchers and teacher-learners, we looked for a methodology to tell this story, always asking ourselves, "What good does it do to learn, teach, create, and write about youth media?" Ethnographers call their signature method *thick description*. In detailed accounts of everyday cultural practices, they interpret how the people they study make meaning in their lives, so the researchers can, in Geertz's (1973, p. 24) words, "converse" with their subjects. Though deeply indebted to ethnographic traditions, in forming this book we needed a way to articulate our "thick *participation*" in the site of our research (Spittler, 2001, emphasis added). Because the truth is, off the page we "converse" with the young people and adults who populate this narrative not only for the purposes of research. We work with them. We have been them. By writing ourselves into our own story in the first person, we challenge accepted views about the unexamined authority of silent authorship (Charmaz & Mitchell, 1996). Given our different backgrounds and viewpoints, we developed a dialogic approach to fieldwork, analysis, and writing.[1]

There are parallels here to producing a radio story. In radio terminology, interview clips are called *actualities*, and the reporter's narration comprises *tracks*. Simple radio stories shift back and forth between these two elements, forming a pattern known in shorthand as *acts and tracks:* interview clip, narration, interview clip, narration, and so on, until the reporter finishes with the final word. But complex stories demand a structure that goes beyond acts and tracks, one in which that predictable rhythm gets layered with and interrupted by sounds and scenes of life unfolding, including events that disrupt the narrator's sure footing and draw the storyteller into the story. In our approach to ethnographic methods, we too move beyond acts and tracks, beyond "their" raw data subjected to "our" analysis. Our personalized accounts connect the cultural and the structural, placing the self and the conventions and eccentricities of storytelling in a social context.[2] We have involved Youth

Radio's students and adult staff members in carrying out this research as field observers, focus group participants, interviewers, archivists, and critical readers. They have shaped both our inquiry process and this textual product, adding a whole cast of characters to the "we" behind our narrative.[3] Thus in alignment with our research methods, and urged to do so by our youth collaborators, we name names. Why should their names be replaced with pseudonyms, as is often the research convention, when we are writing about their creative contributions to a field in which they already have to fight for recognition? We don't, after all, fake names in our citations. The young people featured here have already made the decision to go public with their radio features, revealing themselves to audiences whose size we can only dream about for this book. It would seem problematic, in this light, to deny youth collaborators credit and responsibility for the products of their own creative labor.

In the list of individuals who compose our "we," the primary author, Elisabeth (Lissa) Soep, is Youth Radio's research director and a senior producer in the organization's newsroom. In developing this narrative, she draws on her daily work at Youth Radio over nine years as a participant and an observer, as well as her sixteen years researching youth culture, language, and learning (Maira & Soep, 2005; Soep, 2005a, 2005b, 2006a, 2006b). Throughout this book, when we talk about youth-adult collaboration, Lissa is sometimes one of the adults inside the scenes described. She's the one in the opening vignette, working with Quincy on his commentary about HIV. She started volunteering at Youth Radio while finishing her doctoral dissertation, after hearing a youth reporter on the radio. The experience profoundly transformed both her career pathway and her vision of research, in particular, where it can live and how it can be made. Vivian Chávez is a graduate of Youth News, the program out of which Youth Radio emerged. Now a university professor, she draws on her history as an alumna in her current research and practice in community organizing, violence prevention, and public health. Our last chapter introduces more personal details of what it means to participate in and emerge from this field. There Vivian joins King Anyi Howell, Belia Mayeno Saavedra, Nzinga Moore, Lauren Silverman, and Orlando Campbell with hindsight Youth Radio reflections.

Although never fully out of touch, Vivian reencountered Youth Radio for this book project almost thirty years after having been a student of youth media, when she visited the class where it all starts for young people at Youth Radio. The class is called Core.

CORE CLASS OBSERVATION

It's ten minutes into the ninth week of this twelve-week introductory course. Thirteen young people, a mix of ethnicities, are immersed in dialogue about "prejudice plus power," interspersed with something about "patriarchy and policy" and hip-hop beats. Young people are producing something in a space that holds multiple conversations, computers, adults and youths teaching, reading, and writing. The age range is hard to tell, maybe between fourteen and twenty. They gather around a table, along with three adults and some other folks working at desks scattered in the margins. Two students are writing a commentary. A peer teacher asks to see what's going on, reminding them that they will be on the air at 7:10 PM. I forgot how shy I get in situations like this, watching strangers. Observing, I feel as though I were at someone's house party, just wondering around, without a purpose. A seventeen-year-old peer teacher explains that the students and peer teachers rotate topics—video, music, public service announcements, roundtable discussions, commentary, and news—every four weeks. She explains that she has to be "on her students" or else they will lose focus. I notice how focused she is, multitasking in her roles as teacher, leader, producer. She is doing her job while talking to me about doing her job.

A couple weeks later, I'm back for another observation. I step into a fluid structure for creative activity, which everyone in the room navigates as if it's nothing. Some students gain experience directly on the air through trial and error. Others appear much more advanced and confident. The range in quality surprises me; some are not as "good" as expected. I remember that we did not get to be on the air until we practiced and practiced some more. I am surprised by my judgment. Students are editing, working with technology, and having conversations about tattoos, then back to the editing, back to talking about tattoos. Someone is making beats in the background. The focus is scattered but not distracted throughout the room; there is no front, back, or central location. In spite of how innovative I think I am as a teacher at the university, I expect

students to be quiet and take notes while I talk. Where are these expectations coming from? I write a comment in my notes about how traditional
my understanding of learning is. A handsome young man comes right up
to me and asks what I'm writing in my notebook. His question reminds
me of our age difference and of my role as an outsider. I like being on
the inside. After all, I've been through the program and can relate. But
honestly, everyone around me looks like they know what they are doing,
what they are supposed to be doing, or what they will be doing—except
me. What do I say to this young man who wants to know what I'm here
for? Before I can answer, Training Director (at the time) Gerald Ward II
calls our attention to the board, reviews the day, checks for tasks completed, and wraps up the session commenting on the importance of time
in radio. He says, "This is professional training," and goes on to say that
he has not been late or absent for the show over all the years he's been
with Youth Radio, from the time he started as a senior at Oakland High to
the years he served as a peer teacher, to being hired as staff in a number
of roles. "Time in radio is of the essence," he says, concluding with a hand
gesture we recognize as the sign for money, and once again emphasizes
"being professional." Someone asks a question and the group laughs,
except me because I'm not sure what was said. I smile on the inside,
though, starting to feel on the inside, remembering the community, skills,
and sharpness of youth. Gerald reviews the following week's roundtable
discussion and underscores something about "every voice being heard,
no one feeling marginalized, all sides must be included."

Another day in the life of Youth Radio, no longer feeling awkward,
my values resonate with what's being taught, my body and mind in the
comfort of this environment, which takes off the passage of time. That's
me, a learner, a teacher, a colleague. Observing youth media production
today, I remember who I was back then when I *was* them, what I cared
about, how I learned to care.

YOUTH MEDIA: THE FIELD

Vivian started making media as a sixteen-year-old in the late 1970s.
By that time, the youth media field had already shifted from primar-

ily teaching *about* media to teaching *through* media (Goodman, 2003). Newly accessible equipment, combined with that era's progressive social movements, created conditions for artists, educators, and activists to deploy hands-on production as a means to engage disenfranchised communities of youth. Still, researchers continued to focus largely on young people's media *consumption* patterns, and school-based media literacy— where it took place at all—kept preparing young people to analyze and critique adult-manufactured news, entertainment, and advertising. Even when scholars have taken pains to frame consumption as itself a creative act, they've tended to highlight how young people can critically digest, interpret, and subvert other people's output,[4] not their own—until the last two decades or so, that is. These days, researchers in communications, cultural studies, and literacy are increasingly tracking how young people use new digital technologies to create original media, particularly since the advent of new platforms for social networking, user-generated content, and peer-to-peer distribution, all of which multiply opportunities for youth participation and engagement with media production.

The goals of the field are vast. Individual organizations seek to support positive youth and community development, catalyze expression and new aesthetics, transform markets and industries, and advocate for social justice and civic engagement—and that's just a partial list. Given this huge range of orientations, it's a field that can be difficult to define. And yet definitions, observes bell hooks (2000, p. 14), "are vital starting points for the imagination. A good definition marks our starting point and lets us know where we want to end up. As we move toward our desired destination we chart the journey, creating a map." Early on in writing this book, we thought we might create a map of the youth media field. Then we talked to Sandy Close, executive editor of Pacific News Service and executive director of New American Media. She put it bluntly: "Do not write another publication about the topography of youth media. It's been done. It's boring. Don't do it." Close has developed and launched several groundbreaking media initiatives to promote civic exchange among youth and communities, including *YO, Youth Outlook,* an award-winning literary journal, and *The Beat Within,* which publishes writing and artwork by incarcerated youth.

Researchers have made serious progress in mapping the key models, best practices, goals, and challenges marking the youth media field.[5] What's missing, especially given the serious upheaval taking place today on technological, cultural, and economic fronts, are situated studies of teaching and learning within individual sites that are undergoing change and that are in the process remapping their own terrain. But heeding Close's words, it's not a map we're striving to create here, if maps fix and flatten shifting three-dimensional territories. A more apt metaphor for us may not be spatial but sonic. By tuning into one organization, Youth Radio, we listen for reverberations, dissonances, and silences in the youth media field and across youth culture and education.

We do *not* define the youth media field simply as "for youth by youth" with no adult hands-on involvement, even though youth producers are creating and exchanging content at unprecedented rates completely on their own. Spending more than seventy hours per week using electronic media,[6] American teens are composing fan fiction, designing personal profiles, shooting videos on their cell phones, and engaging and commenting on user-generated content. Wherever and whenever young people can make a digital connection, they are writing, picturing, and gaming themselves into being (boyd, 2007, forthcoming).[7] They do this work, more often than not, physically alone but digitally together. These are tremendously important developments for young people's lives and literacies. And yet, to grasp the pedagogical potential of spaces where young people make and circulate media by themselves, we need to understand how these practices relate to contexts that are expressly designed to promote learning, youth development, and social impact through media production and journalism. Hence we focus here on media production fueled by youth-adult collaboration, which fosters a series of conditions that resonate throughout this book.

First, there is a tension that emerges as young people claim the right to speak unapologetically about experiences over which they hold authority, while at the same time learning humility, which is what it takes for them to embed their voices within the complex narratives that make up any story worth telling. Youth Radio partner Rebecca O'Dougherty, who runs the Appalachian Media Institute in eastern Kentucky, makes this tension concrete when she insists that her students connect their stories to larger issues and legacies in rural America: "So even if they're really upset at the mining company, [I tell them to] be bold, speak out, but they go home and they have family members who work for the mining company or don't feel the same way about corruption."[8] So they have to articulate and challenge their own perspectives by engaging countervailing views. Youth media sees itself as a field that builds young people up, yet one of the most important lessons youth producers can learn is how to critique themselves down. Otherwise, "telling their stories" is really a way for them to impose a sense of what's right and wrong, who's good and bad, what should and shouldn't happen, without insight into their own biases, privileges, and gaps in understanding, and without awareness of how even counternarratives can replicate some of the patterns driving the dominant discourses youth media projects so often aim to critique.

A second tension centers on the field's social justice roots, at a time when youth media organizations increasingly frame their work in entrepreneurial terms. Commercial media conglomerates profit hugely off the same content young people produce inside nonprofit organizations that struggle to get by. Many young producers and their adult collaborators want in on the money being made and on the economic literacy and "hustle" required to convert creative content into valuable intellectual property and living wage work.[9] As Youth Radio's strategic initiatives director, McCrae Parker, has said, getting a story on the air is great, but imagine the positive youth development outcomes of making a down payment on a house. If we're not preparing young people to earn cold, hard cash through their media, or at least through the skills they acquire by producing media, then we just might be setting them up for a few minutes of fame when their stories play on national air, after which they'll go back to bagging groceries or selling CDs from the trunk of a car.

Some veterans in the field are raising cautions about this entrepreneurial turn. Youth media pioneer Keith Hefner, who founded New York City's Youth Communications, says that in his experience "there is a fatal conflict between the entrepreneurial approach and the social justice approach." Students' primary concern coming into his program, he says, "is not that there are people on top and people on the bottom. Their concern is that *they* are on the bottom and they want to be on the top." Money is never the primary goal or motivation for Hefner. Rather, it's to provide young people with the skills and resources they need to decide for themselves what it is that they want to do, whether it's to start their own businesses or become teachers, artists, social workers, or community organizers. That said, more and more youth media organizations are experimenting with ways to dislodge economic disparities not just through critical media stories and career pathways but also through revenue-earning ventures. And that creates "muddy waters," in the words of Jason Mateo, who leads programs at the Bay Area–based organization Youth Speaks, whose poets have contributed to several national Youth Radio stories: "We are going to be community-oriented and at the same time we can't provide for the community if we can't provide for ourselves."

A third tension, and perhaps the hallmark of the youth media field, is the challenge and potential of intergenerational relationships, which connect young people to one another, to their youth and adult mentors, and to the artists, educators, entrepreneurs, and activists who are taking the field in new directions. Silvia Rivera is someone who went from student to general manager at Chicago-based Radio Arte, the only bilingual (Spanish-English), Latino-owned, youth-operated community radio station in the country. She notes that one of the biggest challenges she faces is managing the relationships between young people who run the station and adult authority figures. Youth media producers at Radio Arte and elsewhere constantly defy generational conventions as they create and distribute their work, in particular conventions that have traditionally placed adult white men in positions of running the show. By taking their place at the mic, young people challenge the designation of certain languages and vernaculars as broadcast-ready and others as inappropriate or offensive. They defy the tendency to homogenize whole communities of people, erasing their internal complexity and contradictions. These tensions manifest concretely at Radio Arte, Rivera says: "Some of us speak Spanglish, and some people may feel that it is offensive to speak on the radio like this, back and forth between English and Spanish. Some may prefer standard, proper Spanish. But what kind of Spanish is that?" In youth media, participants see the potential to raise these kinds of questions and redefine communities as both multilayered and interdependent. "Youth media," in Sandy Close's view, "is the story of a generation in search of ways to connect. There is a huge explosion of youth media because young people need community. What makes the field interesting is relationships, youth and intergenerational relationships. This is a generation that has grown up without a sense of community. Their media is their community."

A fourth and final tension driving the youth media field today springs directly from the outpouring of new tools for media production and distribution. With exuberance about unprecedented possibilities come creeping fears about the field's obsolescence. Nonprofit organizations like Youth Radio have always acted as gatekeepers for young people to high-cost equipment, professional expertise, and distribution outlets (Buckingham, Burn, & Willett, 2005). If young people working on their own can now find cheap tools, high production values, and significant audiences, why shouldn't the organizations disband and adults just get out of the way?

Youth media organizations remain crucial for a number of reasons. They provide a platform for collective activity that builds and broadcasts a critical mass of youth voices. They offer opportunities for local organizing with national and international impact. They create places where young people can come together with adults and peers whose paths they might never otherwise cross, whether in America's increasingly segregated high schools or the Internet's stratified social spaces. By engaging young people over time through sustained projects, youth media organizations build leadership and advanced skills. They act as advocates for young people and liaisons to networks of opportunity for broadcast, policy impact, jobs, and higher education. Perhaps most important, they engage young people who are otherwise marginalized from digital privilege. Young people whose perspectives are distorted, neglected, sensationalized, or outright ignored by mainstream media find themselves on the wrong side of what Henry Jenkins (2006a, 2006b) calls digital media's "participation gap." It is in this context, and because of it, that *Drop That Knowledge* was created. We use youth media to reconfigure what it means to learn, teach, and produce new worlds.

And so from here, in chapter 1, we invite readers to reimagine learning as *converged literacy,* which entails an ability to (1) make and understand boundary-crossing and convention-breaking texts; (2) draw and leverage public interest in the stories they want to tell; and (3) claim and exercise their right to use media to promote justice, variously defined—a right still denied young people marginalized from full citizenship as producers of media culture. In chapter 2 we redefine teaching as *collegial pedagogy,* a collaborative practice and a production process. In collegial pedagogy, emerging and established producers jointly create original work for public release, engaging a process that has significant potential to deepen the learning experience for both parties and to enrich the media product distributed to the world. In chapter 3 we rework the notion of media justice by describing what it takes for young people to move from a point of view, which suggests a way of seeing, to a *point of voice,* which demands strategic expression, provocation, and action. In chapter 4 we contribute to *media literacy practice* by sharing concrete methods and tools adults can use to collaborate with young people to produce stories that need to be told. Throughout every chapter we base our discussion on fine-grained, behind-the-scenes accounts of how young people have produced some of Youth Radio's most influential and controversial stories, and in chapter 5, where we close, we offer a playlist with a selection of full scripts from young people you've encountered throughout the book, along with the authors' first-person reflections on their lives in and out of youth media.

The youth-produced scripts contained throughout this book and in the final chapter are not raw data. They contain multilayered analyses of their own, and they tackle the key themes addressed in this book related to youth culture, media, and education. Rather than provide "authenticating details in a narrative already written,"[10] young people's stories drive the narrative unfolding in these pages. By producing these accounts, young people come to see their own experiences and conditions affecting their communities in new ways, asking, "How can I make this a story?" and more subtly, "How can my story affect the thing I'm trying to describe?" Can a story about youth violence reduce youth violence? Can a feature about depression or anorexia or cutting help young people find mental health support? Can a commentary from a young man who dropped out of school help educators reach struggling students? Can a report on standardized testing influence school reform? Is it even appropriate for journalists to aspire to make these interventions? And what happens when the message listeners draw from a story is exactly the opposite of the author's intention? Or when a young person writes beautifully about a specific dimension of living in poverty, the story airs to great acclaim, and the young person returns to a situation that doesn't budge? Or when a reporter speaks in cadences, registers, and hybrid languages that violate the "proper"? Young people and adults at Youth Radio constantly face these thorny questions. The answers are never simple, and yet the questioning itself—messy, controversial, and always incomplete—fuels new learning opportunities for youth producers, their mentors, and their varied publics.

ONE Converged Literacy

It was a classic case of burying the lede, but this time Youth Radio's Finnegan Hamill hadn't even written a story—yet. In 1999 Finnegan was a junior at Berkeley High, taking a break from his Youth Radio peer teaching job to focus on academics, his position at the school newspaper, hockey, and church. But he stayed connected to Youth Radio with occasional visits, especially when he had a story idea.

For almost twenty minutes Finnegan caught up with then Deputy Director Beverly Mire, whose office was the first stop for many students headed into the building on their way to class and for alumni swinging by to visit. Bev remembers covering the usual topics: what was going on at school, the latest Youth Radio news, that kind of thing. Mindful that class would start in a few minutes, Bev says she was about to end their conversation when Finnegan mentioned, almost as an aside, that he'd been "emailing this girl

in Kosovo." A huge massacre had just taken place there, and the bloody
civil struggle was escalating into full-blown international war. NATO was
preparing to drop bombs. News outlets around the world scrambled to
devise an angle on this incredibly complex crisis, and Finnegan had found
a direct line to one sixteen-year-old girl witnessing the run-up to war from
her apartment balcony. And that line came through email, of all things,
itself an emerging medium at the time, at least as a means to connect two
teenagers unknown to each other in real life, separated by a vast distance
in geography and experience. To think Bev could have let Finnegan walk
right out the door, had he not just in time gotten around to his lede.

Bev had previously been a radio music director. She described the
moment she heard about Finnegan's emails as like playing a hit record
for the first time: "A feeling goes through you, and you're like, 'Oh my
God, this is big.'" And it was. *Emails from Kosovo* became a regular series
that aired in seven installments on National Public Radio's *Morning
Edition*, from February to June 1999. President Bill Clinton quoted the
Youth Radio series on March 29, 1999, in his radio address announcing
U.S. participation in NATO's bombing campaign (emphasis added):

> PRESIDENT CLINTON: Three days ago I decided the United States
> should join our NATO allies in military air strikes to bring peace
> to Kosovo. . . . We should remember the courage of the Kosovar
> people today, still exposed to violence and brutality. *Many Americans,
> now, have heard the story of a young Kosovar girl trying to stay in touch
> with a friend in America by e-mail, as a Serb attack began. Just a few days
> ago she wrote, "at the moment, just from my balcony, I can see people
> running with suitcases, and I can hear some gunshots. A village just a few
> hundred meters from my house is all surrounded. As long as I have electric-
> ity, I will continue writing to you. I'm trying to keep myself as calm as
> possible. My younger brother, who is nine, is sleeping now. I wish I will
> not have to stop his dreams."*

Emails from Kosovo was a turning point for Youth Radio. It put
the organization on the national news map, winning the prestigious
Alfred I. DuPont Award, and revealed the potential for youth media to
cover, and even influence, international affairs. The stakes attached to
this particular story were pretty extreme; it was not every day, after all,
that Youth Radio found itself leveraged by the president of the United

States in an emotional justification for war, or that a story's key source faced grave bodily danger. The scale and intensity of this series raised a distinct set of challenges, as we elaborate below. And yet whenever young people produce real media products for real broadcast audiences, the same issues arise in some form: complex decisions related to content, voice, boundaries, balance, impact, control, responsibility, and credit.

It might seem strange to frame the capacity to handle these issues as a form of literacy, and yet that is just what we aim to do in this chapter. We offer a new approach to understanding and promoting youth media learning: *converged literacy.*

As Henry Jenkins (2006b) has argued, in the media world *convergence* describes content expressed through a range of technologies all housed in one place, a website, for example, that features audio, graphics, digital photos, video clips, and a way for visitors to post comments. It's not just that you can find such a wide range of materials in a single location; convergence also makes it possible for a single piece of media to be distributed across a whole range of platforms. You might listen to the same Youth Radio story on your car stereo, through a podcast, by clicking on an online audio link, or by showing up at a community event where the story blares from speakers, the sound filling an assembly hall packed with people.

Literacy, the second key term in the concept we explore here, is a process of making, reading, understanding, and critiquing texts. In today's world, those texts increasingly transcend words on a page (Kress, 2003). Rather than frame literacy as a neutral function of the isolated mind, we locate young people's textual experiments and analyses in social contexts, sometimes face-to-face, and sometimes mediated through digital technologies.

In this chapter we bring together these two terms, *convergence* and *literacy,* to articulate what it takes for young people to claim a right to participate as citizens of the world and agents in their own lives (Ong, 1999). We develop the notion of converged literacy by exploring the processes behind four Youth Radio products. The *Emails from Kosovo* series provides a glimpse into a form of convergence created before the term came into mainstream fashion, revealing some of the educational and ethical challenges that arise when young people's private communication enters the public domain. The *Core Class,* Youth Radio's broadcast media course for incoming students, shows how the program has had to transform both what and how it teaches in order to stay relevant given new developments in digital media culture and face-to-face community engagement. The 2002 feature story, *Oakland Scenes*, mixes poetry and news reporting to examine the sources and effects of escalating murder rates in that city. Here Youth Radio producers reframe a topic that media makers too often use to criminalize young people and deflect attention away from the root causes and effects of persistent violence. In this story, youth expressive culture interrupts that tired narrative. The *Picturing War* story that Belia Mayeno Saavedra reported in the wake of the Abu Ghraib prison scandal examines digital media as a tool for cultural analysis and transformation. The story highlights U.S. Marines' responses to prison torture and the online archives of digital photos they took while deployed in Iraq.

HOW MEDIA MAKES LITERACIES CONVERGE

Convergence is a technological achievement, something machines produce by combining various media platforms in a single presentation. It's also a state of mind, something people imagine into being by learning to think, feel, express themselves, and understand their worlds across image, sound, and text (Jenkins, 2006b). The technological and conceptual shift implicit in the principle of convergence is changing what it takes to create media. There are new rules, and new ways to break them. For example, production in today's media world cannot be disentangled from distribution, so converged media makers need to know how to leverage and sometimes create their own means to circulate their content rather than rely on one-way outlets with automatic audiences. Also converging in today's media worlds are the makers' intentions and interests. Is the point to inspire, to sell, to convince, to mobilize, to inform, to disturb, or some combination? As evident in such developments as consumer-generated marketing (where users co-create ad campaigns) and nontransparent corporate sponsorships (where bloggers accept free gadgets and then plug those brands in their posts), the convergence of various intentions in a single media product can raise new challenges for both producers and consumers, who often have to work harder to find or ignore commercial interests embedded in editorial content. That said, young people increasingly deploy these same commercial strategies to build their own creative brands and draw interest to their original work.

Converged literacy implies that the printed word is just the beginning, or maybe not even the beginning, of what young people need to be able to deal with if they are to participate fully in shaping their lives and futures (Buckingham 2003; Cope & Kalantzis, 2000; Sefton Green, 1999; Tyner, 1998). Scholars such as Shirley Brice Heath (1983, 1986) and Brian Street (1984) revolutionized the study of literacy by arguing that people learn to compose and consume written texts through meaningful social events, such as reading bedtime stories or navigating neighborhood streets. New literacy scholars recognize that young people form some of their most nuanced, persistent, and consequential relationships to texts and narratives outside explicit instruction, but deeply inside interactive contexts: playing hopscotch, doing community theater, mastering video games, talking at the dinner table, rapping, busting poems, or devouring magazines in a friend's bedroom (Finders, 1997; Fisher, 2003; Gee, 2003; Goodwin, 1990; Morrell & Duncan-Andrade, 2002; Ochs & Capps, 2001).

Digital technologies have further stretched literacy to encompass an ability to use a range of tools and programs and to analyze how power circulates through engagements with media (Hull 2003). Young people can use digital literacy as a tool or even a weapon, but literacy can also be used against them, as yet another instrument of exclusion (Alim, 2005). After all, documenting the impressive multiliteracy benefits of launching a blog, creating a profile, or uploading an amateur music video onto YouTube is one thing; it's another challenge entirely to identify what young people actually learn from these experiences, how they benefit, who is shut out from these activities, and what the media project itself contributes to (or detracts from) the public domain. Likewise, Tannock (2004, p. 164) cautions that researchers themselves are often overly eager to "redeem" that which is literate in youth culture: "The academic documentation of literacy among social groups and individuals for whom such literacy has previously been left unrecognized is not in and of itself an automatically enabling or progressive move, but can in fact be extremely disempowering for the subjects of our research." The *Emails from Kosovo* series has been subjected to questions like these, faulted in one online newspaper for exploiting one girl's dispatches while providing a rationale for U.S. and NATO militarism. Finnegan himself, seven years after the NPR series, used his own blog to express some potent critiques of the media machine that made him, for one very intense period in his life, "Kosovo Boy," suddenly caught in his own firestorm of competing adult attentions and agendas. We're featuring his story in a chapter about literacy, and yet Finnegan himself reports in his blog that when Katie Couric asked him back then what he learned from working on the series, "I couldn't think of a damn thing." As evident in this sentiment, when young media producers examine power and its effects, and when their products reach real audiences, the meaning attached to their emerging literacies can be hard to predict and not always what we think.

Three principles of converged literacy drive the design and analysis of youth media learning. Converged literacy is an ability to *make and understand* boundary-crossing and convention-breaking texts; means knowing how to *draw and leverage* public interest in the stories you want to tell; and entails the material and imaginative resources to *claim and exercise* your right to use media to promote justice, variously defined—a right still denied young people marginalized from full citizenship as producers of media culture.

CONVERGENCE IN CORRESPONDENCE: *EMAILS FROM KOSOVO*

After hearing about Finnegan's collection of emails from Kosovo, Beverly Mire says she walked him over to Rebecca Martin, Youth Radio's senior producer, and Ellin O'Leary, Youth Radio's founder and executive producer, to help him figure out how to turn his private correspondence into a public radio story. The emails had an awkward candor and a feeling of tentative cross-cultural curiosity that brought something unexpected to the news the girl delivered through her notes to Finnegan. Still, initially the conversation didn't always delve deeply into the conditions of war and its effects on local youth. Finnegan and his producers framed questions that would reveal new information about the volatile political situation.

As the digital conversation continued, the Youth Radio production team played with different ways to present the emails, experimenting with various sequencing and editing, all the while imagining how to create a story that was true and clear and powerful for an audience meeting two young people for the first time, even as they got to know each other. The team came up with a pseudonym, Adona, for the girl in Kosovo, and after she agreed to allow her words to air on national radio, they asked a female Youth Radio reporter to record Adona's emails for broadcast.

FINNEGAN: It all started because I had the week off from hockey practice. I went to a meeting of my church group; we had a visitor, a peace worker recently back from Kosovo. He brought with him the email address of an Albanian girl my age, 16 year old Adona. She had access to a computer and wanted to use it to correspond with other teens, here in the U.S. I decided to write her a letter when I got back from the meeting. The next day I received the first of what was to be a series of letters from Adona, that would change the way I look at the world.

ADONA: *Hello Finnegan. I am glad you wrote to me so soon. About my English, I have learned it through the movies, school, special classes, etcetera, but mostly from TV. I can speak Serbian as well, Spanish and understand a bit of Turkish. I love learning languages, but I don't have much time to learn them. . . .*

You never know what will happen to you. One night, last week I think, we were all surrounded by police and armed forces, and if it wasn't for the OSCE observers, God knows how many victims would there be. And my flat was surrounded too. I cannot describe you the fear. . . . The next day, a few meters from my flat, they killed this Albanian journalist, Enver Maloku. Someday before there was a bomb explosion in the center of town where young people usually go out. . . .

ADONA: *Hello Finnie. I guess you're ok. And don't worry, your finger will get better soon. Well Finnie (I like calling you that) did I tell you that I am not a practicing Muslim and do you know why! . . . Because, if the Turks didn't force my grand grandparents to change their religion, I might now have been a catholic or an orthodox . . . I think religion is a good, clean and pure thing that in a way supports people in their life . . . . Thanks to religion, I think many people are afraid of god or believe that there is another world after we die, so they don't commit any crimes. Personally, I agree with Descartes when he says that god is imagined by the human mind.*

And just to tell you. You are not making me bored with your e-mails at all, I love reading them. I love to hear about the life there and I am really happy that I have a friend somewhere who I can talk to (whoops . . . write to). Bye, Adona.

FINNEGAN: Adona may not think much of organized religion, but she is very political. She's part of an organized youth movement that blames adults for keeping the war going. She says, as young people, they are looking beyond this war to the future and an end to the killing. . . .

ADONA: *About the NATO thing, you know I feel they should come here and protect us. I wish somebody could. I don't even know how many people get killed anymore. You just see them in the memoriam pages of newspapers. I really don't want to end up raped, with no parts of body like the massacred ones. I wish nobody in the world, in the whole universe would have to go through what we are. You don't know how lucky you are to have a normal life. We all want to be free and living like you do, having our rights and not be pushed and pushed. Finnegan, I'm telling you how I feel about this war and my friends feel the same. Bye. Adona, Kosovo.*

At the time Youth Radio produced this story, for Finnegan to reach out to Adona through digital technology was by no means a given—email was still relatively new—nor was it commonplace to mine emails and other such sources for media content. Recognizing a stash of emails as broadcast-worthy material was itself a key step in producing this series, and counterintuitive given radio's conventional dependence on actually hearing the voices of all characters in any story. Building the narrative around "found audio" (or, more accurately, personal correspondence that wasn't even audio yet, but had the potential to be) meant breaking from the standard formula for a public radio news script. Typically a reporter carries out a number of interviews with characters and experts, usually representing opposing sides of a given issue, gathers scene tape, and then arranges these elements into an outline, composing narration that moves the listener through the various clips. In the *Emails from Kosovo* series the composition is actually much simpler, and yet perhaps that stripped-down quality is part of what made the story work: just two voices lending the series a quality of eavesdropping on (or reading over the shoulder of) young people immersed in a still unfolding conversation.

Yet, although the structure might be simple, the questions and challenges connected to this story quickly proliferated. With so many resources channeled toward this one international series, Youth Radio's adult producers remember that they had to call a special meeting with the youth reporters in the Bay Area newsroom to make sure the young people did not feel that their own stories were being eclipsed. The story dealt with historic political and religious conflict, an ethnic cleansing campaign, militarism, and genocide. But when the broadcasts drew so much attention, suddenly the news reporter became the news story, and that wasn't easy. Neither was figuring out where to draw the line between reporting a story and intervening on behalf of a young person's well-being. Journalism's conventional detachment didn't always apply, for example when Youth Radio backed a petition to get Adona into a safer situation. Moreover, producers had to verify Adona's identity and fact-check her experiences without compromising her safety and without the international reporting infrastructure of a mass-media network. Negotiating relationships with Finnegan's church group, especially after the story became popular, was very difficult. These two nonprofit, youth-serving institutions suddenly found themselves in conversations with mass-media outlets like *People* magazine (which featured the story) and CNN·(which exposed Adona's real name after Youth Radio had worked so hard to protect her anonymity). All these players, each with its own agenda, were then drawn into the public relations and speech-writing machinery behind a U.S. president's foreign policy.

Talk about convergence. As Jenkins (2006b) argues, connecting previously distinct media forms is more than a technological or editorial exercise; the process can disrupt the way institutions usually function and people relate to each other. In this context, organizations such as Youth Radio need to generate new guidelines for the use of personal correspondence in public stories and new clarity regarding where professional broadcast objectives end and youth development concerns begin, a point to which we return later in this chapter. Just as Adona's email messages to Finnegan moved fluidly from popular culture references (her favorite artists were the Rolling Stones, Sade, Jewel, Cher, and REM) to emergency escape plans and political analysis, so too do young people outside war zones (or inside other kinds of war zones right here at home) occupy social worlds where the intimate and the public, leisure and life-

and-death decisions, converge. It is within that space of convergence that Youth Radio works, beginning with a young person's first experience with the organization, the introductory class called Core.

EMERGENT CONVERGENCE: YOUTH RADIO'S CORE CLASS

When Youth Radio started in 1992, students in the program produced single-voice, first-person commentaries recorded and cut (literally, with razor blades) on quarter-inch tape. By 1999, when Finnegan first shared his correspondence with Adona in the *Emails from Kosovo* series, Youth Radio's introductory classes had expanded beyond the commentary, emphasizing multiple media formats and genres. Every week students produced a radio show that rotated among deejayed music segments, preproduced Public Service Announcements, and scripted commentaries and news spots delivered in real time on the air. In the early 2000s, the introductory classes began providing training across these various radio formats while also introducing students to web programming, music production, and video.

Students met twice weekly after school to prepare for their show, *Youth in Control,* airing Fridays at 7–9 PM on KPFB FM. The twenty students in the class were divided into groups that focused on journalism, on-air broadcast, and music. The groups cycled through each of these streams, so that all students experienced every role. Young people who were nervous about reading a commentary or hosting a roundtable live on the radio couldn't opt out of these tasks. When their names appeared on the board (a rundown of the show clock), they'd snap on headphones, lean into the mic, and start talking. Their delivery could be halting, the narrative sometimes predictable, but still, it's never as hard as the first time. All students produced their own music and deejayed segments they programmed themselves, abiding by FCC decency standards. They also created a short digital video project, which they learned to upload to Youth Radio's website. Call it compelled, if rudimentary, convergence: students completed each of these requirements and others, listed on a huge chart in the middle of the workroom, before moving on to specialized training.

On a typical Friday night in 2006, an accomplished drummer and hip-hop producer in his late teens was in the backroom, helping students add percussion and keyboard tracks to the music they were producing. A peer editor, his shirt now untucked from his high school uniform, juggled two commentaries, one about the link between youth violence and the lack of afterschool activities, and the other an analysis of the overconcentration of liquor stores in poor communities. A journalism peer teacher, with her trademark deadpan voice, was telling a reticent commentator that no, she couldn't get another student to read her piece on the air, she'd have to do it herself, and it would be fine. The video instructor, one year out of high school, modeled microphone techniques for students working on an iMovie about how fantasy video games affect young people's real-life behaviors. Minutes before they'd have to record, two students working on a Public Service Announcement about a support group for abused girls were adding believable dialogue to spice up the script.

Alana Germany, a high school senior, sat with her peer teacher to review a list of roundtable questions, which centered on how young people deal with the entertainment industry's unrealistic beauty ideals. Alana was right to be nervous: just a few minutes into her roundtable, one of the young men on the panel started talking about boys and girls in ways she found very troubling (a slight paraphrase: "We all want the big booty and the big titties, you feel me?"), and this was live on the radio. Alana came back to the studio with her jaw set, avoiding eye contact, seeming close to tears. Behind closed doors in the studio, she explained why she was so upset: "Why would he start acting a fool? That makes Youth Radio look bad, and that's on me, because it was my roundtable." A peer in the program who had been practicing her digital editing during the show shared Alana's outrage and stormed out of the studio to tell off her fellow student. All of the peer educators in these interactions were young people in their teens and early twenties, some still in high school, all Youth Radio graduates.

The *Youth in Control* shows that students produced in Youth Radio's Core class were shot through with beautiful bits: unscripted conversations about love or frustration, shout-outs to peer teachers from students dedicating songs to their mentors, and moments when an R & B classic showed up on someone's playlist and soon everyone back in the studio was singing out loud to Marvin Gaye. But these shows also contained their share of cringe-inducing passages, revealing that even the most sophisticated technology users, so-called digital natives (Prensky, 2001, 2006), do not automatically know how to compose a compelling story, respond thoughtfully to live questions, collect usable tape, project a strong personality through the microphone, or fill dead air. Neither do young people necessarily show up with nuanced understandings of social structures or with tools to critique mainstream (or independent, for that matter) media products. James Gee (2000, p. 62) writes that although schools are busily trying to teach young people how to think "critically," that is, to exercise higher-order cognitive skills, it's equally if not more pressing for students to learn how to think "critiquely," meaning to understand that injustice is not inevitable but continually produced, and therefore something we can actually question and resist. Growing up connected to digital technology does not, of course, automatically promote social critique, even if young people today might be more sophisticated than their predecessors were when it comes to recognizing and resisting media manipulations. In fact, several studies suggest that young people's own projects often reproduce stereotypes and predictable media formulas, whether the young producers are working in adult-sponsored programs or peer groups or on their own (Fleetwood 2005; Sinker 2000; Soep 2005b; Tyner 1998).

Just as we can't assume that young people's media products will automatically contain politically astute social critiques, neither can we rely on popular culture to instill converged literacy, even among so-called digital natives—not when some young people can easily leverage personal networks and resources to land internships at media organizations while others are lucky to grab a few minutes on a janky public school computer to check email. That is why, in 2006, a team of adult and youth staff members set out to redesign the Youth Radio Core class to align that introductory training more fully with digital media culture. Two considerations guided the redesign process. First, we prioritized production projects designed to reach significant audiences through various new and old media outlets available in digital culture. Second, we wanted to promote socially relevant and meaningful content, projects that contribute to justice and equity and offer narratives not typically taken seriously by those framing the debates and policies that shape

young people's lives. We wanted to create positive learning experiences
and professional opportunities for young people otherwise marginalized from digital privilege.

With all this in mind, we identified a series of priorities guiding what
our students needed to know and be able to do. Youth Radio students
who had previously focused on the one-time live radio broadcast on
KPFB needed to know how to reframe their media as customizable and
versatile, lending itself to unregulated online distribution and community use at face-to-face events. The organization, which had fought
so hard for on-air credit on national outlets, needed to teach students
to start giving away their work, posting their stories everywhere they
could, targeting niche audiences likely to link to or share those stories
with others in their own networks of friends and colleagues. We needed
to cultivate audiences not just for NPR-style products, but also for projects containing resonant content aimed at youth audiences.

Instead of having students summarize newspaper stories in radio
spots they recited on the air (modeled on the old media "rip and read"
technique), in the new program they would read print stories, record
"person on the street" interviews, host live roundtable discussions building on news themes, and digitize, edit, and upload audio and video
clips and commentary onto Youth Radio's website and other sites for
user-generated content. At more advanced levels of training, in addition
to teaching students the standard public radio–style feature script, peer
educators designed hybrid assignments, for example mixing song clips
and first-person narratives in segments that could air on Youth Radio's
iTunes radio show as well as on websites featuring user-generated song
reviews. Students would need to think beyond digital distribution for
their products, connecting as well with classroom- and community-
based educators eager to integrate youth-produced content into their
own settings for education and community organizing.

Throughout this redesign process, Youth Radio students and staff
broke from comfortable protocols for teaching radio in the old days, back
when an audio story would evaporate into the ether as soon as it aired.
That said, the mission of the organization's media production work has
not really budged; we still were determined to create an environment
in which young people can generate powerful, socially meaningful,

urgently needed content in an environment promoting positive youth and community development. Although the technologies are always changing, the core competencies outlined in Youth Radio's Core class syllabus are, if not platform-agnostic, conducive to remixing to maximize impact and continue to center on preparing young people to tell meaningful stories with relevance to their own lives, their communities, and the wider society.

POETIC CONVERGENCE:
OAKLAND VERSES, OAKLAND VOICES

In 2002 the homicide rate in Oakland was rising at an alarming pace. It seemed a natural Youth Radio story, given that so many students at the main headquarters lived in Oakland and that the violence disproportionately affected young people. Youth Radio had a long history of violence prevention work, both as a youth development organization committed to providing young people with meaningful learning experiences and work opportunities, and as a professional production company covering youth violence through young people's eyes.

So it surprised some of the adult producers when Youth Radio's students and newsroom reporters initially said that they didn't want to cover the situation in Oakland. They resented the fact that so many mainstream media outlets, which in the past had never expressed much interest in the lives of Oakland youth, were now pouring into the community to report on the homicide rate, with daily body counts running like sports scores across newspaper pages. Through a series of impromptu conversations and formal meetings, many of the young people said they didn't want to contribute to this kind of coverage.

But Youth Radio's executive producer, Ellin O'Leary, wouldn't give up on the topic; she had a feeling that the young people could come up with a powerful counternarrative to the news they were offended by, and she felt an obligation to use Youth Radio's position within the national media to draw attention to and reframe such an important issue. After several more conversations with the young people, finally they pinpointed what was missing in the mainstream press coverage. The young people wanted to produce a nuanced account of the effects of the violence on young people and families trying to carry on their lives in a place that felt increasingly unsafe, even as Oakland remained a town they loved and considered home.

Gerald Ward II, a Youth Radio graduate who played a leading role in the organization's broadcast training program while pursuing an undergraduate film degree at San Francisco State University, had lived in Oakland all his life. He was already in the habit of driving a couple of the students home at the end of class on Wednesday and Friday nights, rides on which they witnessed the casualties of violence firsthand. So he decided that on his next trip he'd bring recording equipment. Gerald brainstormed about how he might approach the tape-gathering with students. We wanted listeners to get a sense of what it felt like to walk the streets and how the neighborhood had changed, and he wanted to talk to a range of Oakland residents, including young people and their parents.

Gerald returned the following day with his tape and passed it along to a colleague, who began digitizing it in the studio. Meanwhile, we recorded other conversations at Youth Radio itself during downtime in an attempt to gather as much material as we could in hopes of finding some kind of narrative through-line, a way to bring these voices and scenes together in a story. Young people talked about their personal experiences with violence, the homicide rate, the way the mainstream press was covering it, and also a controversial city proposal to raise the number of police on the streets. The proposal had been linked in the public discourse and in many young people's minds with a "law and order" mentality that neglected violence prevention and diverted support from positive youth programs. One Youth Radio student who was pursuing law enforcement training spoke out in support of the other side of that debate.

Reviewing the tape, it was clear that there were some strong moments and that the young people had shared provocative insights. But where was the story? An unexpected answer came from a nineteen-year-old poet, Ise Lyfe, who came to Youth Radio's studio to record a piece he had written and performed at some poetry slams around the Bay Area. Today, Ise is a well-known spoken-word hip-hop theater artist and the owner of lyfeproductives. At that time, Ise was performing with Youth

Speaks, a nonprofit literary arts program that ran free poetry workshops in classrooms and after school and produced local and national slam competitions.[1] Ise's poem was a retelling of *Romeo and Juliet*, except he recast the characters as Rome and Net Net:

> ISE: *I'm here today to tell a story. A twisted story of ghetto glory. Now, I know you heard of Romeo and Juliet, but I bet you aint heard of Rome and Net Net. See, their story's a bit different. A bit more explicit. So sad, almost all bad. They're young, beautiful and don't even know. Society told him to be a thug, told her to be a 'ho. They victims of a system placed on us years ago.*

Ise's poem resonated with the themes that ran through Gerald's tape, while adding suspense, cadence, and drama.[2] Once we had the poem, putting the story together was pretty easy. We started by dividing the poem into sections where there seemed to be natural breaks, points where we could intercut Ise's unfolding story with clips from the tape. We cut straight from Ise's first verse, transcribed above, to a snippet of conversation between Gerald and Bianca, the student he'd driven home, then back to the poem, then back to the conversation, with ambient street sounds fading in and out to smooth out the transitions.

> GERALD: Where are we right now, Bianca?
>
> BIANCA: 78th avenue.
>
> GERALD: What do you see?
>
> BIANCA: Liquor stores, nail shops, there's a whole bunch of people socializing.
>
> GERALD: This your neighborhood?
>
> BIANCA: Yeah. I try not to go outside at night. Because you never know you might get killed.
>
> ISE: *Let me tell you how Rome and Net Net first met. She was standing at the bus stop, sucking on a lollipop, short skirt, short top—"Girl you need to stop! You wearing summer clothes and it ain't even hot!" Net Net ain't the only one to blame. A number of things make her do what she do. Her mama was never really there. Her dad died when she was two. Yet and still up she grew. And out she grew. Maybe a little too fast because the drunk men on the corner said, "Damn girl, look at your ass." And she laughed, not knowing she being disrespected. She looked up and see Rome coming from the other direction.*

BIANCA: When I get off the bus, all I see, the first thing I see is a prosti- tute on the corner who's pregnant, and who's like probably twenty- something years old and that's just depressing. I mean it's like, dang, she has so much she could do so much more with her life. I mean if the homicide rate keeps climbing and you can't just live, I mean because it's affecting everybody. I mean, you never know if that bul- let is gonna come and hit one of your children.   .

BIANCA'S MOM: I guess right now we're at a point where I don't like my child to be out at night, because stray bullets are everywhere. You know I had a visitor at my home and stray bullets hit the car, and it could have easily been a person, so it's not a very fair situation.

ISE: *Now here come Rome, fronting on his cellular phone, cause his credit got denied when he tried to get it turned on. Looking dumb, with weed in his socks, crack in his gums, he walk down the street throwing up, where you from. He see Net Net, pretends to hang his phone up. He touch his pager like it's being blown up. He said, "Damn, baby girl, what's your name? What's your steeze? Why you got that skirt on, it's only 40 degrees!" She said, "Please!" But she was getting sick, so she sneezed. She said, "Ha CHOO!" He said, "Bless you." She said, "Naw, forget you! You don't know me well enough to be talking about my clothes and all that kind of stuff." "My bad, baby girl, I'm just looking out for your health. By the way, let me introduce myself. My name is Rome. Can we chop it up, talk on the phone?" "No, why?" "Why? Cause you fine, and I know you tired cause all day you've [been] walking through my mind." No, he didn't use that tired line, but . . . She's trippin, so you know what she say? "Okay, that's so sweet. You're the man I always wanted to meet!"*

Here's where we got stuck. The clips were starting to sound redun- dant, the pacing predictable, even with Ise's poem driving the narrative forward. Would it work here to get into some of the debates in the tape about broader issues related to police harassment? Gerald had recorded some pretty intense accounts of racial profiling, and one of the young people working on the piece said he thought it was crucial to include these in the story. But another young person helping to produce *Oakland Scenes* worried that tossing in an anecdote about police misconduct at this point might bog down the story, throw off the pacing, and introduce a whole load of issues that we couldn't work out in this one story. If we included tape from a teenager accusing the cops of violence and racism, wouldn't we then need to introduce a police officer's point of view as well? That would take the piece in a whole different direction, so we opted to save the police tape for a half-hour public affairs show we were developing concurrently to explore the violence in Oakland from a policy perspective.

We called Youth Radio's senior newsroom staff into the studio to listen to what we had so far. They said they wanted to hear more from Gerald, maybe something more personal, to connect with the themes in the poem, a strategy that might also unsettle the interviewer-interviewee dynamic between Gerald and Bianca in some interesting ways. So Gerald headed back into the soundproof recording booth and came out with this, which we mixed into the story right after the passage where Rome and Net Net hook up:

GERALD: My girlfriend and I have only been together 2 or 3 weeks. We come from such the same background in Oakland. Her mom lives on 94th, and I live on, my mom lives on 23rd. It's interesting because when we were younger, I was kinda a square. We could have been friends, but I also could have been someone that she thought was square. I used to carry a briefcase to school and I wanted to be a scientist. Then I wanted to be a stockbroker. I wasn't trying to be a thug at all.

Then back to the poem:

ISE: *Net Net get pregnant. Nine months later, the saddest day of the year, she's holding this beautiful baby girl, but her face drops tears as she sings her daughter a sad lullaby song cause Rome died in a drug deal gone terribly wrong. You see, Rome died, never got to see his newborn baby girl's eyes. Now he's not there to wipe the tears from Net Net's eyes. Net Net puts down the baby, the baby cries. Net Net goes in the kitchen and gets a kitchen knife. Net Net slits her wrists not once, Net Net slits her wrists twice. Suicide . . .*

BIANCA: The only time you talk to your neighbors is if you see them outside and you say "hello" and "goodnight." You never talk about real issues. Things that are important. You can't always like wait around and think that everyone else is gonna do it. You need to take some action for yourself and I think we kinda lost that, our generation.

ISE: *At ten years old, the daughter says both my parents died. At thirteen, she curses the parents she never really knew, "Forget my mama and my daddy, forget him too!" And at sixteen, she's standing at the bus stop, sucking on a lollipop, short skirt, short top, cause ya'll we need to stop. We be wearing summer clothes like it ain't even hot. Leaving our problems to be solved by somebody else. Then we wonder why history always repeats itself. Repeats itself. Why history always repeats itself. Rome and Net Nets in '62, '72, '82, '92, and now in 2002, because through all the madness, we laugh at the ghetto kids on the bus stop. Peace.*[3]

The mixing of Ise's poetics and Gerald's reporting is what distinguished this story from other efforts to draw attention to Oakland's rising violence. Had Youth Radio run the interviews alone, without the poem, we would have been hard-pressed to find a story arc to hold listener interest. Had we run the poem alone, without the interviews, we would not have been able to ground Ise's fictional narrative against the backdrop of the present real-life situation in Oakland.

Converged literacy provides a way to understand the learning process behind this kind of production. Producers needed to open themselves up to genres not typically included in the repertoire of radio conventions, but they also needed to eliminate entire topic areas, such as policy debates and reports of police harassment, which were undeniably relevant to the story but would have sunk it with too much information. The story asked a lot of listeners. No authoritative narrator drew explicit connections between the two interweaving story lines running through the piece, and commuters who usually half-listen to radio news spots on their car stereos needed to pay a different kind of attention to follow the narrative from beginning to end. In this sense, converged literacy spreads from producers to audiences, posing new challenges related to expression and interpretation, forming new relationships between truth and fiction, and reorganizing how young people speak and what goes unsaid. When producers figured out ways to cut between Ise's poem and Gerald's interviews, we were strategically experimenting with the logic governing the broadcast news industry, taking a bet that emotion, lyricism, and make-believe might just convey a stark and undeniable truth, one audience members could get even if they had never attended a poetry slam or set foot on the streets of Oakland. The young producers generated a new kind of story. Those who have traditionally been disenfranchised from digital culture and its expensive appliances emerged here to promote independent media in an age of convergence.

Digital technology has reorganized our lives on intimate and global scales. As the *Emails from Kosovo* series and *Oakland Scenes* foretold, digital technologies and hybrid genres enable young people to frame society's most pressing issues—in those two stories, violence far away and at home—in unexpected ways. Fast-forward two years from *Oakland Scenes*, and young people were once again telling the story of a different kind of war.

OPERATION CONVERGENCE: YOUTH VOICES AT WAR

In January 2004 Youth Radio asked a U.S. Marine in his early twenties to come to our studio in Berkeley to work on a commentary. Our news director, Nishat Kurwa, had read about this young man in an Indian American newspaper. He had joined the U.S. Marines at seventeen and participated in the initial U.S. invasion of Iraq. When Youth Radio got in touch, he had recently returned to the University of California to resume life as a college student, joining his military unit one weekend per month for reserve duty.

While working on the commentary at Youth Radio, this young Marine mentioned that a couple of his buddies back at school had also recently come home from Iraq. I (Lissa) flew down to the campus shortly thereafter for a one-day scouting trip to meet the other young vets and explore the possibility of producing a full-blown story—with multiple characters, scene tape, and more—about young military personnel readjusting to college life as Iraq war veterans. There, I met Ed and Luis. The Marines took over the mic and interviewed one another about their time in Iraq and what it had been like to come home. Ed was a senior and art major. He drove a humvee as part of a combined anti-armor team, and he described his role in the war as "kill[ing] Iraqi bad guys." In his dorm room, Ed opened the closet and pulled out a portfolio filled with artwork he'd taken from a girls' school in Iraq that had been blown up.[4] Because he was an artist himself, Ed said the pictures helped him understand "the historical context" surrounding the war for Iraqis and gave him insight into "what they're going through."

Luis was just a freshman, still on active duty. He didn't like talking about his time over there. It was weird, he said, coming home from his deployment to a dorm where the sounds of gunfire and bomb blasts rang through the hallways, blaring from the video game consoles in nearly every room. All three of the young Marines shared photographs they'd taken throughout their deployments, many of which hung on their bedroom walls. Their units had compiled hundreds of pictures, they said, which they circulated among themselves and to friends and family members through CDs and email attachments.

Shortly after this scouting trip, photos of detainee torture leaked from the Abu Ghraib prison in Iraq, setting off a huge international scandal. The photos pictured male Iraqi prisoners, many naked, simulating sex acts, piled on top of one another, and attached to leashes and wires, with U.S. soldiers looking on, sometimes posing, sometimes snapping pictures. I contacted the Marines to see whether I could come back for a second visit, this time with Youth Radio reporter Belia Mayeno Saavedra, to hear more and look at the photos these Marines had brought home from Iraq.[5] Ed had uploaded his photo collection onto a website he designed, where he added captions containing his own commentary on what he saw and did while deployed.

It was a challenging day, as we tried to make sense of handmade drawings and letters closeted in dorm rooms, snapshots and emails archived on personal computers, and memories digitized on minidisk in order to produce a story that shed new light on a crisis that had captured the attention of the world. Some of the most vituperative debates in the U.S. press centered on who deserved blame for the acts pictured in those photographs: young, low-level prison guards or their higher-ups. Notably, reports of the abuse had circulated for more than a year before the photographs surfaced: "It was the photographs that made all this 'real' to Bush and his associates. Up to then, there had been only words, which are easier to cover up in our age of infinite digital self-reproduction and self-dissemination, and so much easier to forget" (Sontag, 2004).

Citizens around the world struggled to analyze the relationship between the photos and other texts and narratives vying to tell the story of an unfolding war. The Bush administration rushed to contain the scandal by framing the abuse at Abu Ghraib as a reprehensible, unauthorized aberration carried out by a handful of misguided soldiers. There were many in the United States and elsewhere who balked at this argument, describing the torture of Iraqi prisoners as "neither exceptional nor singular" (Puar, 2005, p. 15). Interestingly, although the Marines went to great lengths to distance themselves from the behaviors of the young men and women in U.S. uniforms captured in those photographs, they aligned themselves with arguments, often emanating from those deeply critical of the war effort, that the Abu Ghraib prison guards' actions were anything but exceptional. Only civilians watching the war on TV from the safety of living-room couches would be surprised, the young men maintained, in what became the opening scene of Belia's story.

Picturing War, by Belia Mayeno Saavedra

Part 1

BELIA: A year ago, Former Marine reservist Ed [last name] returned from Iraq, after taking part in the U.S. invasion. Now he's back at University of California at Riverside, a twenty-six-year-old art student. Here's what he says about the stories of prison abuse coming out of Iraq. . . .

ED: *It's like Chris Rock said, I wouldn't do it, but I understand. I'm not saying I approve of it, but I understand the conditions that led up to them doing it.*

BELIA: Ed's buddy Luis [last name], a shy twenty-one-year-old, resumed his freshman year at Riverside when he returned from Iraq a year ago.

(Sound comes up . . . bit of quiet laughter, Luis: "Oh yeah, I remember that, but you know what happened. . . . ")

BELIA: Luis was a field radio operator for a logistics unit in Iraq. . . . He says sometimes they had to round up Iraqis and detain them. And that when you see someone as your enemy, and you feel like they're going to kill you, you start to look at them with hate. At some point, Luis says, you're going to lose your judgment, even if it's just for a minute or two. And it's up to you to know how to manage it, he says. He tells this story.

LUIS: *I think we picked up prisoners, and put barbed wire around them. I recall one of the corporals offering me an opportunity to go in there and abuse some of them. I think it was Corporal —*

MARINE: *No, don't name him.*

FEMALE VOICE: *No. Don't.*

MARINE: *Don't name him.*

LUIS: *He said, Hey, [last name], look, there's one of those Iraqi guys. Wanna go in there and kick em? I thought about it for a split second, but then I guess my judgment came into play, and I said, that's not the right thing to do. Just go back to my five-ton, and if I'm called upon to do something, gotta do my job.*

BELIA: When you ask him about what happened at Abu Ghraib, Luis says the soldiers responsible should be treated harshly, possibly including higher-ups. But like his buddy Ed, Luis says the abuses don't really surprise him.

LUIS: *People see it on TV, they're not living it, so they find it surprising, "oh, this is obscene." But then, you tell me one thing that happens during war that is not obscene.*

Just weeks after the first pictures of prison torture came out, the Youth Radio interviews revealed that prisoner abuse was by no means isolated to Abu Ghraib or carried out without supervisors' knowledge. Luis did not share pictures of prisoner abuse, but he did describe it. More than that, he was just about to reveal the name of the corporal who reportedly invited him to "go in there" and kick "one of those Iraqi guys." His fellow Marine stopped him: "Don't name him. . . . Don't name him." No surprise there. But the Marine's voice is not the only one you hear if you listen closely to this moment in the story. You can also pick up another voice, a female one, mine (Lissa). I too say, "No. Don't." I had to listen back to the tape a couple of times to believe I had actually done that—stopped Luis from naming a higher-up in his chain of command who had allegedly instigated detainee abuse.[6] Maybe I thought I was protecting the story; we'd had military higher-ups kill pieces in the past.[7] Or maybe I thought I was somehow protecting Luis himself. That's never the explicit goal in Youth Radio's production model. We approach young people as agents whose voices should be amplified, not vulnerable populations in need of our benevolent protection. But if the media production process itself creates risk for young participants—whether they are sources, as was the case here, or reporters like Belia—that complicates the question of responsibility. If a youth media organization's mission is to serve and promote youth voice, to what extent are participants, young people and adults, obligated to try to prevent negative consequences for young people drawn into any given media story?

When faced with a question like this one, it may seem beside the point to invoke literacy. And yet in many ways literacy is precisely the point here, because literacy is what all of us implicated in this story depended on, in our personal and collaborative decisions about what stories to tell and how to tell them. Making those decisions required converged literacy to the extent that we were working across media forms (sound, snapshots, websites) and navigating various institutional contexts as well, seeking ways to comply with and sometimes subvert protocols governing mass-media outlets, military chains of command, and youth development agencies. In the end, we strove to tell this story in a way that framed individual young people's actions within larger cultural and political contexts. Belia and I kept coming back to this question: How can we make this story about these young men, but not about these young men, about the role of torture and abuse in the context of militarism, about new ways that soldiers are documenting their wartime experiences, and about the experiences of young people selectively recruited for war (Mariscal, 2005)? That is a lot—perhaps too much—to ask of a four-minute radio story produced and broadcast in a matter of days. And yet that is the least we should ask of a larger body of work, from Youth Radio and the youth media field, covering the most difficult and important issues confronting young people at any given moment in history.

These issues, and the literacy required to understand and act on them, have grown ever more complicated as a result of new digital technologies, as further explored in the second half of Belia's story.

Picturing War, by Belia Mayeno Saavedra

Part 2

(*Bring up computer sound . . .*)

BELIA: And as we've seen over the past weeks, the graphic images of war are not only televised, they're digitized. After Ed [last name] was called to Iraq, one of the first things he did was stock up on camera supplies.

ED: *We spent a lot of time patrolling, driving around, so I'd whip out the camera, real quick, take a picture. I mean, we wouldn't be taking out the camera when we were doing anything mission-critical or important. But I mean, half the time we spent on the road, we got to see a lot of Iraq. . . . But I just took the pictures as a record of my travels, I guess. Because me going to Iraq, going to war and back, was the only real adventure I'll ever have. (laugh)*

BELIA: These reservists say, when they come home from Iraq it's normal for them to scan their pictures onto a computer, email them around, or burn them onto a CD. It's a digital yearbook of a military unit's shared experience in Iraq. Ed put *his* photos on the web.

(Bring up sound. Ed: "Here's—okay, we're gonna go in, and it says—and here's a link to it . . . ")

BELIA: Some of the pictures are just pretty shots of the desert and the ruins in Babylon. But many of them are graphic shots of charred dead bodies, or truncated torsos lying in the sand. The photos show us *what* he saw, and the captions he added tell us *how* he saw it. Ed and his fellow Marines nicknamed one burnt corpse "Mr. Crispy."

ED: *When I first saw dead bodies, I was like, I've never seen dead bodies like that before, so out of curiosity, I whipped out the camera and stuff. I was in the car, we were still driving the whole time, I didn't get out and say, oh, Kodak moment. Just gave it to my driver, my guy on top, the gunner, take pictures, basically what it was, you find your photo ops when you can. . . .*

BELIA: Ed points to another shot, one of Americans in camouflage giving candy to Iraqi children, and his caption reads "Hey kids, here's some candy. Now make sure you don't sneak up on me tonight or I'll have to shoot you."

(Bring up sound. Ed: "So here's a picture of blown up tanks, big old statue of AK 47s on an Iraqi flag, that's pretty good. . . . ")

BELIA: Ed's grisly photos and captions are disturbing. And what may have started as a personal travelogue is now part of a growing stream of images soldiers are bringing home, changing the way the world sees this war.

In youth media practice and literacy theory, we often frame technology as a means of social connection and a tool with which young people can exercise agency.[8] Ironically, though, the young Marines also seemed to rely on technology for evidence of innocence, a way to *disavow* connection and *deny* agency. Ed insisted that in snapping pictures, he wasn't really doing anything, except witnessing: "I just took it as I saw it . . . like a news reporter who takes pictures and brings them back home. . . . " Like a news reporter, and also like a tourist with a gun. Ed described his visit to Babylon this way: "Pretend Disneyland is empty, and you got your M-16, and you get to check it out, but you still gotta be careful, because someone could come out of Space Mountain and kill your ass."

Although Ed described his photography as a hands-off documentation exercise, the captions on his website told a different story. Clearly he
was doing something by juxtaposing his commentary with the photos.
During our visit, Ed booted up his computer and launched into a tour of
his site, "My Spring Break 2003." The image on the front page depicted "a
bunch of girls wearing burkas and bikinis holding up AK 47s, and then
in the background is a picture of oil burning in the water, and then the
mountains are burning in the background."

Ed's website begs the question, Was he exercising converged literacy
here? He deployed digital technologies, combining and juxtaposing various forms, formats, and genres, to express an experience he had lived
through, one that challenged the mainstream media's representation
of the war in which he fought. He exploited new media methods of
distribution for his photographs and commentary, inviting comments
and participation from visitors. In these ways, Ed exhibited some of the
very skills and habits many contemporary educators and media scholars
advocate, as we tout the virtues of digital media production. And yet the
product of his particular experiments was deeply troubling, shaped and
disciplined by forces that destroy young people's lives.

Further complicating these issues is Ed's own way of explaining the
purpose of his website. "The point of the captions, it was a critique of
my spring break, and everyone else's," he said. Belia and I kept trying
to push him on this point, but we couldn't quite figure it out. What was
he trying to critique? In the end, reflecting back on our own story, we
have asked ourselves the same question. To what extent can a story like
this one function as a kind of critique, even if some of the perspectives it
revealed conform to rather than challenge ideologies that make life more
dangerous for young people who are already marginalized?

This line of questioning cuts to the heart of the relationship between
converged literacy and engaged citizenship by highlighting the fact that
such a relationship is never straightforward or guaranteed. What distinguishes a place like Youth Radio from an individual young person uploading photos or creating a blog is that Youth Radio is a collective effort to
promote critical thinking, support positive youth development, convey
underreported and media-distorted community experiences, and contribute media products marked by journalistic rigor and compelling analysis.

That is not to say that every story in Youth Radio's archive achieves these ends. Some might even argue that Ed's website, by virtue of its uncensored representation of war (compared to the tightly controlled mainstream press), might in fact do more than the Youth Radio report to provoke new avenues of dialogue. But in creating that story, Youth Radio producers aim to promote an informed and rigorous public discourse grounded in truth and evidence, while at the same time supporting a meaningful learning experience for those involved, young people and adults, whether they agree with one another or not. It is in these ways that convergence in the technical and textual sense can transform into a kind of literacy.

For Belia, exercising that literacy meant thinking deeply not just about how she framed the story overall, but how she chose her individual words. In preparing this story, she struggled to find the right adjective to describe the photographs Ed brought back from Iraq. In the popular discourse, "horrifying" seemed the word of choice to characterize the Abu Ghraib photos.

BELIA: But in the interview, Ed kept saying, "You have to love the war, because if you don't love the war, you're gonna go crazy." And I kept hearing that over and over in my head as I was looking at the things he did and his website, and the ways he talked about the war. His perspective was disturbing, it did disturb us. But the use of "horrifying," something about that felt very removed, like, "Oh, look at that horrible thing that person is doing over there that I have nothing to do with." Because even though I didn't send him to Iraq, in the larger scheme of things, living as an American citizen and benefiting in certain ways from the military industrial complex and all the "isms" and crazy things we're all pulled into just by virtue of where we live and who we are, I think that "horrifying" and other words that were more removed or felt more distant were maybe a little too passive. But we did have to choose something that showed, it's not like this was okay with us.

In reflecting on her word choice for this story, Belia emphasizes her own connection to the story she reports, explicitly refusing a position of passive detachment. And this, perhaps, is among the most important achievements a young person can work toward in a project geared to promote converged literacy: claiming a right to participate, as an active agent, in living, telling, and framing every historical moment's defining stories.

CONCLUSION

In this chapter we have framed converged literacy in three ways. The first centers on production: an ability to *make and understand* boundary-crossing and convention-breaking texts, such as radio stories composed from digital correspondence (*Emails from Kosovo*), music clips (Youth Radio's Core class), spoken-word poetry (*Oakland Scenes*), and photos with captions uploaded to the web (*Picturing War*). These stories defy expectations and reach beyond superficial meanings and modes of representation. Preparing young people to tell these kinds of stories means approaching media education with new rigor and a different set of standards, as we can no longer settle for outcomes that support critical consumption or production in the old media landscape. This work requires continually redesigning curricula to stay relevant to youth and their varied engagements with digital culture and politics.

The second dimension of converged literacy centers on distribution: knowing how to *draw and leverage* public interest in the stories you want to tell. In producing each of the stories featured here, young producers and their adult collaborators described new relationships: between a boy in Berkeley and a girl in Kosovo; between Rome and Net Net; between U.S. Marines and the Iraqi youngsters they pictured as both enemies and recipients of liberation. These individual relationships, captured through sound, image, and word, had wider cultural implications related to militarism, love, and violence. Producers were able to draw public attention to these issues by framing them in new ways and by distributing their stories across a range of outlets, including radio, web, and community forums. In the case of *Emails from Kosovo* and *Picturing War*, the world was already obsessed with the specific topic of each story: the conflict in the former Yugoslavia and the abuse at Abu Ghraib prison in Iraq. Young producers seized on this public preoccupation to bring new facts, insights, and analyses to those themes. *Oakland Scenes* was different. The national mainstream press at the time paid little attention to the mostly black and brown young people dying every day in Oakland, except perhaps through sensationalized coverage, so the challenge for this story was to create public interest in a topic of pressing, though persistently overlooked, importance.

This brings us to the third framing of converged literacy presented here, which centers on impact. Converged literacy entails the material and imaginative resources to *claim and exercise* the right to use media to promote justice, variously defined. None of the stories described in this chapter sacrifices journalistic rigor for the sake of a political agenda, but all reveal that young people can tell stories that support equity and enfranchisement. Each disrupts narratives of exclusion that promote the self-interest of those already occupying positions of privilege and power. We emphasize resources here because it makes no sense to add "converged media literacy" as yet another requirement young people need to meet if they are to qualify as full-blown citizens, without addressing the vast disparities in their access to the tools, networks, and experiences that prepare them to exercise that citizenship. When young people are only selectively initiated and integrated into the processes and practices of converged literacy, their lives and stories are missing or misrepresented in the public sphere.

Convergence, as we have said, means that media forms that used to inhabit separate spaces now coexist in single sites. Spoken-word poetry intercuts with street corner interviews. Digital photographs illustrate military diaries and undermine efforts to suppress the most obscene dimensions of war. Convergence has also changed the rules of the media distribution game. To be media literate today means knowing not only how to produce rich content, but also how to create demand and the imperative for audiences to share and disseminate what you've done across their own dispersed networks and to stay in the conversation during the story's digital afterlife. These conditions for media production and distribution raise new intellectual, ethical, and political challenges about the value of converged literacy's products, for the young person who made them and for their varied audiences. A piece of media might contain all the technical elements of convergence and yet contribute very little to anyone's literacy, if literacy implies a capacity to understand and critique the way the world is organized by virtue of being textualized. It is in the combination of the two—convergence and literacy—that there is the greatest potential for making change.

TWO Collegial Pedagogy

In the winter of 2004 National Public Radio contacted Youth Radio with a proposal. Researchers had released findings from a national poll about sex education and abstinence. Show producers preparing reports on the study invited Youth Radio to create a companion story from the perspective of young people. The matter was taken up in the newsroom's editorial meeting, where young reporters and adult producers gathered for an hour or so to check in and develop new story ideas. Each week a different young person facilitated the meeting, and when adults wanted to comment they raised their hands and requested permission.

The topic of sex education and conceptions of abstinence drew spirited engagement. Young people described their own ideas and shared perspectives from their friends, parents, and social adversaries at school. One high school senior designated members of a clique at her school "virgin ho's," setting off knowing laughter and eye rolling from the young people and puzzled looks from some of the adults, who needed help understanding the term. Virgin ho's are, we learned, girls who freely and frequently engage in every form of sex but intercourse and still act self-righteous because, technically, they aren't "having sex." Labels like this one heated up the discussion. The young people argued about which behaviors were deemed appropriate for girls and which for boys, and how those disparities made life difficult for young females. The group also touched on definitions of abstinence for gay and lesbian youth, whether it was possible for a teen couple to stay together if only one was a virgin and aimed to stay that way (consensus was, probably not), and whether abstinence-based education really tempers sexual experimentation among youth (again, probably not). Evidently the topic of abstinence had significant potential as a Youth Radio story. Young people were in a strong position to contribute knowledge informed by their own experiences, their social networks, and their research into wider social trends and public policy.

This editorial meeting captures the first moments of the first stage of Youth Radio's production cycle: finding and framing the story. Although young people initiate most Youth Radio stories, in this case adult journalists solicited a youth perspective and shared the potential for reaching a huge audience. Youth Radio's senior producer, Rebecca Martin, fielded the initial request and helped the young people think about ways they might approach the topic, pointing to some of the most surprising data in the national abstinence study.[1] From that point, young people played a leading role in determining the specific form and tone of the story. As they continued to talk and began gathering tape, the teen reporters framed the topic as one they considered worthy of exploration and eventual broadcast. The angle: the disconnect between definitions of abstinence by youth and adults. Whereas the majority of adult respondents to the survey said touching disqualifies a young person from the status of being abstinent, the young people producing the story had different definitions:

SANOVIA: My mom and I talk about sex all the time. So you'd think she, of all people, would know how I define abstinence.

MOM: *How WOULD you define abstinence? (Laughter) I don't know. What do YOU think?*

SANOVIA: *Mom, answer it, how do you think? Mama, just say it.*

MOM: *I don't know!*

SANOVIA: Well here's the deal. I believe you can do everything leading up to sexual intercourse, including oral sex, and still be abstinent. Most of my girlfriends in high school seem to look at abstinence the same way I do. But not everybody. Ask seventeen-year-old Krystle Martin how far you can go, and still be abstinent. . . .

KRYSTLE: *Definitely kissing. Because that's still pretty innocent. And probably to touch one another, but that probably would be where it stops.*

SANOVIA: A lot of adults disagree. Can you believe that 63 percent of them say if you touch each other, you're NOT abstinent? And talk about old school—40 percent say passionate kissing is off limits, too. Even Krystle's definition isn't uptight enough for her mom.

KRYSTLE: *Well . . . she's not really like hip to a lot of things, or updated on a lot of things. Maybe she would think being abstinent is like being completely separate from a boy—no contact whatsoever.*

As evident in this excerpt from the finished script, Sanovia Jackson's frame for the abstinence story helped dictate whom she interviewed, how she handled the national research data, and what stories she *didn't* tell, despite the temptation to include every interesting tangent related to teen sexuality that came up in the editorial meeting. Framing the story and collaboratively looking for an angle is usually the first step in creating a radio feature, but this process recurs and extends through every phase of production. As with any creative undertaking, very often young people's initial plans for a story's main focus shift midcourse, when they find or lose a key character, fail to uncover sufficient evidence for a trend they wanted to report, or face an editor who sends them back into the field when a script misses an important perspective or scene.

Through all of these iterations within a single story's development, young reporters collaborate with adults in a process we call *collegial pedagogy*. In collegial pedagogy, emerging and established producers jointly create original work for public release, engaging a process that has significant potential to deepen the learning experience for both parties and to enrich the media product distributed to the world. That said, collegial pedagogy also raises serious challenges for young people and adults. It entails collaboration across differences in power as it manifests through age, position, and experience, and sometimes race, class, and gender. Relentless deadlines and mutual creative investment intensify the undertaking for all involved. While these factors bring young people and adults together in a shared undertaking, they never cancel out, nor should they obscure, the very real institutional, historical, and cultural forces through which power circulates in any collegial relationship and any pedagogical relationship, particularly those with high stakes attached.

The process of collegial pedagogy, as a form of youth-adult partnership, kicks in at Youth Radio at an intentional developmental moment, not right away. When incoming students first arrive at Youth Radio, they enroll in introductory classes centered on the production of a live weekly radio show, and their main instructors are all teens themselves. While adult staff members design curriculum, direct the training department, and oversee classes, the actual teachers are peers, many still in high school and all recent Youth Radio graduates. This core training provides a crucial foundation that ignites young people's interest, as well as providing them with basic skills. It is not until young people advance to professional internships in Youth Radio's various departments that they begin collaborating more intensively with adults. This is the phase of learning that takes center stage in this chapter. One key goal in collegial pedagogy is that, through intense youth-adult collaboration, young people develop the technical, creative, and intellectual capacities that enable them once again to step away from heavy adult involvement. They increasingly work independently to produce broadcast-ready stories for major national outlets while maturing into adult journalists partnering, from the other side of the dynamic, with students following in their footsteps.

In this chapter we develop the concept of collegial pedagogy as a crucial and largely overlooked dynamic for teaching and learning through joint media production. We situate this process against the backdrop of learning theory, identify the conditions that bring young people and adults into productive collaborative relationships, and explore collegial pedagogy's contributions and vulnerabilities as a way to organize teaching and learning. The structure of the chapter follows the production cycle itself, glimpsing a series of Youth Radio stories at key moments of framing, gathering tape, scripting, editing, broadcasting, and living in the aftermath of a story's release. We focus especially on six stories: Sanovia Jackson's feature on abstinence, Sophie Simon-Ortiz's report on military marriage benefits, Nzinga Moore's story about students who opt out of standardized tests, Simon Hadley's reflections on the status of free speech in high school in an era of war and controversial homeland security, Rachel Krantz's critique of the new college entrance exam, and Rafael Santiago Casal's poem about the commodification of youth culture.

THEORIZING THE PRODUCTION OF LEARNING

Collegiality implies a relationship in which two or more people jointly engage in a significant task for a shared purpose, with collective responsibility. Sometimes colleagues work separately but in parallel; at other times they share space, time, and tools and metaphorically conjoin their minds and imaginations. Pedagogy, the art, profession, or study of teaching, traditionally embodies teacher-focused education. We use the term to connote a process of teaching and learning beyond classroom methods and activities. In a project such as Sanovia Jackson's abstinence story, collegiality and pedagogy converged in ways that unsettle some basic assumptions about learning as typically theorized in school settings and academic subjects. Adult producers did not, in any obvious way, stand up and "transmit" information, although clearly their professional expertise as journalists and educators shaped Sanovia's process. Even singling out Sanovia as a "recipient" of learning fails to capture the reality here. In the editorial meeting, the adults were the ones who needed an education in youth culture terminology, and Sanovia's peers at that table, and later on the other side of her microphone, shared in a collaborative learning process that informed the story and eventually the public. Once Sanovia started scripting her story, she worked side by side at the computer with an adult producer to arrange and write around her interview clips. Encroaching deadlines and daunting broadcast standards intensified the sense of urgency around her project and added a projected audience: the ultimate evaluators, who carry varied perspectives that can never fully be known. In these ways, Sanovia's process violated the most traditional conceptions of teaching and learning, where the teacher holds and hands over knowledge, and the learner receives that information and then awaits a teacher's evaluation and grade.

Contemporary education theorists have, of course, developed more imaginative ways to conceptualize learning than those reducing human development to information transmission and acquisition. In particular, we are indebted to three approaches that reimagine learning as a product of community practice, critical pedagogy, and positive youth development.

First, Youth Radio students, interns, and instructors can be seen as participants in a "community of practice" (Chaiklin & Lave, 1996; Lave & Wenger, 1991). Following this line of thinking, novices like Sanovia develop skills, understandings, and knowledge through joint activity with more experienced others. Young people begin participating at the edges of a given activity, and with time and practice they grow into a fuller role, needing less and less guidance from others. For Sanovia, this community of others included her peer educators in the introductory and advanced Youth Radio classes, where she learned the basic skills of commentary writing, news reporting, field recording, and digital mixing. That group distinguished itself from school-bound learning communities in that the teachers who coached novices like Sanovia through the production of a weekly live radio show were her own age, with uneven levels of expertise themselves. The community of practice forming around Sanovia's abstinence story also included her fellow newsroom interns, adult producers, and eventually radio editors from one of the nation's top news shows.

The notion of learning as something communities create, rather than something teachers transmit, goes a long way to help illuminate and explain how young people's minds and creative products develop through hands-on collaborative work in this kind of setting. Yet the framework of community participation fails to capture the mutuality of joint production in collegial pedagogy. Young people and adults at Youth Radio do not metaphorically co-construct a learning environment. They literally co-create a media product through an intricate co-compositional process shot through with opportunities and risks, as we explore here. Under collegial pedagogy, young people and adults actually make work together, revealing their investments and vulnerabilities to one another in concrete ways. Several factors are at stake at a place like Youth Radio *for both youth and adult participants,* including journalistic integrity, professional reputation, personal and political commitments, intellectual and creative development, and the intended and actual impact any given story has on its audience. The adult producer cannot create the story without young people to identify topics worth exploring, to find and interview characters, and to experiment with novel modes of expression and ways of using words, scene, and sound. At the same time, young people cannot create the story without adults to provide access to resources, equipment, broadcast outlets, and institutional recognition and to share the skills and habits developed through years of experience as media professionals. Young people offer a key substantive contribution that the adults cannot provide, a certain kind of access, understanding, experience, or analysis directly relevant to the project at hand. That is a major point of the youth media field after all: to contribute insights and challenging perspectives to a mainstream media that too often ignores the experience and intelligence of youth. Yet adults not only oversee or facilitate the learning experience surrounding a given media production experiment; they actually join in the production process itself.

Second, collegial pedagogy borrows from critical pedagogy, as both our thinking and Youth Radio's methodology draw on the work of Paolo Freire and other theorists who link teaching to transformative social action in the interest of oppressed communities (Darder, 2002; Darder, Baltodano, & Torres, 2003; Giroux, 1992; McLaren, 1989; hooks, 1994; Shor & Freire, 1986). Freire's legacy has pushed progressive educators to frame the student-teacher dialectic as a relationship of mutual humanization (a potential rarely achieved under the dominant "banking model" of education, which treats learning as a commodity exchange). Working in the spirit of critical pedagogy doesn't mean that the politics of any given story are obvious. Sanovia's abstinence story does not aim to topple the Bush administration or even Bush's sex education policy, nor does she address every social critique raised in the editorial meeting, in which young people discussed gender inequities and the exclusion of lesbian and gay youth from sex education. But Sanovia's story does turn scientific findings into social questions, while also unsettling standard media conventions that would, under normal circumstances, assign an adult to report on teen sexuality, quoting maybe one or two young people, if any.

Moreover the student-teacher dynamic that critical pedagogy is so concerned with misses something crucial: audience. When producing for significant audiences, the student-teacher dyad necessarily expands to include other young people and a massive pool of listeners with shifting positions, perspectives, and influences. Surely audiences can radicalize youth media pedagogy. When distributed widely, young people's projects have the potential to influence public debate and even social policy. But audiences can also squelch a young person's message, in particular when mass-media outlets, with their own complex institutional, political, and commercial interests, broker access to listeners. Young people and adults at Youth Radio are literally colleagues, both earning paychecks to work together and to generate products for real audiences, one as supervisor and one as intern, and this reality shapes their moment-to-moment interactions. Collegial pedagogy reorganizes conventional relationships between teachers and students, and yet it by no means eradicates the shifting distribution of authority characterizing any pedagogical arrangement, including one defined by youth-adult collaboration.

Third and finally, collegial pedagogy draws on a framework of positive youth development, which plays to young people's strengths and counters the tendency to criminalize and pathologize young people, especially those who are poor and black or brown, while demonizing their families and trashing their communities (Kelley, 1998). And yet in their zeal to honor young people's assets, positive youth development proponents can sometimes fail to account for the severity of conditions some young people face, including economic and political abandonment and racism (Ginwright & Cammarota, 2002). In some cases, the desire to celebrate young people's lives contorts into a process of fetishizing "youth voice." Soon adults worry that if they question or critique young people's projects in any way, they must be abusing their power (Ellsworth, 1992; Orner, 1992), pursuing a fantasy of "authentic" youth experience, which often translates into a sensationalized portrayal of racialized urban youth (Fleetwood, 2005). Youth Radio does not hand young people tape recorders and "give them voice" to tell their stories. In collegial pedagogy, young people share the production process with multiple collaborators, including peer educators, Youth Radio's adult producers, editors from outside outlets, and audiences. For some of Sanovia's interviews, she sat in a recording booth and shared interviewing responsibilities with an adult producer; only later did she take over and handle those conversations on her own. When it came time to script her story, she worked with a producer to review her logs and compose an outline for her first national feature. Young people at Youth Radio are the key players in every phase of production and distribution, but they never carry out the work alone. Sometimes the pressures that influence their editorial choices are considerable, causing them to question whether they are making choices at all. Formal and informal checks and balances, as well as bottom-line policies—young people always maintain final editorial say over their own projects—are necessary to ensure that young people drive both process and product, even if they work hand-in-hand with adults.

CONDITIONS FOR COLLEGIAL PEDAGOGY

Our research and participation in relationships marked by collegial pedagogy have revealed three conditions, or underlying principles, that support this mode of teaching and learning.[2] The first is an ongoing process of *collaborative framing*, which has already begun to emerge through Sanovia's abstinence story and which continues to evolve as young people and adults together confront obstacles, challenges, and unexpected curves in a story's developmental trajectory. The second condition is *youth-led inquiry*, requiring that young people guide the story's execution. They form and pose the questions, and although adults continue to play a supporting role, sometimes modeling inquiry before stepping back, the youth reporters drive the process of finding and figuring out what a story needs and what they need to understand to tell that story. Third is an orientation toward *public accountability*. Certainly much of the intensity surrounding youth media learning drives toward the moment of delivery, when producers digitally feed the media to the broadcast outlet and the piece airs. But throughout the production process, young people and adults continually ask themselves and one another, Why is this story important? What can it accomplish in the world, both positive and negative? In what ways can it live beyond the three or four minutes it takes to play and potentially exert meaningful social impact? Collegial pedagogy creates an expectation that the work advances from a single young person's gut reaction or raw testimonial into a mediated social intervention, with strategic thinking about the potential intended and unintended consequences of the story young people and adults collaboratively produce. In the end, however, young people ultimately are accountable to themselves, as storytellers, artists, thinkers, and community members. Even when their editorial choices are highly personal—not about pleasing an audience, but sometimes quite the opposite—under collegial pedagogy they need to find the language to express a rationale for those choices, in public, to convince collaborators that their judgments are right.

Collaborative Framing

The abstinence story provided a snapshot of the first condition for collegial pedagogy: collaborative framing. Finding a frame is an essential starting point that launches the cycle of preproduction, production, post-production, and distribution. In this case, adult journalists handed the broad topic of abstinence to the newsroom. More typically, young people wrack their brains for ideas. Sometimes, when they're lucky and paying attention, hot topics surface from encounters in their everyday lives.

That's what happened to nineteen-year-old reporter Sophie Simon-Ortiz, setting in motion a particularly challenging investigative report she produced in 2005. The war in Iraq was in its third year, and Sophie was interning in Youth Radio's newsroom. She had already contributed to the organization's ongoing series, *Reflections on Return*, stories from the youngest veterans coming home after Iraq deployments. One evening during that time, Sophie was at a party, where she started talking with a friend of a friend. Days later she sat down with her newsroom producers to share this young woman's story. The woman was married to a U.S. Marine she barely knew. He was her college roommate's little brother, living on an enlistee's salary, when he discovered an easy way to boost his monthly wages, plus get a waiver to live in an apartment off-base. The military awards higher salaries and added perks to married personnel, usually more than a thousand dollars per month. He needed a wife. So the Marine contacted his sister's roommate and proposed marriage—for money, not love. He would get the boost in pay, and she would get a cut of his added salary plus guaranteed world-class health benefits. Considering that more than 30 percent of young people in this woman's age group were uninsured, and she was about to age out of her parents' policy, the arrangement looked like a pretty good deal. Soon they headed to Vegas for a wedding at the Hollywood Wedding Chapel. Then the Marine got orders to ship out to Iraq.

> WIFE: *I asked him, "Are you afraid?" And he was like, "Well no, you can't be afraid, 'cause you get paralyzed." So, as we were getting into the war, it was like uhhhhh, I don't really feel like an outsider to this quite so much. Like those tax dollars, some of them go to me. I am part of the defense budget.*

Sophie arranged to interview the young wife. Before their scheduled meeting, Sophie worked with producers to come up with questions and prep equipment. Then she interviewed the wife in her bedroom, sitting on the mattress, flipping through the couple's wedding photo album. It would be hard (and possibly troubling) to imagine an adult reporter achieving this level of informality with a subject in an investigative piece on sham military marriages, but that's not how Sophie framed the story, at least not in the version that aired. Sophie's first steps after the interview were to log her tape, pick the best clips, and then arrange them into a single-voice narrative, which included this excerpt:

> *My fiancé kept assuring me that there were a lot of people in his training group doing the same thing, and that it was tacitly smiled on by their supervisors, and that even some of his supervisors had indicated to him that they had had a similar thing going on and then they got divorced when they met people they wanted to spend their lives with, so that pushed it over the edge for me. . . .*
> *I only just recently started to redeem this health care coverage and that is super awkward. Imagine going to the gynecologist and being like, "I need this birth control and I'd like a full battery of STD tests," and they're looking at*

you funny, like "What are you doing while your husband's out defending our country?" (pause). I love scams, you know, what can I say?

I (Lissa) was one of Sophie's producers on this story. The two of us went back and forth about closing the story with the line "I love scams, you know, what can I say?" It made a strong impact, based on responses from colleagues we brought into the studio to hear the rough cut. Clearly the wife took some delight in scamming a government she regarded with suspicion, and yet Sophie worried that if the piece ended there, the broader implications of the story might get lost. Some listeners might just dismiss this young woman as a jerk; others might cheer her personal politics but miss the deeper message.

Youth Radio's executive producer, Ellin O'Leary, and our national editor raised additional concerns. Sophie was interested in the health care angle of the story, the lengths to which young people have to go to obtain reasonable coverage. But with only one character, this version of the story didn't establish the scale of the phenomenon Sophie was describing. She needed to show that this marriage was not just an isolated young woman cheating the system for benefits. And so Sophie embarked on an intense period of research, reviewing precedent-setting legal cases and interviewing military and civilian attorneys, a sociologist specializing in military family life, other young military personnel, and public affairs officers from various military branches, all to establish that the case she had discovered was part of a larger social trend.

Then there was the matter of anonymity. Sophie needed to verify the wife's identity and story without revealing her name or that of the active duty Marine she'd married. Protecting a source's anonymity is a basic journalistic tenet, with particular significance in the case of young people, who are making judgments that might very well have unanticipated consequences far down the line. Sophie first had to find out the wife's last name—no small challenge, because the first name the character had given Sophie turned out to be a nickname, and Sophie hadn't asked for her last name (an oversight she's likely never to repeat!). Sophie was able to find one online full-name reference to a student with the girl's nickname that seemed to fit but that would never cut it as a bullet-proof identity check. Luckily, when Sophie called the university both she and the young wife had attended, she happened upon a fairly lax receptionist who confirmed enrollment of a student bearing the full name Sophie had found. The next step, which you'd think would be far more difficult, was actually easy. Sophie plugged the student's name into a database of Las Vegas marriage certificates, and moments later the record popped up on the screen, with husband and wife named in full.

"What if the consequences of this story are bad for kids?" Ellin pressed Sophie to consider. Youth Radio's news director, Nishat Kurwa, responded, "What we do is report on youth, and that's not always a rosy picture." "My priority is contextualizing it," Sophie said. "Otherwise, it's not worth putting my ass on the line, or hers [the military wife's]." What if Sophie's notes were subpoenaed? That might sound paranoid, but Ellin said to Sophie, "In a way, you're forging a path. What are the steps we need to take, even if the risks are remote?" Reflecting on the present state of media culture and why Youth Radio had not as yet faced a situation quite like this one, she noted, "It's a different time. There's a chilling effect." No one in the conversation was willing to let that effect freeze Youth Radio's ability to produce investigative stories, especially one that so clearly embodied the organization's commitment to promote youth-driven enterprise reporting. Sophie had discovered a little-known phenomenon and carried out the original research to compose a compelling account. But the frame needed to be just right. In the end, "I love a scam" appeared nowhere in the final piece, which ended instead like this:

WIFE: *I asked him, "Are you afraid?" And he was like, "Well no, you can't be afraid 'cause you get paralyzed. So, as we were getting into the war, it was like uhhhhh, I don't really feel like an outsider to this quite so much. Like those tax dollars, some of them go to me. I am part of the defense budget.*

SOPHIE: And not a small part. The military is spending 36 billion dollars per year on its health care system for military personnel and their families. That's double what it spent in 2001. And while there's no hard data on how many of these couples are families in name only, most everyone we spoke with said the trend was rising.

KEVIN: *It exists and it exists moreso than most people would believe.*

SOPHIE: That's Kevin Walters, Army specialist from the 82nd Airborne, who served in Afghanistan and Iraq. He says he wouldn't get married for convenience himself, but he understands why others do it in these trying times. . . .

KEVIN: *And if you're doing something to help yourself and help another, then it's really not such a bad thing. It's one of the only things the military can't control. I'm sure they wish they could.*

PAO RAINES: *Using this illusion of marriage as a means to an end is really inexcusable.*

SOPHIE: Lieutenant Kyle Raines is with Navy Public Affairs. He says just last year, some sailors stationed in San Diego were accused of marriage fraud. And after a court martial proceeding, one was demoted and discharged from the Navy. But conviction was only possible because this particular case involved falsified documents. Without that, says Lt. Raines, the military has few weapons.

PAO RAINES: *If you have a legally binding marriage, it's just that.*

SOPHIE: So the wife I talked to isn't worried about any major consequences. But she has faced some awkward moments, redeeming health care benefits with her husband far away.

WIFE: *Imagine going to the gynecologist and you're like "I have my husband's medical insurance and I need this birth control" and they're kinda looking at you funny (laughs) like "What are you doing while your husband is off defending our country?"*

SOPHIE: She says she didn't expect these kinds of encounters . . . or that marrying a soldier for healthcare . . . would somehow bring her closer to the War in Iraq.

The production process behind Sophie Simon-Ortiz's *Military Marriage Benefits* story reveals some important dimensions of collegial pedagogy as it manifests through collaborative framing. When young people collaboratively frame topics for themselves, they unlearn familiar commonsense truths and open up multiple points of view. Cross-cultural communication skills are not only invoked in theory but are applied in a range of settings, from on-the-street interviewing to newsroom and community meetings to pitching to outside editors. At Youth Radio young people learn to seek questions behind answers. Their comfort zones are challenged through dialogue with others, whose basic assumptions and lived experiences are, in some ways, different from their own.

Youth-Led Inquiry

The second key condition that supports and fuels collegial pedagogy is youth-led inquiry. In moving through the stages of her story, from a single interview to an investigative feature, Sophie worked with adult professionals in various capacities, all of whom made serious, high-stakes investments in the form and outcome of her reporting. She conferred and sometimes directly collaborated with her immediate producers, senior editors at national media outlets, and even her interviewees, whose trust, honesty, and candor she needed to tap in order to get strong tape. Framing was a continual process, as Sophie collaborated with her production team to contextualize this story within larger social issues, rather than allow it to center on one individual's personal choices. That took a tremendous amount of reporting legwork. Her producers helped identify experts and arrange interview logistics and sometimes asked a few follow-up questions in the studio, but Sophie conducted every interview. She was the one who uncovered the press release about unprecedented spending on military health care, flagging it as a key statistic for the story as well as a news peg that might help make the case for the story's relevance when we pitched it to outlets. It's important to note that Sophie was nineteen at the time. She had interned at Youth Radio since the summer before her sophomore year, and she had gone through a journalistic boot camp of sorts as a member of the Youth Radio team covering the Democratic National Convention. She was very skilled, and this training enabled her to lead the reporting process to the full extent, beginning with her instinct to listen for stories everywhere and all the time. Many young reporters working on their first national stories require more hands-on support and involvement from adult producers to face the moment-to-moment challenges of research, interviews, and scripting. Yet even in those cases, under collegial pedagogy young people drive the inquiry process, and their own learning, as they produce stories for significant audiences.

By guiding inquiries like this one, young people learn to contextualize their own experiences within broader considerations, having to ask themselves again and again, Where does this idea fit? What else do I need to learn? What can I use? Even in the midst of an interview, their challenge is simultaneously to solicit information and compose the larger narrative inside their heads, always anticipating how the voices and scenes they include will operate within the finished piece. They draw on immediate resources—for example, perspectives from their friends or observations from their schools—and link to wider debates that circulate around them, ultimately talking back to the very policies that most directly affect their lives and their generation.

In Sophie's case, every interview except her taped conversation with the wife took place in Youth Radio's studio, enabling her producers to listen in and provide feedback and follow-up questions as necessary. When young people carry out interviews in the field, however, very often they are on their own, and yet collegial pedagogy continues, as evident in another national story. This story reveals what can happen when young people's capacity to lead an inquiry comes into question, when they encounter adults who need some convincing.

In 2001 the newsroom was investigating the effects of standardized tests on students and teachers in public schools around the country. There was a great deal of interest across the United States in students who were opting out of state standardized testing. Much of the public focus centered on young people from privileged school districts whose parents claimed that testing was forcing teachers to relinquish valuable class time, sacrifice meaningful projects, and "dumb down" the curriculum in order to teach to the test. Parents in those districts were organizing to find ways for their children to opt out of the tests.

Meanwhile community groups not drawing nearly as much attention were trying to expose test-related injustices and inform students in underresourced public schools about their right to refuse to take certain tests. One Youth Radio reporter, Nzinga Moore, took on the story of finding out what happens when students in high schools serving primarily poor and working-class families opt out of state tests. The reporter knew she would need to talk to students who took the test as well as those who opted out. She arranged to gather classroom scene tape at a city public school on test day and to talk with teachers, administrators, and a university-based national expert on measurement and school accountability.

Before Nzinga headed to the school campus for her interviews, we did some research on legal protections and guidelines for reporters conducting interviews on school campuses. We learned that for news reports, a journalist was legally free to enter a school campus and record interviews with minor students if they knew and appreciated that they were talking to a journalist and that their comments could be broadcast or published, and so long as the interview did not disrupt the educational process.[3] We reviewed these guidelines carefully with Nzinga, discussed the various gray areas she needed to think about as she prepared for the interview, and considered both the ethics and the effectiveness of her approach. For example, although Youth Radio is committed to producing hard-hitting education stories, the organization depends on goodwill from school teachers and leaders as key decision makers in recruitment sites, fellow educators, and story sources; it was critical to protect Youth Radio's reputation of journalistic integrity in school circles.

Nzinga was in the school library, recording her interview with a student who had obtained a waiver to opt out of the test, when the school principal entered the scene.[4]

PRINCIPAL: Who are you?

NZINGA: I'm Nzinga Moore with Youth Radio. . . .

PRINCIPAL: Are you authorized to be here?

NZINGA: Yeah.

PRINCIPAL: By whom? . . .

NZINGA: It's not against the law or anything. I talked to [name] and asked them. I set this up with [student's name].

PRINCIPAL: You set it up with [student's name]?

NZINGA: She's not taking the test. I already talked to [name], a security guard just checked to make sure I was here—

PRINCIPAL: But I'm the principal. The thing is, I want to know who you authorized this through.

Here Nzinga led an inquiry process that got her into some trouble with a daunting figure: the woman running the school where she was gathering tape. She abruptly had to shift gears, from interviewing the student to being interviewed by the principal, and yet she took steps to hold her ground throughout the questioning. The principal's first concern in this exchange was, quite understandably, a question of authorization. As the leader responsible for her students' safety and well-being on the school campus, she wanted to know who had allowed Nzinga to initiate and record the conversation, regardless of its content. Nzinga's initial response, "It's not against the law or anything," asserted her legal rights as a journalist, but she immediately then named specific others known to the principal—someone at the front office, the student, the security guard—making herself *not alone* in determining that the interview was appropriate and allowed to take place. She began to situate herself, in other words, among the principal's known colleagues, as a way to bolster the legitimacy of her presence. But it did not suffice to name individuals. The principal's question suggested not just a person but a process of authorization, which she went on to elaborate.

NZINGA: Who I authorized this through?

PRINCIPAL: Yeah, who did you ask for permission to come here?

NZINGA: Oh, it's a public school. I didn't think that I needed—

PRINCIPAL: You do, you need my permission.

NZINGA: I asked my editors and everything, and they said by law—

PRINCIPAL: Who's your editors?

NZINGA: Lissa Soep and Rebecca Martin. We can go talk to them right now—

PRINCIPAL: Well we can't, because I'm in the middle of doing something else. But you have to understand that everything has to come through me, okay, with my permission, and so I'm going to stop this right now until we go through the right process.

NZINGA: And what's that?

PRINCIPAL: Well, you could contact our public information office, that's what I have all reporters do, and if they authorize you to come on here, they'll call me and say it's okay, and then we'll make it work.

Nzinga contextualized her work in two ways: locating the interview in "a public school," which carried specific implications for access, and then situating her inquiry within a journalistic framework, naming her editors, who had informed her of her rights. The principal spelled out what she deemed the proper bureaucratic process for school site interviews. Striking in this move on the principal's part was her affirmation of Nzinga's status: "That's what I have all reporters do." She used Nzinga's own logic to insist on a certain protocol. It seems worth noting here that the principal had an opportunity at this point to belittle Nzinga's status by pointing to her age.[5] Instead, the principal addressed Nzinga as a fellow professional trying to do her job. At the same time, however, she continued to dispute Nzinga's methods.

NZINGA: Okay, because it was my understanding that it's okay for me to come here, because we're a youth program, and we're just trying to talk to young people and see—

PRINCIPAL: But all the young people are taking the test. And [student's name] I know has a waiver so she's not taking the test, but so you're only getting [student's name]'s side. So I want you to call—

Here was the first moment when the principal indicated her awareness of the content of the interview. But first, Nzinga shifted her frame a bit, from a focus on journalistic professionalism to her participation in a youth program: "We're just trying to talk to young people." In making this move, Nzinga described a scenario to which an educator might have a hard time objecting. (Who can find fault in kids just talking to other kids—about something substantive, no less?) The principal, however, voiced some concerns, raising questions about the reporter's objectivity; she described Nzinga's interviewee as an exception, one side of the story.

NZINGA: Well, what happened is, we're getting both sides of the story, but this is the side we also need. We talked to an analyst from Stanford University and he gave us a very objective point of view about the testing and about taking the test.

PRINCIPAL: Do you understand that you didn't go through the proper channels to be here?

NZINGA: I'm not sure what the proper channels are, because it was my understanding that we could just come here and do the interview and just talk to students, but it's okay, I'll—Can I have your card?

PRINCIPAL: I don't have a card. I can give you my name and you have the school phone number (the principal says her name here). . . . Now the thing is, you're just here to interview [student's name]?

NZINGA: Yes, that's all—

PRINCIPAL: You can finish your interview with [student's name]. And then the next time you want to come on—because I'm interested in youth, in Youth Radio—I want you to follow procedures.

NZINGA: Okay.

PRINCIPAL: Okay? Thank you.

In this final stretch of talk, Nzinga aligned herself with another source of authority. She was not talking only to other young people, after all. We were consulting experts from prestigious universities and abiding by the same journalistic ideals of even-handed storytelling the principal had invoked. Nzinga's response here seemed a turning point in the conversation. The principal shifted gears to focus on what Nzinga understood, rather than what she was allowed to do. Requesting someone's business card is one of the most recognizable professional, even collegial gestures, as well as a way to foreground the principal's specific role in potentially shutting down the interview and leaving open the possibility of further contact. In the end, after reinforcing the limits of what she was approving, the principal allowed the interview to continue, so long as Nzinga understood that next time she would need to "follow procedures."

This interaction between Nzinga and the school principal shows a different facet of collegial pedagogy, wherein the young reporter needs to actively establish her legitimacy as the one leading the inquiry. That said, it's impossible to know whether this principal would have treated an adult reporter any differently had she encountered that person interviewing a student on school grounds. Youth Radio producers have long suspected that our reporters' youthfulness sometimes actually helps them get good tape in tightly controlled places because officials might underestimate the young person's ability to reach a significant audience. It's a striking paradox. Teens whose bodies, voices, and fashion choices match stereotypes of youthful offenders incite fear when adults cross paths with them on the street or when their stereos thump bass lines from passing cars. When these same young people enter social institutions as reporters, carrying microphones and asking questions, adults sometimes underestimate their power. Maybe they aren't afraid enough of the potential impact of a young person's story—an odd circumstance that can actually work to young people's advantage when they're looking for candor, disclosure, and unguarded truth.

In any case, whenever young people leave the confines of Youth Radio's newsroom, their learning enters a different, often more challenging phase.

Had one of Nzinga's producers accompanied her to the school, the encounter with the principal would no doubt have been quite different. Instead Nzinga had to navigate this tricky interaction entirely on her own. She had to mobilize what she had learned inside Youth Radio (and elsewhere) to fight for her story and for the clearance to continue her inquiry.

Public Accountability

Nzinga's story ended up airing on National Public Radio. Reaching millions of listeners in this way constituted a serious accomplishment, for her and for the organization. Nonetheless, broadcast is not the end-all and be-all for Youth Radio stories; it simply ushers these cultural products into a new phase, that of public circulation. Even pieces that do not go out nationally air somewhere: on a website, on iTunes radio, or on one of our local outlets. Stories don't meet their full audiences until the very end of the production cycle, after the topics have been framed, tape gathered, scripts written and edited, and audio mixed. And yet a sense of audience accountability hovers over every stage. This imaginary audience presence raises the stakes associated with every choice young people make, forcing them to think beyond the studio, and even beyond the broadcast, to consider what their work will do once it enters the world. Under collegial pedagogy, young people work with adults to imagine a life for their work outside themselves and their own personal self-interests, holding themselves and one another accountable to the immediate and longer-term impact of their joint productions.

Young people are accountable to various publics, including audiences, adult mentors, and family members and friends whose opinions matter to them. Very often young people work one-on-one with adult producers to review story outlines, scripts, and audio mixes. Discussion might center on something as particular as the timing of a breath or the length of a pause between clips, or as large scale as whether the story makes any sense or carries any emotion or contains anything we haven't already heard a million times before. Occasionally editing takes place in a public forum, with multiple participants weighing in, not always harmoniously, on a story in development.

In 2003 a Youth Radio graduate came by the studio to tell the newsroom about a scandal that had recently taken place at a local high school. Two students, both first-generation Southeast Asian immigrants, had been discussing President George W. Bush in class, and they allegedly made some comments they intended as jokes, but that their teacher perceived as threats. According to reports, one of the students, using a common slang term for someone who is confused or wrongheaded, said, "Bush is whack!" But the teacher reportedly thought she heard "Bush should be whacked," in other words, killed. According to the young man telling us the story, the teacher called the Secret Service, whose agents arrived at the school within hours to interrogate the two teenagers involved, without legal counsel present or parental notification. The young man also reported that the students were terrified and intimidated, and there were even indications that the Secret Service agents threatened to deport their parents if the students did not cooperate.

One intern in the newsroom, a high school student named Simon Hadley, was infuriated by this story, which seemed especially troubling in light of post-9/11 immigration sweeps. After reviewing local newspaper coverage (which was strikingly scant, given the nature of the events), Simon decided that he wanted to write and broadcast a letter to the teacher who had turned in her students to federal agents. A draft of that letter is excerpted here, in which he calls the two students involved by the pseudonyms John and Billy.

> Dear [teacher's name],
> How could you report two sophomores in your class, little John and Billy, to the U.S. Secret Service Agency for talking mess about Bush? Just in case you don't know how they feel, well let me tell you how little John and Billy feel. The April 23 interviews with federal agents left them scared and upset. And I'm pretty upset, too. . . .
> What I want to know is, how do you report students for saying something in a discussion you started off? I think the U.S. Secret Service Agents . . . need to investigate you. Cause judging by your actions, something is really wrong with you. I mean, if I was to throw a soda can on the floor, what are you going to do? Are you going to call the U.S. Secret Service Agents on me? I don't think so.
> You are supposed to be a teacher. Students are supposed to feel free to say whatever they want to say around you. And you have betrayed that trust. You should not be able to have a class at all. And if any of

those students were smart, they would hurry up and get out of your class immediately. So they won't get reported to the U.S. Secret Service and threatened to have their families sent back to where they came from (like what happened to Johnny and Billy). . . .

What I want to know is, how is it that when you call the U.S. Secret Service because you say some teenage boys in your class made a threat to the president, those officers can rush on down there right away? But when someone calls the police cause Helen's husband is beating her and her children, by the time the police get to the scene of the crime, Helen and her kids are all bruised up and healed?

Simon drafted his letter independently and then worked with an adult producer to refine the writing and his central arguments, with the idea that the letter could be featured on Youth Radio's website and possibly aired on our local morning radio show. The first wave of this editorial process focused on basic grammatical and compositional considerations, as well as more conceptual issues. For example, a frequent point of discussion at Youth Radio is how audiences tend to react when they hear the voice of an angry teenager on the air. Very often, young people generate their best material when they take on topics they feel passionate about. That said, we have found that straight-up angry commentaries sometimes backfire. Like it or not, adult listeners are good at tuning out what they hear as a teenager's rant, and they may be quick to empathize with other adults they see as being attacked.

This wasn't the only issue Youth Radio's deputy director, Beverly Mire, raised when she reviewed Simon's piece. Did we know enough about the context of the event itself, the facts of the case, the teacher's point of view, or the students involved to draw the kinds of conclusions Simon put forth in his letter? What would be the impact of printing or airing a letter like this on those directly involved in the scandal, on Youth Radio's reputation, on Simon's own personal, political, and intellectual development? We discussed these questions in an editorial meeting, which itself grew quite heated. Gerald Ward II, a young man in his early twenties who led Youth Radio's training program at the time, was a graduate of both Youth Radio and the school district in question. "When I first heard [what happened at the school], I was really mad," he said. But he wasn't sure that Simon's mode of expressing that anger was the most effective tactic. "You want people to say, 'I'm feeling this point,'" Gerald said, and sometimes a full-on attack on a single individual is not the best way to bring about that kind of response from listeners. Another student thought the personal insults in the letter were distracting; she wanted something "more mature than just going off," especially as Simon hadn't spoken directly to anyone involved. Instead of stopping with a single attack piece, she said, why not produce a half-hour show dedicated to the larger issue of civil liberties in high school, with Simon's letter being one part of that story? Simon agreed to talk with some young people who had actually witnessed the event and to try to get a fuller sense of what the teacher was thinking when she made that phone call to the Secret Service. It turns out, as reported in the show Youth Radio eventually produced, that the teacher had not intended to name her students or even her school, but only to inquire about her legal obligation to report a case like this. Simon worked with Senior Producer Rebecca Martin to turn his letter into a story that integrated music, clips from interviews with students who had actually witnessed the Secret Service agents' arrival, and some passages from his original commentary.

SIMON: If you were a teacher, how could you report two of your students for talking mess about President Bush? It's just amazing that the Secret Service decided to come to [the high school] and start some drama right before the end of the school year. Everybody and their momma is talking about it, including me. The bad news is the principal, the teacher, and even the students interrogated by the agents are not giving interviews. But the good news is [the school] has a lot of students, so it wasn't hard to find three young people who had something to say.

(Music Bridge: "I'm talking 'bout freedom . . . ")

DANIEL: Well, my name is Daniel Jackson, I go to [the high school], and I'm seventeen years of age. I didn't know the students personally, but yeah, I was present when it took place.

SIMON: You seen it?

DANIEL: Yeah.

SIMON: Did you see what the Secret Service people looked like?

DANIEL: Like one dude was a little hefty and had on his suit, his little ear piece, and all that good stuff. Sunglasses in his little pocket. Other dude was kinda tall, slim, your average Joe.

SIMON: *As a student personally, what do you think about [teacher's name]?*

DANIEL: *As a teacher, she's a pretty good teacher, I don't really talk to her, besides getting the assignments and doing the homework, I don't really pay attention to her, have conversations. But besides that, she's a real cool person, I think, so that's why I thought it strange.*

SIMON: *Really?*

DANIEL: *Yes.*

SIMON: *You couldn't see her, basically, doing what she did?*

DANIEL: *No, she's real down-to-earth. She's not lost her mind. You know . . .*

SIMON: But is she really crazy? Everybody has their own opinion on the subject. I always thought in the real world, what's said in the classroom stayed in the classroom. Even when students don't like their teachers—I know I didn't like all of mine—they still want teachers to understand and protect them.

The development of Simon's story reveals the third feature of collegial pedagogy: public accountability. In the immediate aftermath of hearing about the scandal surrounding this teacher's actions, Simon responded with an unrestrained piece of writing. As evident in the final paragraph of his original letter to the teacher, this was an opportunity for Simon to make connections between the event itself and larger social forces, for example, those that keep police out of poor communities when protection is really needed and yet bring law enforcement into hostile confrontations with poor teenagers under questionable circumstances.

That would have been enough, had Simon been accountable only to himself. But the editorial process held him accountable to a larger public. Framing a deliberate public intervention requires multiple forms of data and the support of a learning environment within which a young person uses available resources—technologies, modes of expression, and expertise from peers and mentors—to turn an initial response to a given situation into an effort to influence and unsettle that state of affairs. In the context of collegial pedagogy, Simon joined with peers and adults to subject his own reaction to further interrogation, asking himself what he was trying to say, how his story could have an impact on the circumstances he described, and what possible responses his work might engender, including those he had never intended. Slowing down, doing the research, and being proactive instead of reactive draw out a more

complex topic and more interesting story. One-dimensional representations of reality are quick and relatively easy to put together. What is
immediate is what is apparent; thus we ask young people, and ourselves,
for a more complex version of reality, one that presents multiple perspectives that challenge the obvious with evidence-based arguments and
rigorous reporting.

Simon, by the way, wasn't thrilled with this editorial process. He
was fond of his inflammatory letter to the teacher and didn't love the
idea that his personal opinion wasn't enough and that he would need
to solicit interviews from other young people directly involved in the
incident at the school. Interviews took him outside his comfort zone.
Before working on this story, Simon had created a humor column, *Simon
Says,* for Youth Radio's website, where he provided irreverent and often
controversial responses to teens' earnest questions, and he had also written some personal commentaries, always delivered with his trademark
cheekiness. This story was the first time he was asked to bring other
characters into his narrative and to modulate his tone to match the
topic. As any writer knows, submitting to an editorial process is rarely
frustration-free, and yet the ability to solicit and apply feedback is a key
lesson young people need exposure to if they are to participate fully in
meaningful creative tasks and develop multiliteracies through a range
of expressive modes.

Equally important as learning to accept criticism is knowing how and
under what conditions to push back. In 2005 the College Board released a
new version of the Scholastic Aptitude Test (SAT) that included an essay
section in addition to the usual pages and pages of multiple-choice questions. High school senior Rachel Krantz had just taken the new SAT, and
she came into Youth Radio to write a commentary about it. In her story
she argued that the new writing portion further privileged people like
herself, who had attended elite schools. An excerpt from my field notes
at the time describe what happened after I (Lissa) read Rachel's draft.

> What was missing in the piece, I thought, was any first-person, insider
> sense of what the test was actually like, and I told Rachel that. I said,
> Look, there's something you have here that no adult has—you actually
> just took the test. But I have no sense of that here. She cut me off mid-
> sentence and said, All that stuff will make it too long. She went on: I

know you guys, for a lot of our stories, the point is to be the cute young person who shares their experience. But this is a piece where I want to just make a point. Adults do that all the time in the media, so this is a case where that's what I want to do. I asked, But is that good radio? Is that what you want to listen to? Adults going off on their opinion or analysis with no narrative? . . . That said, her remark about us wanting "cute" kids to tell their stories stung. . . .

We ended up with RK adding just a few very short lines with specific details about the test (the question posed in her essay section, and what she meant by "grammatical," using a concrete example, in her description of the new writing section). She said it seemed to her the writing section was really a way for test makers to judge whether test takers could "correct" ebonics "mistakes."

Months after this commentary aired on a local outlet, I asked Rachel what she remembered about it and whether she might want to elaborate on her thoughts about the editorial process. Rachel acknowledged that for this topic, adding some narrative to her analysis of the SAT made the piece more interesting for the listener, and that the conversation sharpened her argument. But more generally, she said, "I am sensitive to the fact that it's a little condescending to ask me to make it a personal story, as if I don't have a political perspective that's not necessarily based in experience. . . . A part of me appreciates that you're trying to push me to see how the political is personal because it is, but I am sensitive . . . to the desire to compartmentalize. I don't think you do that, but you know what the stations want. It's kind of safe to keep youth in this voice."

Youth media producers like to think that by introducing young people's voices to mainstream coverage we are acting boldly. Rachel says sometimes "keeping youth in this voice" actually plays it safe, not going far enough to challenge the limits imposed on young people's participation in public debates. It's a tricky balance that adults at Youth Radio talk about all the time—how to help students shape stories for broadcast without compromising their vision—and the ground here is shifting as more and more outlets for youth-produced content emerge, creating new opportunities and challenges for youth-adult collaboration.

We were reminded of these challenges when Youth Radio asked seventeen-year-old poet Rafael Santiago Casal whether he'd consider contributing one of his poems to a series on youth, money, and marketing that the newsroom was producing for a national show. Today Rafael is the creative director of First Wave, the hip-hop theater-based performing arts program at the University of Wisconsin, Madison. At the time he worked with a literary arts program called Youth Speaks, a leading nonprofit presenter of spoken-word performance, education, and youth development. Rafael delivered this particular poem in a head-spinning rush of words and images, shot through with sexual metaphors and profanities. In the poem, he railed against the style industry, which he said uses child labor to commodify and sell youth culture back to kids at a price they cannot afford. His words also took aim at conformists who fall prey to the homogenizing effect of mass consumption. Rafael started with a mocking reference to "the man with fashion sense," who had the bright idea to tell kids what they need, creating "a million martyrs" identically dressed in sagged jeans, major league team jerseys, silver chains, and two-hundred-dollar shoes. Later in the piece, Rafael moved from "the man" as the target of his condemnation to a corporation he gendered as a "damn fine" female who offers sex with just this catch: "you got to brand it and lavish and ravage your own / image after we ho ya and handle your own every dollar / until everyone marches to the same beat." He linked these media manipulations to a kind of "mental incarceration" not unrelated to the forces that "ended in the unfortunate / substantial transformation of our pentagon into a quadrilateral." Rafael concluded with an image of his own body controlled by the manipulations he described, an ironic message given the penetrating critique he had just produced:

> From BET to MTV we got PYTs marketing sex appeal the
> all mighty breast appeal[6]
> It sells, yes but reflects poorly on the women ya feel
> Got us thinking woman? Oh you mean woo-man here to woo
> the man from the man to the man just to do the man lie
> down dick ride and screw the man please she fuckin
> rules the man this is just the plan they planted
> embedded empowering them through the image in women
> and men til corporate America owns my dick, they tell
> it where to be what to do and how high to go so
> frequently that i don't own it anymore I feel lied to

We move to their currents like a tide pool
A million martyrs marching to the same beat
What an eye full

Youth Radio producers were struck by the power of the poet's message and the intricacy and lyricism of his imagery. We also had to consider the broadcast standards we would face in pitching the poem to our outlets' editors, who were used to dealing with news reporting and business-related features and commentaries, not poetry. Through email we shared our feedback with Rafael. He would need to consider shortening the poem to fit standard slots. Federal Communications Commission guidelines prohibit cursing and graphic sexuality. And we suggested that radio listeners on their afternoon commute might find the subtlety of some passages hard to follow.

In response to this emailed critique and suggestions for revision, Rafael basically declined to participate. Perhaps we had missed the message of the poem, he said, which was about media manipulation of a personal truth. Was that not what we were asking him to do by requesting significant edits? The poet's response set off an exchange of subsequent emails and face-to-face conversations, during which we figured out a way to work with his piece, given our editorial considerations and his insistence on the integrity of the message. The version of the poem Rafael recorded for Youth Radio aired, largely unchanged, on a local weekly public affairs show, not the national one. Only the profanities, which would have disqualified the poem from broadcast on any network, were eliminated from the artist's original. This does not, of course, mean that young people's raw voices should be left as is, without the benefit of thoughtful response from peers and adults, only that these kinds of decisions need to be made on a case-by-case basis and that even a final outcome with few changes to the finished work can sometimes mask a more complex process of youth-adult collaboration.

This episode underscores the complex relationships among young people, adults, youth-serving institutions, and public cultures that shape collegial pedagogy. What drew our interest was the content of Rafael's poem, from a vantage point of a listener and as a curator of youth content. But in his response to our critique, Rafael brought us inside his message, forcing us to reflect on our editorial methods. The process pulls adults inside the learning experience. Young people and adults jointly and reciprocally—not always painlessly—learn from and assess one another, always with an eye to a future for the unfolding work, its public release.

CONCLUSION

Sanovia's exploration of abstinence, Sophie's report on military marriages, Nzinga's inquiry into standardized testing, Simon's reflections on free speech in classrooms, Rachel's response to the new SAT, Rafael's poem about youth culture industries—all of these narratives circle around a familiar theme: youth voice. Although media producers and theorists tend to romanticize youth voice as individual, authentic, and pure expression (see Fleetwood, 2005, for critique), we draw attention instead to the complex ways young people and adults collaboratively frame projects. Even through youth-led inquiry, adults continue to play important, if supporting, roles. Young people hold themselves accountable to various publics as they decide what they want to say and how they want to say it. In this sense they strategically modulate their voices, joining their own experiences and analyses with a chorus, not always harmonious, of others. The collection of stories described here further complicates youth voice as raw, autobiographical testimonial by virtue of the range of genres and styles evident in this collection of Youth Radio narratives. These stories contain elements of investigative reporting, policy analysis, personal expression, commentary, and poetry. The boundaries surrounding these forms blur, as young people intentionally violate many of the standard compartments into which we often place, and sometimes force, media stories. It comes as no surprise that these experiments give rise to especially intense youth-adult collaborations, as emerging and experienced producers explore new terrain. Collegial pedagogy can generate powerful products through challenging learning processes. In identifying roles for themselves in young people's creative pursuits, adults face the challenge of finding ways to support young people's varied voices rather than "keep them in this voice"—in other words, the voice adults are most ready to hear. Only one of the young media producers featured in this chapter was a poet, but all strove to achieve in their narratives what Audre Lorde (1984) describes as poetry's capacity for illumination, a way to "give name to those ideas which are—until the poem—nameless and formless, about to be birthed, but already felt."

THREE Point of Voice

Fuck the News. That was the original title Anyi Howell chose for his commentary condemning the shield law, a provision that protects news gatherers from having to reveal confidential sources or turn over notes and raw tape. It wasn't the *New York Times* reporter Judith Miller's case that got Anyi interested in the shield law, but Miller's story did draw national attention to this otherwise obscure journalistic privilege. While Anyi was working on his story, Miller was locked up for refusing to name her source that broke a CIA operative's cover. The case blew up because the CIA agent in question was married to a former diplomat, who questioned the claim that Saddam Hussein possessed weapons of mass destruction. There were suspicions that Miller's source was an executive branch insider who leaked the CIA agent's identity to retaliate for her husband's actions. The U.S. government had leveraged the erroneous WMD intelligence as the single most important "slam dunk" rationale for the war in Iraq.

Anyi's ire about the shield law had nothing to do with Judith Miller or the war in Iraq. At least initially. He smacked up against that law on his way to work. Early one morning in the spring of 2005, he was walking with a Youth Radio colleague, Elmer Clark, through a Bay Area subway station en route to a staff retreat. Some local TV producers were on the scene recording interviews with commuters about a string of robberies at the train stations, and while taping, the cameraman happened to capture a confrontation between the police and two riders, both young black men. Anyi wanted to use that footage in a story he was producing about racial profiling. Invoking the shield law, the television station refused to hand it over. Anyi felt especially entitled to that footage, and angry about the station's decision to withhold it, because the person on the other side of the police pistol at the station that morning was Anyi himself.

> ANYI: *He was trying to put me in handcuffs. I'm like, "Leave me alone." "When I tell you to do something, you do it." He went through all my pockets, basically telling me he didn't give a fuck about my rights. I was telling him, "This is not how you approach a citizen," and I kept asking him, "What's the meaning of all this?"*

Even with handcuffs snapping around his wrists, Anyi had the presence of mind to pose a question about youth citizenship. Moments later, he says, he turned to the television cameras that happened to be rolling at the time and insisted, "I'm a media member. I want a copy of this tape!" and then he stated his Youth Radio email address and affiliation. He never received the tape, but the gesture was significant nevertheless, and not only because Anyi's journalistic credentials tangibly shifted the dynamic around his detention. Beyond that practical effect, adding media to the citizenship question aptly reflects today's reality. Young people's uneven access to meaningful roles as media producers has everything to do with their engagement as full citizens and agents of social change.

In chapter 2 we argued that literacy entails the material and imaginative resources to *claim and exercise* the right to use media to promote justice, variously defined. In this chapter we use Anyi's experience at the subway station that morning, and a series of related media projects, to describe what it means, and what it takes, for young people to develop a "point of voice" through media production in an era of proliferating outlets for youth-generated stories circulating within and way beyond the confines of mainstream broadcast media channels.

POINT OF VOICE

Point of voice combines two phrases, *point of view* and *youth voice*, that youth media practitioners, policymakers, and theorists, ourselves included, invoke all the time. The idea of claiming a point of view acknowledges the value of young people's particular and diverse perspectives, while recognizing that everything they, and all of us, see is shaped, enabled, and constrained by the specific vantage point we occupy. Without abandoning principles of rigorous reporting, espousing a point of view suggests that a detached perspective is not always the best or even a possible way to get to the truth. Truth itself, once revealed, has a point that can cut through silences, misunderstandings, and lies to generate new insights and actions.

In media production, though, claiming a point of view is not enough. Making media means translating a vision into a statement; hence our shift from *view* to *voice*, from seeing to expressing, from taking in the world to speaking out the word (or the picture or the sound). By invoking voice, we find ourselves in tricky territory. It's nearly impossible to avoid the term *youth voice* in any conversation about youth media work, and yet the phrase is sometimes misleading in its implications. The trouble starts with the cheerleading spirit many of us who work with teenagers tend to bring to youth voice. The broader public persistently regards youth with fear, if not thinly veiled disdain, framing young people (particularly working-class youth of color) as criminal, pathological, apathetic, chaotic, disappointing.[1] Perhaps in reaction to this view, we adults who want to align ourselves with young people can sometimes overplay their goodness and power. Youth voice no doubt has serious potential as a site for solutions, and certainly we are among the first to insist that young people need a voice in policymaking procedures, public debates, cultural narratives, and community organizing. The problem is that many of us rush to youth voice as an answer instead of a starting point that raises a slew of new questions, none simple.

Adults are often gatekeepers to resources and decision makers. So what happens when young people and their adult collaborators don't see eye-to-eye about what's best for youth? How can young people who exercise their voices through media maximize the impact of their stories, given massive changes in the media landscape as it relates to business, politics, education, and culture? What are the potential consequences for young people whose stories, because of today's permanent search- able digital archive, never go away even if their points of voice radically change? And what opportunities are available, and not available, for young people to go beyond one-off media stories in ways that actu- ally transform their own personal trajectories as well as the cultural narratives and social institutions that structure their lives? What is the relationship, in other words, between youth media expression, social action, and justice? These are the questions raised, not answered, when young people assert a public point of voice.

YOUTH MEDIA JUSTICE

The relationship between media, action, and justice is shifting in fun- damental and confusing ways. It's a time of unprecedented consolida- tion *and* proliferation of media platforms, and never has it been harder or easier for independent voices to reach audiences. On the one hand, with the approval of the Federal Communications Commission (FCC) and what the sociologist Eric Klinenberg (2007) describes as its rampant "re-regulation," media conglomerates have taken over local print, radio, and television outlets around the country at striking rates; in the two years after the U.S. Telecommunications Act went into effect in 1996, Klinenberg says the number of media companies owned by individuals dropped by seven hundred. Debates about whether and what kinds of regulation are needed to protect "net neutrality," the U.S. government's warrantless wiretapping programs, and who gets to own (and monetize) newly available and highly valuable airwaves as television goes digital have yet to be resolved. Although major news agencies sometimes use their huge reach to inform and entertain at clutch moments, editorial staff at big news agencies face enormous pressure to make profits for shareholders by boosting stock values, which de-centers public interest as a driving force shaping content and resource allocation (Henry, 2007). Moreover the line between editorial and paid content is blurrier than ever. Even spaces that seem independent aren't always, and it can take some serious digging and savvy to know precisely what you're dealing with when you consume or even make today's media.

On the other hand, powered in part by the advent of citizen journalism and online self-publishing venues such as blogs, social networking sites, and user-curated outlets, the public has never had access to a richer array of options for telling their own stories and framing knowledge and the news. Perhaps as a result of these developments, the media reform movement is picking up new energy, as is evident in the public's successful challenges to the FCC (McChesney, Newman, & Scott, 2005) and in a huge range of transnational and grassroots organizing campaigns that leverage the media for social justice efforts related to issues from environmentalism to gender and racial equity, indigenous and immigrant rights, and military policy. Media justice and reform proponents fall along a huge continuum. Some approach the issue from a national policy perspective, organizing to change government regulations. Others work locally, like those at Prometheus Radio, who help communities around the country build and license low-power radio stations. Some media reformers work to expose the insidious ways that corporate interests and partisan agendas shape what gets on the air, or investigated by enterprising journalists. Others aren't terribly interested in objectivity at all; they unabashedly leverage the power of the media as an advocacy tool to mobilize the public to take action. For proponents of a free press across this spectrum, new media production and distribution practices and relatively cheap technologies make it much easier for newsmakers without training or expensive equipment to have their say. Whether anyone's listening, that's a different story.

Where do young people fit in this mix? Here too we hit contradiction after contradiction. Young people are singled out as casualties of media privatization, to the extent that they find themselves ever more alienated from media ownership. Yet they constitute the single most coveted commercial market, and in this sense wield considerable power to sway what gets on the air. Young people lead the world as media innovators, redefining how we form identities, find friends, play games, make decisions, and learn. Yet they are also the population most likely to struggle for access to meaningful roles and tools of media production. Based on such measures as faith in the government and conventional public institutions, young people are trending downward as dutiful citizens. Yet in terms of civic engagement in informal, issue-specific, peer-to-peer mobilization efforts, "actualized" youth citizenship is on the rise (Bennett, 2007).

Our aim here is not so much to take a side with respect to these contradictory statements about youth and their relationship to media and justice. Rather, we build from a position, grounded in our own and other people's research and practice with youth, that media production *can* provide a way for young people to develop agency and a sense of citizenship, especially around issues of equity (Duncan-Andrade, 2007). What we offer is a concrete focus on *how* a group of young people, in real-world circumstances, hammered out a point of voice for themselves, facing new obstacles while leveraging new opportunities, at a moment of danger and possibility. Without in any way diminishing youth voice (if we didn't believe in it, we wouldn't do this work), we do want to complicate its cheerleader politics, which too often assume (1) that expression in and of itself turns things around for youth; (2) that young people speak in authentic counternarratives; and (3) that the proliferation of digital outlets means never having to compromise.

Assumption One: Expression in and of itself
turns things around for youth

While police officers were mistaking Anyi Howell's car for a stolen vehicle, he says he turned to the television crew capturing the encounter, as if they were broadcasting live, and spoke directly to the camera: "Email me at Anyi at Youth Radio dot org. I'm with the news." As soon as Anyi said that, the cameraman asked the police, "Did you tell these men why they're being detained?" "Hell no, they didn't," Anyi says he shot back in reply. It turns out that the on-air TV correspondent on the scene had done some work with Youth Radio's founder, Ellin O'Leary, so hearing

"Youth Radio" set him off too. He pulled out his cell phone and called Youth Radio to let us know what was happening. The staff member who got the call immediately drove over to the MacArthur Street station to see what she could do. Once her colleagues were cleared and released, she drove them to our staff retreat—late, but they made it.

Anyi says he started producing a radio story in his head while the incident was still playing out. That's partly why he was so eager to get his hands on the television footage—he could already hear how it would sound in his story—and why he was furious when a morning news producer refused, invoking the shield law for the station's "own protection." "I'm like, 'Dude, I was victimized,'" says Anyi. "'Who are you protecting?'" But it wasn't just his story Anyi was thinking about; he would also contact the police department's Division of Internal Affairs to launch an investigation into the handling of his detention. The TV tape was prime evidence. Or so he thought. This was months before Judith Miller's arrest, but when her imprisonment put the shield law in the national spotlight, Anyi's frustration reached a new level, which he expressed in a commentary with the revised title, *No Shield Law (Fuck the News* had no chance with the FCC). He had this to say on the commercial talk radio station KCBS, where Youth Radio has a weekly one-minute slot, about the television producers who refused to turn over their tape of his altercation with the police:

> The journalism community is up in arms about "Shield Law" protection.
>
> I'm King Anyi Howell with a commentary from Youth Radio.
>
> Even as someone working in journalism, I am completely against shield law protection for commercial media sources. A few months ago I was at a BART train station and was profiled by a police officer, wrongfully accused and accosted for stealing my own vehicle. The entire incident was captured by Fox's KTVU news cameras.
>
> My naïvete led me to believe that the KTVU tape would shed light on what I view to be an epidemic in this country: police mistreatment of minorities and racial profiling. However, the station representatives said even though the footage exists, I wouldn't be able to watch it or use it. They told me the shield laws allow them not to release copies of footage to anyone, at their discretion. Unfortunately, the Shield Law is a two-way door that swung and hit me right across the backside.
>
> For Youth Radio, I'm King Anyi Howell.

That swinging door did serious damage, because Anyi says he had naïvely assumed the TV reporters would hand over their tape, "journalist to journalist." In his mind, their refusal eclipsed all the success he had experienced in Youth Radio's newsroom: "I was feeling enraged with this whole industry," he said, convinced that commercial outlets were perverting journalistic privilege designed to promote risky reporting, when in his view they were invoking that same protection to obscure rather than expose the effects of criminalization on targeted U.S. populations.

All this complicates the assumption that expression in and of itself turns things around for youth. Writing a commentary about the shield law was a first step in Anyi's effort to push back against racial profiling, and its significance was not trivial. The fact that Anyi could experience his run-in with the police through the eyes and ears of a journalist, and not just a citizen rendered a suspect, shifted his treatment by law enforcement and witnesses. That's major. If more young people had a sense of themselves as actively producing the stories of their lives (as well as having the material resources to do so), they would possess a fuller array of tools and strategies to deploy against unjust or harmful treatment (and to prevent that treatment in the first place). In forming his critique of the shield law, he added a provocative perspective to the mix of voices weighing in on that policy—not arguing that the law shouldn't exist, but highlighting an underrecognized consequence of it. By linking the everyday experiences of racialized youth with national policy and international warfare as well as the state of the free press, he made an important contribution to raging public debates.

Nevertheless, Anyi's effort to tell his personal story and to analyze the effects of racial profiling over years and generations for young black men was hardly empowering, at least at first. In the initial stages of his media production work, Anyi says he felt more and not less constrained by forces outside his control, more and not less defeated in his attempts to change his own circumstances and those around him, more and not less keenly aware of the limits on his power, doubly *un*protected by law enforcement and journalistic privilege. Clearly, telling the story in a single commentary wasn't enough. Still he didn't get his tape. Still the officers at the subway station weren't disciplined for their actions, nor did Anyi receive an explanation that satisfied his desire to understand why, despite his objections, they may have been following standard rules of conduct. Still young men were targeted, again and again, for walking, driving, talking, or just being black or brown. Still, Anyi said many young people in his world felt safer with their own guns than 911:

> ANYI: Not because we're bad, renegades. It's because you [the police] have damaged the relationship with the community. We're not gonna call a landscaper who constantly fucks up the grass, even if the grass is out of hand. We're gonna go out there ourselves with some scissors.

To form a point of voice, young people need sustained opportunities to make meaning and media from their experiences—not to stop at a single story, a single burst of expression, a single chance to reach an audience. Media production is nothing if not iterative, and so is any effort to create social change. The one-shot approach not only limits the impact of the product; it also stops the learning process at a point when there is more to say and do.

As if Anyi needed further evidence of the continued strain in youth-police relations, just a couple of months after his confrontation with the police, there was another incident that hit especially close to home, against the backdrop of generally rising tensions between youth and law enforcement. One Friday evening a Youth Radio peer teacher was escorting some Youth Radio students—scripts, CDs, and playlists in hand, exuding preshow nervous energy—from the organization's head-quarters to the radio station where they broadcast the weekly *Youth in Control* program, about a block away. The peer teacher says that three police cars suddenly circled around him, with cops coming at him with guns raised, yelling to get up against the car. He told the cops he was doing his job, that they could call his colleague to verify that he had just left Youth Radio and was en route to KPFA for a live show. They ignored that information. The police had received a tip that a young black man in a red shirt was in the area, wielding a gun. The peer teacher was a young black man wearing red. Never mind that he was on deadline and responsible for a group of teens going to work. He was a suspect. Just like Anyi. Just like Elmer. To respond to and ultimately try to change a situation as complex as this one takes more than a single youth voice.

Assumption Two: Young people speak in authentic counternarratives

It was definitely a setback for Anyi not to get permission to use the television footage in his radio story, but he moved forward anyway, imagining ways to describe what happened to him and Elmer at the subway station as part of something larger: the experience of racial profiling as a rite of passage for young black men in the United States.

Even though this confrontation was what Anyi describes as "the most significant" altercation he'd had with the police to date, it was hardly the first. When he was ten, a cop stopped him and his uncle on the street. They were looking for a twelve-year-old around Anyi's size. The officer let them go, but not before repeating to his uncle, "Are you sure he's been with you all day?" After the cop pulled away, Anyi's uncle predicted, "You're going to fit a lot more descriptions when you get older." Anyi's dad also grew up with racial profiling, telling his son in an interview for the story, "It's not right. There's other ways to handle what they do without making it appear like they're going after one segment of society." Anyi interviewed many people for his feature, but even with all these perspectives he sensed that the story needed another element, something that captured the emotion behind his message, not just facts and opinion. So he invited the young artist Dahlak Brathwaite into Youth Radio's studio. Dahlak had written and performed poetry about racial profiling with an organization called Youth Speaks. Dahlak recorded a poem Anyi then used as a motif running through his narrative.

> *Red, white and blue lights blaze the sky like it's the fourth day of July*
> *but it's not the 4th day of July. It's a Friday night in the winter*
> *fuck firecrackers, these crackers fire at niggas*
> *born black and your birth right is the fear of what the boys in black and*
>   *blue do*
> *you aint even got to know what happened in the past to know what might*
>   *happen to you. . . .*
> *Innately inserted into the black subconscious are three kings*
> *You got Martin King, Don King and Rodney King*
> *One spoke of the American dream, one lived the American dream and the*
>   *other got put to sleep and thus had the American nightmare.*

Working with his producers, Nishat Kurwa and Ellin O'Leary, Anyi went through rounds and rounds of edits on his story, finally putting together a version that ran more than six minutes—that's long for radio—combining his own narrative with the poetry and interview clips. He posted the piece on his personal MySpace page. He played it on the Youth Radio iTunes radio show, following up with a panel discussion about the issue with some young Bay Area artist-activists. The story aired on Youth Radio's Saturday morning music and public affairs show on KPFA, the nation's first community-supported radio station.

But still, Youth Radio was having a hard time getting the story on a national show. The story didn't sound like something you'd typically hear on public radio. Anyi's bold rhetorical style, the topic, and the unconventional narrative structure probably all contributed to the challenge of getting it on the air. Finally, producers of a national program said they wanted the story. But there was a catch: they didn't want the poem.

By the time Anyi reached this point as a commentator, he had been working in Youth Radio's newsroom for a couple of years and he was not one to compromise easily on his writing. Doing edits with Anyi could be challenging; like many talented writers, he was extremely passionate about what he said and how he said it, and it took a lot of convincing to get him to consider changing even a single word. Many of us in the newsroom expected that cutting the poem would be a deal-breaker for Anyi. But he surprised us. The piece finally aired on NPR in July 2006, with no poetry, and Anyi's editorial sign-off:

DNA of the Black Experience
Youth Radio
Anyi Howell

> The first time I fit the description of a suspect, I was ten. And the more I was stopped for conversations with police . . . the more I began to make adjustments in my life. I had to learn not to stand outside the house with nondescript cups, or ride four deep to the club. Some of my friends like to keep all the registration papers in their glove box ultra updated. Others get nervous about how many people in their backseat are wearing ballcaps.
>
> For as long the term *racial profiling* has been around, fools have been denying the phenomenon exists. But I contend every black man in America at some point will be racially profiled or harassed by the police. It's a part of the DNA of our experience in the United States.

One morning last spring, while I was parking my car at the BART train station, a police officer looked at me and ran my license plate. He entered a false number, and my Oldsmobile Royale Brougham 88 came back as a stolen Honda. So now, I'm a car thief. My friend Elmer and I weren't prepared for what happened next. . . .

ELMER: *Our conversation was interrupted very rudely and abruptly. . . .*
In the distant background, I hear a voice of an officer in the back saying
"Everybody move aside" . . . and I turned around to see the barrel of the
officer's gun face to face and he tells me to step back and stand on the
concrete. He was like, "Brothers like you guys, I know how y'all get down,
stealing cars." . . . He's not talking to us like citizens—he's talking like we're
convicted felons he's delivering to Massachusetts for multiple murders.

The BART Police Officer realized his mistake on the triple check, and after embarrassing himself, he let us go. That wasn't the first time a police officer came at me sideways. But I was floored by the reality that an officer's simple mistake was enough for him to approach me at gunpoint.

The situation is so bad, I know brothas who are putting magnets and stickers on their cars that read, "Support Our Troops" because they think displays of patriotism will stop them from getting profiled. That strategy would only work if you could slap a "Caucasian" bumper sticker on your black self. But please believe when I got my new car and went to the auto parts store, I bought a case of oil, transmission fluid, and a couple of American flags. You know, just to keep my car running.

When you go from being a black boy to a black man, you start to understand police will use deadly force on you. I could sneeze and get shot to death. The next time police harassment happens to me, I'm demanding a certificate of release. It's a document saying a person was detained but not arrested—and then let go. Almost like a receipt for racial profiling. More than just another story to add to my experiences with out-of-pocket police.

For NPR News, I'm Anyi Howell.

The process of producing this story challenges the assumption that young people speak in authentic counternarratives. Several times throughout this book we have drawn on Nicole Fleetwood's (2005) critique of authenticity imposed on racialized youth in particular and their media products. The absolute premium placed on authenticity can reduce the value of young people's creative expression to its realness, rawness, and representativeness of a particular kind of cultural narrative America wants, a narrative describing sensationalized violence, essentialized otherness, and heroic individual survival. Youth media programs can be complicit in supporting this kind of narrative, even in cases where participants strive to deploy media as a tool for social justice work. And because the public rarely glimpses the process behind media products they consume—even those created by youth—the behind-the-scenes negotiations and institutional considerations that shape the voices young people present to the public often remain hidden.

Multiple voices run through Anyi's story: the views and experiences of young people and adults, expressed through prose, poetry, and snippets of conversation. That quality alone challenges the idea that a singular authentic truth drives the narrative. Moreover the voices that actually show up in the story are only some of the perspectives shaping its finished forms. Peer and adult editors inside Youth Radio, as well as those at local and national media outlets, also co-created Anyi's narrative, as did the Federal Communications Commission, digital media's emerging platforms, public radio's conventions, and nonprofit organizational norms. You might see these various outside voices and forces as censors constraining Anyi's authentic expression. That view is worth serious consideration, to the extent that peers, adults, and public policies can all play a role in squelching or softening perspectives deemed dangerous or threatening. One response would be for adults to adopt the posture of *protecting* young people from the pressures these forces create. Another, the one we favor, is *engaging* young people in multiple opportunities to take on, navigate, and reflect on the challenges they will invariably come up against when they have something powerful to say.

Anyi told his story in various versions. Which version was most true, most authentic? That's not the point. Finding, framing, and claiming a point of voice entails not producing a single complete narrative, but knowing how to transform what you have to say across a range of audiences, styles, and opportunities for social impact, without losing the core message. It's not about bending to every audience or outlet demand, but about learning how to leverage various platforms to reach targeted publics and how to draw the line when necessary. Anyi was willing to lose the poem for one version of the story, but only because it played fully, curse words and all, in other places. He refused, however, in any version, to let go of the bit in the final paragraph about a "certificate of release," even if the average national public radio listener, who is white and affluent, is a lot less likely than Anyi to find himself or herself needing to obtain what he considers a "receipt for racial profiling." To Anyi, that one piece of concrete, useful information needed to be in the story no matter where it aired, no matter who was listening, in order for him to make *his* point.

Just as the assumption that young people express themselves authentically can lead to trouble, so too can the widespread expectation that they consistently speak in counternarratives, meaning that their stories predictably contain a social critique. Certainly both of Anyi's stories considered here counter dominant positions. But their critique is unpredictable and sometimes counterintuitive. The *No Shield Law* commentary took a position that challenged not some abstract oppressive power structure, but Anyi's own immediate colleagues in Youth Radio's newsroom, which saw itself as a hotbed of critical media literacy. His perspective also challenged the reigning sentiment among professional journalists. At the time of Judith Miller's arrest, major professional journalism associations rallied their members and most prominent colleagues to sign petitions, lobby legislators, and lead protests passionately defending the very law Anyi had criticized.

Whenever adults join forces with youth producers to make media, they should be prepared for the critique to boomerang back to themselves, and that's not always comfortable for adults who want to align themselves with youth. And yet moments like this one, which center on disagreement between youth and adult colleagues, are among the most powerful learning opportunities and tests of a media organization's independence—but only when young people retain final editorial say. When discord happens between youth and adults engaged in collaborative storytelling, both parties need to clarify their positions in a convincing way. It is a process that in the end informs their independent and joint work moving forward, imprinting future media products and methods.

The feature on racial profiling as a rite of passage for young black men functioned as a kind of counternarrative, but arguably, the removal of the poem took away one register of that critique. Anyi made the call that it was worth it for him to reach the massive NPR audience even with a version of the piece that was incomplete. It was still *his* story, he says, and it didn't hurt that the link on the NPR website drove traffic back to Youth Radio's own site, where listeners would find the long version in all its glory, poetry and curse words and long clips and all. When other Youth Radio students and emerging producers reflected on Anyi's process with this series, some expressed frustration that he had to compromise at all to get his story on national air. They contended that our struggle should be to change the norms governing mainstream media's production values and narrative sensibilities, not accommodate them. No one argued with that effort as fundamentally crucial, but there isn't a media producer in the world reaching massive audiences who doesn't face some version of the dilemma Anyi confronted.[2] Arming young people marginalized from digital (and other forms of) privilege with the wherewithal to make strategic judgments on their own terms, with their various communities in mind, seems a crucial step toward media justice.

Assumption Three: The proliferation of digital outlets means never having to compromise

Getting *DNA of the Black Experience* on national and local radio and across the Internet via iTunes and MySpace was a victory for Anyi and Youth Radio. And yet the moment when Anyi felt a great sense of accomplishment with respect to his racial profiling series took place off the air entirely.

While Anyi and his newsroom collaborators prepared various media projects addressing troubled youth-police relations, they also connected with a community organizer to plan and cohost a live forum at Youth Radio. At that event, a local chief of police joined Anyi, Elmer, other Youth Radio students and staff, along with local public officials, press, advocates, and concerned community members. "I was aware that it wasn't only how police had harmed us," Anyi said about the planning stages for the forum, "but also how the community can disregard the law. I wanted it to be an open discussion." The forum planners were well aware that this focus on dialogue rather than condemnation had strategic value. "I knew if I *framed* it like that," Anyi said, "it would be easier to bring them to the table."

Elmer, who moderated the forum discussion, launched the event by playing the long version of Anyi's story. Then he opened up the conversation, raising prepared questions and handing over the mic to audience members. He led with a general question about the sources of mistrust between youth and police. The chief of police mentioned some basic misunderstandings about what officers actually have a right to do on the street.

> CHIEF: There's a standard established by the courts when officers have reasonable suspicion that someone is involved in crime. They have the right to detain that person and compromise their liberty for a little bit while they investigate whether a crime took place and what the circumstances are. Many times, innocent people find themselves in circumstances where there's reasonable suspicion that they're involved in criminal activity.

The Youth Radio peer teacher who'd been detained by police en route to the *Youth in Control* live show took this opportunity to speak up. He described what had happened to him, the three squad cars sirening around him, ordering him up against the car, guns pointed. "There's a way to do it, and there's a way not to do it," he said.

> PEER TEACHER: They just stopped the car out of nowhere in front of me, and told me to get on the car. . . . In a situation like that, someone could panic, reach for their ID, and since you got your guns drawn on him, you're just gonna start shooting at him, in fear that he has a gun.

> CHIEF: I can understand and appreciate that perspective. But think about it from the perspective of a police officer who wants to go home that night, who doesn't want to get shot by the armed robbery suspect he's about to encounter on the street. We train our officers that when you're confronting somebody who might have a gun, you draw your weapon, you issue very specific commands, like "Get down on the ground!" We train a great deal about how to do that in a way that is safe for the officer so the officer does not put himself at unnecessary risk. . . . Sometimes when we have those encounters, it really *is* the guy who did it, he's got the gun in his back pocket. If you don't come out with the gun in your hand, put the guy down on the ground, and do everything you need to do, the officer puts himself at risk of getting killed. So I expect that the officer will take that person down in a safe manner.

The chief went on to say that, in addition to a protocol for arresting a person, there is also a clear set of procedures for letting that person go, a process called *disengagement*. After a detainee has been cleared of suspicion, the officer is supposed to explain what just happened, treating the now former suspect "with respect and dignity," the chief said. At this point, a young person in the audience challenged the chief. In his experience, that style of disengagement rarely happens. Usually, he says, you're handcuffed, put on the ground, and then once you're cleared, you face "the disrespect of them just saying, 'It's no big deal.'" The young person said it's that kind of behavior that gives citizens the idea that police consider themselves "higher than the law."

Reflecting back on the forum later, Anyi said knowing that he and Elmer were able to create a "safe space" for questioning the chief of police like this, and for the chief to have to answer, made the whole event worthwhile.

Through his series of works on racial profiling and youth-police relations, Anyi explored and exploited an impressive array of platforms for getting his story out, including social media websites, broadcast outlets, old-school community meetings, national conferences, and university classrooms. In this sense, he positioned Youth Radio's work squarely in the space that media scholar Henry Jenkins (2006b) describes as "convergence culture": not a fully disembodied virtual universe, but a world "where old and new media collide." Amid the brouhaha surrounding digital media's possibilities, it is crucial to remember that face-to-face encounters bring an array of people into a single room who otherwise may not come to see, hear, learn from, and challenge one another on pressing social issues like the ones Anyi, Elmer, and their peers raised at their forum.

Anyi's final outlet for this series was a print magazine to which he contributed an article describing his process of producing these various media products. The headline was *Multiple Platforms Means Never Having to Compromise.*

> Having succeeded in getting my piece aired on multiple local stations and posted all over the web, I was satisfied with outlets getting whatever version suited them. To me it was akin to their audience getting the TV edit of a movie instead of the director's cut. . . . It is definitely a

better feeling to give a feature life on multiple platforms than to pitch a story to a single outlet and have to bend over backwards to try to conform the expression of your ideas to that outlet's audience.

Anyi makes a persuasive point. With persistence and support from his producer, Nishat Kurwa, Anyi was able to tell his story on his own terms in several places—MySpace, the youth-police forum, his KPFA show—so that the national version without the poem didn't feel like much of a compromise at all. With the advent of more and more media outlets where users create and curate content, young people can now get their stories to "millions of users," as Anyi says in his article describing MySpace traffic. They are no longer dependent on professional journalists to tell and disseminate stories on their behalf.

But in the spirit of collegial pedagogy, we want to push back a bit against Anyi's argument. Our first concern has to do with the difference between actual and hypothetical audiences. How many of those millions of MySpace users are visiting Anyi's personal homepage? What is the likelihood that the chief of police who attended the youth-police forum is among those visitors? How many digital producers like Anyi who, unlike Anyi, are fully dependent on social media outlets with no access to a broadcast entity like NPR, are actually getting attention for their work outside a small circle of friends? And who among those producers are people most likely to be targets of racial profiling and other forms of social oppression and exclusion—people who are young, poor, and black or brown? If the latest data from the National Center for Educational Statistics are any indication, answers to these questions are troubling; key measures of digital access and participation reveal persistent gaps among youth based on factors of class, race, geography, and family educational background (DeBell & Chapman, 2006). And despite the fact that social media sites have the potential to democratize media production and distribution opportunities, new media researcher John McMurria (2006) found that there is "far less diversity than broadcast network television" among the top one hundred rated and most frequently viewed videos and heavily subscribed channels on YouTube.

Our second concern pertains to impact. We would add to Anyi's headline a very important *if: Multiple Platforms Means Never Having to*

Compromise If and Only If . . . you are either a person who happens to occupy a position of digital privilege, with regular and unfettered access to high-tech tools, connectivity, and know-how, or a person who is part of a network of others who can bring your collective resources, intelligence, and influence to leverage media outlets to express your point of voice without compromise, and with credit.

Having a network of others to pursue multiple platforms of expression for your work might *lessen* the compromises you need to make, but you will also face new compromises characteristic of the digital media age. With only user-generated websites at your disposal, lots of good stuff gets buried. The methods for determining what content rises in the ranks of social media sites are guided by what Surowiecki (2004) calls the "wisdom of crowds" (i.e., amateur users who visit those sites). That sounds pleasingly democratic, but the method says nothing about who is actually participating in those crowds and in what ways. Subtle, challenging political commentary has to compete with the sensational, the silly, and increasingly the sponsored (i.e., social media content backed, sometimes not transparently, by "big media" companies and marketers).

A main reason Anyi was able to reach the massive NPR audience was because he had learned to write for that audience through rigorous training, because he had access to broadcast-quality recording and editing equipment, and because he could get in the door through the institutional relationships and pathways that had been built, over years of hard work, by young people like him and adult collaborators. A main reason he and Elmer were able to convene a well-attended youth-police forum featuring local citizens and law enforcement officials was because they had the backing of a prominent community-based organization; because they possessed public speaking, hosting, and planning skills; and because they had access to networks of others who could help pull off such an event.

Revisiting Anyi's headline, perhaps a different spin on the title gets closer to the point we're reaching for here. The proliferation of digital media platforms means youth media producers, young people and adults, can never *afford* to compromise in their pursuit of collaborative networks to support young people's most challenging perspectives. The fewer resources young people bring to production by virtue of digital privilege, the more dependent they are on intentional initiatives to get behind their points of voice and to link those perspectives to concerted work for social justice.

CONCLUSION

The first assumption we challenged in this chapter held that expression in and of itself turns things around for youth. Our discussion highlights the importance of providing sustained opportunities for young people to produce one story after another, moving beyond a single burst of expression to form an ongoing and always developing body of work. The second assumption contended that young people speak in authentic counternarratives, and we have seen that their points of voice are always mediated and strategic; only at their own peril should adults think they can predict what young people will say and that adults will always want to rally behind it. Adults working with youth should be prepared for unexpected arguments, including those adults might not want to hear, and should have a plan for how to sustain conversations among youth and adult collaborators and their audiences while the story is evolving and after it gets out. The third assumption presumed that the proliferation of digital platforms means youth producers no longer have to compromise to deliver their messages to significant audiences. The work described here underscores that those platforms need to include the neighborhood street corner and community stage, along with the social media website, iPod, or mobile phone. Moreover, young people need the backing of collectives, formal and informal, to leverage power and influence, especially to expose unfamiliar experiences, reveal threatening actualities, and advocate for unpopular positions, as they cultivate and communicate their distinctive points of voice.

AFTERWORD

If Youth Radio were ever at risk of taking for granted the range of independent media outlets for young producers, events taking place through the winter of 2007 would have brought that complacency to an end. A recent program graduate was in town and asked if he could guest-deejay a music segment on Youth Radio's Saturday morning show on KPFA. Arrangements were made. Since Youth Radio's earliest days, KPFA had provided airtime for student shows (through its splitter station, KPFB) and hired graduates in significant numbers; it is also the nation's oldest listener-supported free-speech radio station. The Youth Radio alumnus wanted to include on his playlist a song about police brutality called "My Favorite Mutiny" by the conscious hip-hop group The Coup. The Youth Radio producer on hand that Saturday morning asked the student several times whether he had the radio version of the song, knowing that the uncut version contained several curses on the FCC's list of forbidden words. The student reassured his producer that the track he downloaded was a clean radio edit. It wasn't, and it was too late before both of them realized it. A string of swear words went out on the air. It was a serious mistake, but no one expected the severity of the response: cancellation of the show, despite a shared mission to provide a platform that broadcasts independent and challenging community voices. Representatives from KPFA sent the cancellation letter three weeks after the show, saying they couldn't risk the possible FCC fine should anyone report the mistake, and that their decision was final. Anyi had been one of the show's main hosts.

We share this story here, at the end of a chapter on point of voice, to underscore the contradiction contained within the present moment. Never has it been easier or harder for young people to reach audiences. Never have noncommercial outlets experienced more pressure from government re-regulation and other threats to their survival, including the very digital platforms many of us regard as promising spaces for independent expression and collective social action. Never has there been a greater need for young people to contribute to the public debates and decisions affecting their lives and social worlds. And never has there been a stronger imperative—just as more and more young people get locked up and shut up—to make sure that they can connect to the kinds of tools, networks, and experiences they need to formulate and disseminate something worthwhile to say.

FOUR

Drop That Knowledge

THE FIGHT

It was the second week of the winter 2007 Youth Radio Core class. Sixteen fidgety high school students gathered around the big table at the center of the main room, gigantic backpacks stashed underfoot, chips and salsa strewn across the tabletop. Jason Valerio, the Core class director, called for everyone's attention. One of the peer teachers started reading through the radio show rundown displayed on a dry-erase board, announcing which students would be deejaying in the first hour, who would recite commentaries, who would read the news. Then Jason's office phone rang and he ducked out to take the call, leaving the peer teachers in charge.

Noticing Jason's absence, a peer teacher named Jennifer flipped open her cell phone and dialed a friend, her chatty voice competing with the instruction at the board. Cell phone usage at Youth Radio is not allowed, and whipping one out in the middle of class is considered pretty outrageous. Bill, another peer teacher, reprimanded Jennifer from across the room, "Jennifer, you shouldn't be on the phone!" She glared back, telling him to leave her alone, it was an important call. Their voices escalated. The other peer teachers and students looked freaked out, eyes darting around the room. Bill and Jennifer kept yelling, and then Bill grabbed the phone from Jennifer and threw it at her. "He broke my phone!" Two other peer teachers broke up the conflict, drawing Jennifer and Bill in separate directions out of the room.

Strained silence. Giggles. A few "whatever" looks. "Here's what I have to say about what just happened," said Brandon, another peer teacher. "It was fake." Jason came out from his office and called for a round of applause for the performers. Then he asked everyone to take out notebooks. It was time to interview the "eyewitnesses" in the room and write a story about the fight, the students' first news reporting exercise. Leon, another young staff member, took over at this point, going over to the board to write down the "4 W's and an H" (Who, What, Where, When and How), and to introduce the inverted pyramid, the journalistic convention of leading with the most important information and narrowing down from there to the less crucial details.

"The fight" is one activity Youth Radio uses to teach the basics of media production.[1] In this chapter we present a series of behind-the-scenes stories that contain models for teaching media production to young people across a range of settings. We begin with an overview of the cycles of production any producer goes through to create a story, with observations about how innovations in digital media have disrupted linear progression from preproduction through production and postproduction to distribution. Next comes discussion of the ethical dilemmas that invariably arise when young people define their own story topics and reach significant audiences. Ethics and editorial considerations have grown more complicated for young producers, given the advent of peer-to-peer distribution channels and a permanent searchable digital archive, which we comment on here. The chapter then advances through a range of genres—the commentary, the interview, the feature—offering concrete methods to introduce young producers to these narrative forms and revealing some of the distinct opportunities and challenges each presents for young people and audiences. Key across all genres is how the story is framed, in radio-speak, through a host's introduction and back announce, as well as its afterlife, which includes audience response and extended use. We end by analyzing the implications of these methods not only for educators who work with teenagers, but also for university professors, ethnographic researchers, and professional journalists eager to integrate youth media into their practices and products.

PHASES OF PRODUCTION

Whether they're working on commentaries, interviews, or feature stories, producers move through four phases: preproduction, production, postproduction, and distribution. The process looks different depending on the product as well as other factors, including topic, audience, timeframe, technology access, and point of view. But you can't make a story that reaches an audience without moving through the tasks marking each of these phases.

Preproduction

During preproduction young people identify story topics, characters, sounds, and scenes. They prepare a three- to four-sentence pitch for their stories to present at an editorial meeting attended by peers and adult producers. To get clarity on their own investments in the topics they've selected, they often free-write on their story ideas. Research in this phase goes beyond web searches; having actual conversations usually leads to new angles and ideas. Young producers set up interviews, come up with questions, and prep and practice with their equipment until they're ready to start gathering tape.

Production

During production students interview characters and analysts. They record *ambience* (naturally occurring sound) as well as *scenes* in which

Table 1   Phases of Production

Preproduction	Production	Postproduction	Distribution
Identify a topic	Record source material (sound, images, data, interviews)	Log	Frame story for broadcast
Research		Arrange	
Frame		Script	Share with audiences
Envision		Edit	Repurpose for various outlets
Outline		Critique	
Plan			Manage response and extended use
Practice			

something meaningful happens, advancing rather than simply illustrating the story. Sometimes producers collect found audio (e.g., voicemail messages, clips from home videos) and create or download music that resonates with the themes they're exploring in their stories to add texture and mood.

Postproduction

In postproduction young people log all recordings: the interviews, scenes, beds of ambient sound, even the music. With guidance from peer educators and adult producers, they comb through logs to pick their best clips, then arrange those elements in an order that makes sense logically and narratively. Next they simply write around the clips, composing their own narration in such a way that introduces each character and scene, makes transitions, fills in missing information, and draws the story to a conclusion. Once the script is written, critiqued, and approved, young people record their narration (a process called *tracking*) and then import all the audio elements into a digital editing computer program. They use that system to mix their stories, arranging and layering the audio bits to match the script.

Distribution

Youth Radio students have a guaranteed audience; their stories air on various local and national outlets, as well as through online channels, including our own website, MySpace, Facebook, podcasting, and iTunes radio. Particularly with national outlets such as NPR, whose audiences number in the tens of millions, getting a Youth Radio story on the air can entail several rounds of arduous editing with the outlet's show producers. It's not easy to get stories on national radio, yet massive audiences (more than 26 million for NPR) can motivate and intensify learning, and through public release young people can influence pressing social, cultural, and policy-level debates. Today's media landscape offers a proliferating array of distribution options: social networking and peer-to-peer websites, blogs, public access stations, the school newspaper, and community events. A key dimension of distribution entails preparing for and handling audience response, repurposing material for multiple outlets, and priming stories for extended use (e.g., when policymakers, advocates, educators, health providers, peers, and fellow journalists comment on and apply youth-produced content based on their own agendas).

CIRCLES OF PRODUCTION

Digital media culture has shifted the order, pacing, and gatekeeping mechanisms that have traditionally governed these four production phases. In light of these changes, rather than a predictable sequence of steps, the production process has become a cycle without a prefigured beginning or end, nor a fixed pathway through.

Due to the proliferation of consumer-curated media outlets, a contributor to a website might start with the fourth phase, distribution, by grabbing existing digital content and making a case for why that story belongs on a website's front page, turning dissemination into an act of creation. A video game player or fan fic writer might start at the third phase, postproducing someone else's media by changing an existing game's code or retooling another author's narrative, thus transforming the media experience into something new.[2] The widespread availability of everyday media (e.g., home videos and digital photos, archived voice-mail recordings) can launch a creative project at the second phase, mid-production, with recordings in hand, around which the maker only later frames a narrative. These and other examples demonstrate that media production doesn't necessarily start at the beginning, if we imagine the beginning as a process of pulling an original idea out of the air. Rarely does the process march forward without lots of stopping short, reversing course, and circling back to start again.[3]

FOUNDATIONS FOR LEARNING

Two forces move young people through the production cycle, regardless of the point of entry or pathway they follow. First, there's the urgency to tell the story, which is why it's so important for them to find renewable interest in the topics they've selected and to care about the story's poten-tial impact on the world once it goes public. Second, there's the scaffold-ing that propels their learning forward. Like any other producer, young people will soon lose focus and engagement if they sense that they are no longer developing new skills and understandings, no longer building or deepening relationships that matter to them. The notion of converged literacy we discussed in chapter 1 is crucial here, to the extent that it lends specificity to what young people garner from media production in terms of personal growth and social impact. We have framed converged literacy as an ability to *make and understand* boundary-crossing and convention-breaking texts, *draw and leverage* public interest in the stories you want to tell, and *claim and exercise* the right to use media to promote justice, variously defined, a right still denied young people marginalized from full citizenship as producers of media culture.

This framework for converged literacy outlines a set of questions edu-cators and young people can ask themselves as they evaluate any learning experience: Does the experience provide young people with opportuni-ties and skills to break conventions while still understanding the rules of the game? Do young people play an active role in not only generating raw content, but also tailoring and delivering that content to existing and emerging audiences? Is the media production work contextualized within a larger ambition related to justice? By this we do not mean that personal essays or political analysis should blindly push unexamined agendas; social justice work can entail opening avenues for expression for those whose experiences would otherwise be ignored, distorted, or used against them. Exposing hidden information, or simply sharing honest, uncensored, unpopular, or controversial perspectives, contributes to a fuller public discourse. What's important is to create conditions in which young people can debate the fraught relationship between media and justice and position themselves as influential producers in that mix.

Youth Radio has based its conception of media literacy on the accumulated knowledge of countless young people, producers, youth development experts, educators, organizers, and scholars who have informed Youth Radio's model by way of hands-on involvement and publication of texts cited throughout this volume. While young people produce powerful media in a range of learning environments, we have identified nine factors that promote youth engagement in projects relevant to converged literacy and beyond. Young people engage their minds, imaginations, and passions when:

1. They participate in active learning and hands-on production.
2. They work with real deadlines and real audiences and outlets.
3. They know that their involvement in any given project doesn't have to end when that project is complete; that they can stay involved, escalating their skills and intensifying their responsibilities.
4. They have final say over what they release into the world, but they have to listen, negotiate, and sometimes fight for their vision.
5. They find recognition for what they know and how they communicate, as ends in themselves and as means to engage with new conversations and discoveries.
6. Activities are industry-relevant and linked to innovative formats and well-suited technologies.

7. Pedagogy balances peer teaching and youth-adult collaboration.

8. They can get where they need to be, their workplace is safe, and they're not hungry.

9. Students and teachers connect their everyday work to goals related to equity and social impact.

Even with these conditions in place, when young people are invited to explore topics that matter to them, controversy often follows and ethical questions arise.

ETHICAL STORYTELLING: SOME QUESTIONS

How do you maintain a firewall between the editorial and business sides of youth media production? Is it worthwhile to pursue stories from a youth perspective that might reflect poorly on young people, and if so, why and how? Do you offer protection for young people who might face trouble for going on record about their experiences, and if so, in what forms?

Firewall questions are rarely straightforward, and it is always a good idea to sit down with a group of adult and youth producers to discuss specific scenarios in which pressure from funders or outlets or even an editor's personal politics might encroach upon content, and together answer, "What will we do?" It's a question more and more professional and veteran journalists find themselves revisiting, as newsrooms fight to protect investigative desks and other costly efforts from rampant cost-cutting. The stakes are high for next-generation journalists, who will need to find new solutions to the challenges they will surely face when they can't take for granted a "church-state" divide between the editorial function and the bottom line.[4]

The question of perspective is equally daunting. If a youth media project aims to counter the mainstream press's tendency to criminalize and pathologize young people, why create content that makes young people look bad? Framing is crucial, as we have seen in discussions of stories throughout this book. Youth Radio editors feel strongly that difficult stories are among the most important to tell. The commentator whose father is gay and who grapples with his own homophobia, the young woman who's not sure if she's ready to grow her naturally wavy hair into dreadlocks, the young man who condemns the shield law protecting journalists' anonymous sources because he says journalists use it to protect racist police—these kinds of stories reveal complexities in young people's lives and invite deep discussions among youth producers, their adult collaborators, and audiences.

The question about protection highlights the tension built into Youth Radio's dual mission, as a youth development organization and an independent production company with an explicit policy that, when those two functions come into conflict, the first trumps the second. Easier said than done. No one can fully predict what will happen when a piece reaches its public. For a story about a girl whose family used a fake address to enroll her in a decent public school, we not only used a pseudonym, but we also digitally altered her distinctive voice. That story aired in 2003, and many broadcast outlets since then have tightened their guidelines for using anonymous sources. Youth Radio has walked away from broadcast opportunities when an outlet insisted on using a source's first and last names and when we collaboratively determined that doing so would present too great a risk.[5] Overall, adult editors do not see it is as their role to make decisions on behalf of young people about the stories they want to tell, but only to facilitate tough conversations about possible intended and unintended consequences of making any given story public, and about how a young person might frame a narrative in such a way that steers listeners away from problematic or erroneous interpretations. It would be naïve, though, to claim that anyone can fully control how audiences receive any story, and that is perhaps among the most important lessons young people learn when they produce media for public release.

This lesson has grown even more urgent as a result of the searchable digital archive that now serves as a permanent repository for youth-produced content. The implications of that archive became very concrete when Youth Radio graduate Belia Mayeno Saavedra admitted that she cringes when she has to tell potential dates her last name because she knows the first thing they'll do when they get home is Google her, and there they'll find, at the top of the results list, a commentary she wrote as a teenager about being mixed race, offering an outdated perspective on her own identity and racial politics. As educators, we face new responsibilities to facilitate a process whereby young producers project five, ten, even twenty years down the line to determine what it will mean for something they say in their teens to follow them into perpetuity, leaving them very little control over who sees it or how it is used. Given Youth Radio's methodology of collegial pedagogy, it's never our approach to do that advanced thinking for young people, but we do want to engage in that thinking with them and help make sure it happens. Our collective jobs have gotten a lot more challenging, and interesting, now that a radio story no longer "evaporates into the ether" as it used to, as Youth Radio founder Ellin O'Leary puts it. Today's digital archive contains new surveillance mechanisms as well as evidence for the increasingly commonplace due diligence work of citizen searchers (be they employers, college admissions officers, or possible lovers). Young people are called on to respond to these new conditions through a kind of ethical forecasting. They learn to hinge present-day decisions on an imagined future for their work, its potential to cause harm and do good. Although not without risk, this kind of work is what is required today to produce meaningful media projects that go beyond the status of an assignment handed in to a teacher and filed away in a locked cabinet of completed work.

Ethical considerations arise at every stage of youth media production. It's wise to create space for discussion of these issues from the very beginning, before young people have identified story topics, a process that itself doesn't always come easily.

WHAT MAKES A GOOD STORY? TIPS FOR FINDING TOPICS

You're sitting in front of a group of young people. You want them to come up with an idea to work on for a commentary, a story, or a show. You ask them what they care about, what makes them mad, what people don't get about them, what happened to them that day, that week, that year, that changed them. They stare blankly back at you. "My life is boring," some of them say. "Why would people care?" Or the opposite extreme: "No one will believe me" or "What's happened to me is my business."

You shift gears. You ask them about a policy issue, a social controversy, a recent news event. Some of them reiterate something they read online or picked up on last night's news or heard around the dinner table, but it doesn't go much further than that. What can you do?

You can start by stirring things up. Have students take a critical look at the way they, their issues, and their communities are portrayed (or ignored) in mainstream media, and then challenge them to come up with something better, more nuanced, true. Youth Radio uses these strategies across its various programs, perhaps most intensively at Camp Sweeney, a residential facility for incarcerated young males, where the organization has offered weekly classes for about ten years. Typically the class begins with a media literacy activity that sets young people up to create something different from what's already available to them. Sometimes the activity is about demystifying the media industry as a whole, with an analogy that taps into what the young men already know. If the recording industry is like professional sports, Youth Radio Youth Programs Director Erik Sakamoto says to his students at Camp Sweeney, who's equivalent to the players? The general managers? The owners? Once the students have worked through this analogy, they investigate the net worth of various superstars of music and sports, examine how the sponsorships and contracts allocate rights and profits, and reality-check the likelihood of ever ascending to the level of a Jay-Z or Kobe Bryant. Mapping the media industry landscape in this way then opens a discussion for young people to identify channels through which they can enter and share their stories. In a subsequent session they might use lyrics from a song such as Lil Wayne's "Tha Block Is Hot" to explore how popular music promotes or downplays "hood realities," and then bring that to a discussion of gentrification and local government's role in urban renewal and the displacement of poor families. That discussion may prompt a conversation about what young people as media producers can do about the changes in their communities, and why it's important for them to be thoughtful and strategic in how they define and represent their turf. And then the writing begins.

However the process starts, the point is to find a connection between stories that exist and stories that need to be told. Another way to pull that off, developed by Senior Producer Rebecca Martin, is to begin with a critical reading of the daily paper. We encourage young people to look beyond the front page for stories; some of the best stories are in the back pages, with just a few lines of copy. We ask them to pick a story and find a new angle to move the story forward. What is the youth spin? Some stories, such as federal budget negotiations or corporate corruption scandals, may seem to have no youth element, but they do. We urge young people to think creatively about finding the youth side of the story. We discuss how to cover a story differently from other outlets. Education stories are a perfect example of stories that directly affect youth but often don't include the perspectives of youth, or include students only through a sprinkling of token quotations. That's where youth-produced coverage can be transformative. We get young people to think about their audience. Are they aiming to explain dimensions of youth culture to adults? Or do they want to reach other youth? Do they want to address like-minded listeners, or convince an audience that initially opposes what they have to say? These decisions shape the topics they choose and how they will approach their story. The last step is to work creatively with assignments. If the young people get stuck, we might suggest they underline three short lines from the article that speak to them in one way or another (they love the lines, they hate the lines). They can spend five minutes free-writing (pen never leaves the page; fingers never stop tapping the keyboard), integrating those three lines into a first-person commentary or spoken-word poem. Another option is to have them investigate a new story from the point of view of someone they think is missing from the article. In this way, the young people find a new angle on an unfinished story.

This activity is a good way to launch discussion of point of view and genre (the writerly conventions of a print article compared to the conversational tone of a radio report or the personal opinion driving a commentary; also, truth versus fiction). It grounds young people's discussions in something concrete, a specific set of events and people that gets them thinking about a new story they want to tell. They might notice unanswered, or unasked, questions, assumptions implicit in the reporter's angle, or contradictions between the article and their own experiences. The print piece that launches the discussion doesn't have to come from a newspaper. Some young people might choose an academic text as a point of departure for stories that build on or counter the article's central argument.[6] A very serious story may be embedded in a popular culture phenomenon, such as a reality television show or the lyrics of a controversial song. In any case, the next step in pursuing the story is for the young people to figure out what they need to find out and what they already know. Answering the first question launches the research process; answering the second question can usefully come in the form of a first-person commentary.

THE COMMENTARY

A commentary is usually one to two minutes long, which translates to no more than one full single-spaced page. Starting with a commentary is a way for young people to write down their own thoughts and opinions, to explore why the topic interested them in the first place, and to shape something of a narrative arc that may or may not turn out to frame a fuller story with multiple voices and scenes. Often the commentary stands alone as a strong piece for publication or broadcast.

Commentators share experiences that are personally meaningful, perhaps counterintuitive, and resonant with larger social themes. Commentaries don't have to be objective, but they are reality-based and should take into account opposing points of view (and the contested issue of objectivity can be a provocative subject of discussion for teachers and students doing commentaries for the first time). The best commentaries aren't political rants or personal diatribes, nor do they stick to generic observations. Through commentaries, young people articulate perspectives grounded in compelling evidence, which might come in the form of lived experiences, references to research, or bits of dialogue with people they've encountered in their everyday worlds. We ask students to work through the following steps:

1. Write about issues that inspire passion in you. Draw on your own experience to bring new insight to an issue people are struggling to understand or think they already understand. You could respond to a school shooting by talking about how you were an outcast and overlooked by adults in your school. You could write about the U.S. crackdown on border crossing from the standpoint of a teen from Appalachia who understands what it's like to believe you have to

leave home to make a living. Youth Radio's Emily Schmooker wrote a commentary about body image by describing how a comment meant as praise actually hurt her feelings, made her mad, and changed her life:

"I just wanted to thank you for going up there and doing what you're doing . . . and showing that us fat people can dance." That comment was supposed to be a compliment from the middle aged audience member who approached me after a performance when I was fifteen. But to me, he was just an older man watching my body, telling me who I was, and molding me into something that I didn't want to be. Of course all teenagers have insecurities, but up until that moment I never considered myself a spokesperson for fat people . . . just someone who loved to dance and act. As a matter of fact, I had never even considered myself a fat girl. Now, I had the weight of all fat people on my shoulders.

2. Find a strong hook, or lede, and remember that in radio you don't have a lot of time, so clarity and economy of expression can make or break your story. Really spend time crafting that first paragraph. You'll rarely get it right the first time. When Pendarvis Harshaw first sat down to write a commentary about his friend's death in 2006, the loss was still raw. His first draft began this way:

I was in the San Francisco Airport with two co-workers heading to New York for the first time in my life. I had turned my phone off the day before and hadn't checked my e-mail in days. The trip couldn't have come at a better time: I needed the fresh air.

The week prior to my trip, I was sitting at a New Media Awards banquet in San Jose when I received a phone call that my childhood friend had been murdered. "Willie's dead," my big partner Mal told me . . . . Then I threw my phone.

In this draft Pendarvis described an airplane ride, a hospital scene, and a lyric from the rapper Nas before getting to his point, which centered on a relationship he saw between "babies and bullets" in his community. The final version of Pendarvis's story, which aired nationally a few months later, was quite different. It started like this:

I met Will when we were in seventh grade. That same year, a female classmate of mine became a mother at age thirteen. Not too long after she gave birth, my partner Norro was murdered in Stockton. That was my first time experiencing both extremes. Up to that point, the biggest drama had been fistfights, or getting jumped—but death, that was only for old people. At the time I didn't realize it, but seventh grade was my introduction to a teen life in East Oakland.

January 26 of this year, my friend Will was murdered. The church was crowded for his funeral, wall-to-wall with familiar faces, some of which I hadn't seen since middle school. It seemed like everybody was wearing hooded sweatshirts silk-screened with Will's photo. Will was my boy, and to be putting on a button-up and these hard bottom shoes to put him in a casket . . . it just didn't seem real.

In Pendarvis's second draft, he unburied his lede. Every memory surrounding Will's death carried weight for Pendarvis, down to the song on his iPod that helped him mourn. But those details would not necessarily resonate with listeners. His editor, Youth Radio graduate and News Director Nishat Kurwa, worked with Pendarvis to transform a chaotic flow of events and emotions into a compelling story released into the public sphere.

3. Use concrete examples, images, and stories in your writing. If you are talking about getting along with your parents, describe specific incidents or arguments when your communication worked or broke down. In another example, one young soldier returned from the Iraq war with posttraumatic stress disorder, and he talked about going to all the welcome-home barbeques "numbed out . . . like you're watching a black and white TV, you're just not there." In a commentary about her struggles with depression and hypomania, Belia Mayeno Saavedra filled her narrative with detailed images that drew listeners inside a deeply personal and sometimes chaotic "war inside her brain":

I remember the first time I really started to feel out of control. I had a strong urge to translate the opening passage of a Raymond Chandler novel into Theban script and transcribe it all onto my closet door in multi-colored soap. I still remember the satisfaction I felt when I saw the rainbow of nonsensical characters zig-zagging all over my walls. But just like all the other times to come, like when I bought five identical dresses . . . or spent hours in a train station staring at the ground because it looked like the floor was breathing . . . when I tried to silence my mind by obeying its wild demands—I didn't feel better for long. And even worse, all of my beautifully dreamed plans didn't even make sense to me a few days or weeks later. Amazingly, I didn't even know I had a problem. It never occurred to me that other people don't live like that. But I recognized the dark mood that always came after my sprees wasn't right. When I was fifteen, I had terrible insomnia for months. I couldn't sleep, eat or concentrate. I filled my bed with kitchen knives to scare away the sadness—but it wasn't quite as comforting as I thought it would be. So I started mixing gin and pain-killers squirreled away from my parents' cabinets. It was the only way to rest and get a break from myself. I wasn't suicidal. I just wanted to go into a "mild" coma so that maybe one day I could just wake up and the tumult inside of me would be over.

4. Express yourself conversationally. Write the way you speak, and read your scripts aloud as you write. Don't just mouth the words. Say it out loud. On your first try, you might sit with someone who can listen to you tell your story and type it out for you to be sure it's conversational. Think about the rhythm and pacing. Vary sentence length. If you write poetry or make music, give your commentaries a lyrical sensibility. At the same time, think about your audience, and if you want your story to reach a wide audience outside your immediate community, consider how to introduce colloquial expressions in ways that enrich your narrative. Youth Radio's Anyi Howell has a special knack for finding that balance:

As far back as I can remember, my grandmother, a retired Oakland High cafeteria manager, has gone all out during the holidays to decorate her home in East Oakland. . . . Santa's sleigh and his reindeer were on the roof, along with carolers. Inside, a miniature Christmas town, complete with an ice skating rink, sat in the front window for neighborhood to see. Together, my grandparents put days into the details, placement, and positioning of the Christmas statues, lights, and decorations. When they plugged everything in, thousands of lights would illuminate the scene—leaving me in awe. . . . People would say, "That's YOUR grandmother? Yeah, I know that house—I always bring my kids by there." Nothing could make me more proud.

But this year, for the first time in my life, there will be no decorations. My Grandmother decided to quit because spineless chumps from the neighborhood steal her displays right off the front lawn and damage her crafts. Because of its reputation for violence and homicide, some proudly call my grandmother's neighborhood the Murder Dubs. The vandalism has taken a toll on her spirit.

As a young black man, I know life is hard out here. Some of us are hungry and poor, and we face aggressive racism on a regular basis. I understand the anger in the hearts of my people, but why take it out on my grandmother? . . . What these youngstas don't realize is that the folks they're hurting are the same ones who understand them and what they're going through best. When the police go upside the heads of one of these young brothas, it's these seniors and long-time homeowners . . . who organize and attend rallies to support these fellas. There was a time when a common sense of respect and consideration existed among all of us, even hustlers and street criminals. Today it's gone—either because it is no longer given, or it is no longer demanded. When this mutual honor and respect is restored, the Christmas spirit will return to the Dubs. And Santa Will Dance again in my grandmother's yard.

5. Don't be afraid to use humor and show attitude. That's Youth Radio's Quincy Mosby's trademark. But the best is when humor mixes with substance, as in Quincy's commentary about rappers breaking into the movie business. In just over two minutes he moves from light pop culture observation to a deeper cultural critique. A select few emcees make great films, Quincy says, but they're definitely the exceptions. And the damage isn't limited to the box office:

Most of these films have the same clichéd and regurgitated scenes of toilet humor and pointless sex that don't advance the plot in any way. And they create an image of African Americans as overly promiscuous marijuana addicts and criminals. The dialogue in these bombs is stereotypical and just plain offensive. "Yo dogg, wassup!" It's like the screenwriters think those are the only words hip hop artists know. Do they think if a rapper utters words with more than one syllable, his brain will implode? I can't promise that won't happen, but I'm pretty sure it's not going to. What's really demoralizing about these films is they're often either "hood movies" with a rapper co-starring as the jive-talking friend, or, like Eminem's 8 Mile, loose biographies about a struggling hip-hop artist trying to make it big, but being pulled down by the streets. Honestly, how hard is it to pretend to be yourself? Believe me, I do love hip-hop and my black brothers and sisters. And everyone has a right to express themselves artistically. But where's the personal pride?

6. Fact-check! Even though commentaries are written in first person and can be opinion-based, you still need to verify sources and the

information you report. When commentator Pendarvis Harshaw said that "the N word" originated in U.S. slavery, Youth Radio got verification in writing from an African American studies professor. When one student wrote a commentary stating that cutbacks in municipal transportation funding doubled her commute time to school, an unhappy representative from the transit office called the next day to ask specifically what bus line the student rode, gathering evidence in hopes of refuting her claim. Incidentally, working with young people to notice and analyze which facts, claims, and sources of authority editors do and do not trust can itself serve as a provocative exercise in critical media literacy.

The commentary is a great place to start the narrative process because it doesn't require a lot of advanced work. After students come up with an idea, we tell them to start writing. Very often the writing process itself generates new questions and curiosities, which can then lead producers to want to hear from and write about someone other than themselves.

THE INTERVIEW

Interviews challenge young people to move beyond their assumptions about the topics they care about and to analyze responses in ways that further their stories and respect their interviewees while keeping the focus on telling the truth. The first step for interviews is booking: finding the right person to talk to, whether for a one-on-one conversation, a feature story, or a roundtable discussion. This step is crucial, as it determines which perspectives will end up on the air and which will be left out. In addition to issues of balance, there's also on-air personality to consider. Sometimes a young person has no choice but to book an individual by virtue of his or her position in a given field—the nation's authority on military law, the leading expert on dating violence—but more often than not reporters can choose among multiple contenders, and they are well served to preinterview those candidates to find the one likely to be the most compelling and persuasive on the air. Preinterviews are short and not recorded. Students should not ask every question they plan to pose in the actual interview, or else the answers may sound rehearsed. We ask young people to come up with three or four key questions that will give them a sense of what this person will contribute to their story or roundtable. Then it's time to reach out and make some calls. But first, students can rehearse the interview process based on an activity Senior Producer Rebecca Martin designed.

Booking

THE RULES

- Divide students into teams.
- One team member will participate in each round as a booker.
- Adult producers and other students will serve as interviewees.
- Team members will be scored on their performance based on
  — Greetings: Are you polished, and does your tone match your interviewee's?
  — Pitch: Are you clear and convincing in how you describe your project?
  — Manner: How confident and compelling are you?
  — Questions: Do you ask topical questions? Do you probe for more information?
  — Closing: Have you been clear about next steps?

SOME BOOKING TIPS

- Ask people you trust when searching for guests. Make sure you know the backgrounds and agendas motivating your sources for contacts.
- Write out questions before preinterviewing anyone. Write a two- to three-line description of the story or show you are booking. Write important details you'll need, such as the day and time you are trying to book and location information.
- When cold-calling organizations or businesses for guests, don't give up just because you are told no. Ask if there is anyone else you can talk to. If possible, sidestep the public affairs office, and if that's not possible, make sure always to be nice to the gatekeepers who determine your access.
- The first person who says yes isn't always the best person for your interview.

- Just because someone is chatty doesn't mean he or she will be a thoughtful guest.

- Be sure the guest is a reliable source and offers other resources on the topic. Always consider a person's potential biases.

- Think about how you want to frame the "youthiness" of the story. Sometimes Youth Radio reporters emphasize that they're part of a journalism training program. That angle taps people's eagerness to contribute to youth-initiated projects and learning. At other times they highlight the organization's track record of national broadcasts and high-profile awards. That angle taps people's interest in reaching and influencing significant audiences. It all depends on what you think will be most effective and resonant with your potential interviewees. But no matter what, you are ethically and legally bound to let people know that they will be identified by name and recorded for possible broadcast.

- When finishing a conversation, don't promise anything. Tell guests that you need to check in with your producer, and warn them of possible changes in the show.

Once you've booked your guests, analysts, or characters for your story, the next step is to come up with interview questions. Young people conducting interviews for the first time should role-play the conversation in advance, with a peer or adult producer acting the role of the interviewee. As with the booking exercise, have fun with this. Assign the "interviewee" different personality characteristics: talkative, tight-lipped, obnoxious, offensive, nervous, condescending, dominating, tangential. Come up with a signal (a buzzer, a bell, a pointer) to make the interviewee switch character on demand throughout the role-play. Stage the interview as a performance in front of your full group, and then debrief together about what worked and what didn't. This way, the group learns from one young person's preparation.

Interview Tips from Youth Radio's Newsroom

GETTING STARTED

- Always remember to ask for name and age (where appropriate), and get permission to use your interviewees' voices and names in your story.

- Start with easy questions, ones your subject should feel comfortable answering, so you can build a rapport. It can be effective to start with general questions, and then move to specifics. (This approach works as long as you have ample time. If there is a chance you'll be cut off after just a few moments, jump right to the most important questions.)

- Let your interviewees know that you'd like to be able to use their answers without hearing your questions, so ask them to answer in full sentences. For example, if you ask, "At what age did you first meet your biological mother?," ask them to answer in a way that includes the question: "I met my bio mom for the first time when I was twelve years old."

- Before you start the interview, make a checklist of the information you absolutely must get from your subject and bring that list with you.

- Brainstorm the kinds of things that make you feel inspired to disclose aspects of your own life, and try to create those conditions in your interview.

- Make sure you can answer these questions: What's your story about? (Keep the answer brief.) Where will it air? (Don't make promises unless you're 100 percent sure.) Will you edit what I say? (The answer is usually yes.) Can I approve my clips? (The answer is almost always no.) Who else are you talking to? (Be careful about protecting others' confidentiality. You're not obligated to disclose other participants.)

GETTING INTO IT

- Think about what you want to reveal about yourself, how you can make the interview a real conversation and not a grilling. (But be careful to avoid speaking over your subject; that can make it harder to use the tape.)

- This one's obvious, but easy to forget: avoid yes / no questions! Frame your probes in ways that elicit stories and vivid details. Don't hesitate, at any point, to say, "Can you give me a specific example or memory of what you're talking about?" or "That's really interesting. Can you say a little bit more?" or even, "I'm not sure I understand. Can you bring me back to that moment . . . ?" "Walk me through that."

- Try not to lead the witness. Don't ask questions that reveal your own biases, or make your interviewee feel pressured to answer in a certain way (unless you are intentionally being provocative, but then be careful that you frame the responses fairly in your story, perhaps by including your question on the air as well).

- Even if you have a detailed list of questions, make sure you really listen to your interviewees as they speak. Make eye contact and respond to what you hear, not only what you came prepared to ask.
- Always a great follow-up question: "And then what happened?" Remember that the best tape comes from characters telling specific stories that bring you into the details of their lives, not articulating generalized positions or simplified points of view.

FINISHING UP

- Review your checklist of crucial information and make sure you covered everything before you say good-bye.
- At the end of the interview, ask subjects if they have anything to add. (That question often yields the most interesting material!) Make sure to get their contact information and ask permission to get in touch again if anything further comes up.[7]

These guidelines apply to a range of contexts, but interviewers face special challenges when they are called on to facilitate multiparty discussions, for example, when they host roundtables on public affairs shows. Booking roundtables means not only looking for great individual participants, but also considering how each perspective fits into a larger whole. When young people take the role of host, they disrupt persistent power dynamics that too often relegate them to the position of answering rather than asking questions—and that's assuming they have a place at the table in the first place. We ask students booking a panel to consider likely and unlikely participants, with special attention to those not typically invited to the discussion, who they think have something crucial if unexpected to offer.

Once the panel is under way, hosts need to manage each panelist's air time, paying attention to balance and focus, even when participants (including the host himself or herself) bring very different conversation styles and agendas to the table. It's important for the host to come prepared. Youth Radio panels usually center on a theme, such as adoption, interracial dating, standardized tests, or rites of passage. Hosts need to study up on the key debates associated with their theme and to have a sense of where each of the panelists stands. Still, the best hosts learn not to grandstand or feel they need to prove everything they know about the topic being discussed. Although it can be useful for hosts to share details that are relevant and even sometimes personal about their own lives, they are there to facilitate disclosure among guests, and to listen. Really listen. With experience, hosts learn to make sure their key questions are addressed, but also to allow the conversation to move in an entirely different direction than anticipated, based on the genuine encounter they co-create with their guests.

In most cases, an interview or roundtable discussion plays out as a direct conversation between a reporter or host and subjects. But not in every case—and divergence from this norm can actually generate great radio. Youth Radio's Los Angeles bureau chief, Sara Harris, worked on one story with Jorge Nunez, who was born in Mexico but moved to the United States when he was two years old. As he grew up, Jorge got into trouble and was eventually locked up in the California prison system. Partway through his sentence, Jorge, who says he spoke Spanish "like a white boy" and had spent his entire life in Los Angeles, copped a plea and agreed to be deported back to Mexico without a hearing: "They drove the bus right to the border, and opened the gate. I was free. But I was in Mexico." Jorge's mother and his two kids were back in the United States, now a forbidden destination for him. When his daughter turned five, he bought her a Dora the Explorer doll for her birthday, but he couldn't be with her to celebrate. Sara, his Youth Radio producer, could. Sara recorded Cynthia Marie as she opened up the doll and kept rolling tape when Cynthia called her dad on the phone. Then Sara went back to Mexico to play the tape for Jorge, and she recorded his reflections on the conversation. They cut together these cross-border elements to produce a key scene in Jorge's story, with the doll's automated soundtrack audible in the underneath:

CYNTHIA: *(on tape) Hello! . . . my birthday is now-now.*

JORGE: When my daughter got on the phone, it was like. . . . She said, "I'm five," and I said, "Man, you must be bigger than me now! Are you real tall?" And she was like, no. And I was like, you're five, and she was like, no but . . .

CYNTHIA: *(on tape) How old are you?*

JORGE: I was like, you know who I am? And she said, "Yeah, you're George."

CYNTHIA: *(on tape) Yeah, you're George. George.*

JORGE: I said, "I'm you're daddy."

CYNTHIA: *(on tape) My dad.*

JORGE: And I was like, why don't you call me daddy? Then she was like, "I don't know."

Jorge's story is an extreme case of collaborative interviewing, in which Sara Harris, the adult producer, transported audio and served as proxy interviewer in a country to which Jorge could never return. This strategy of passing recordings back and forth and scripting around clips to tell a cross-border story is one methodology in what Sara has dubbed "audio postales." The technique doesn't have to involve international travel to yield powerful moments. Young people can record in one place, then bring that tape to someone else and record his or her reactions to it. By intercutting between these two scenes, they can produce passages in which two distinct points of view, two geographies, two moments in time unfold together.

For many Youth Radio stories, not only those dictated by extenuating circumstances, like Jorge's deportation, adult producers participate actively in interviews. Especially for first-time reporters, the adult producer can provide coaching to make sure that together they cover all the necessary narrative ground while capturing sound that is clean and of broadcast quality. Cassandra Gonzalez, another one of Sara's students at Youth Radio LA, reflects on an added benefit of having Sara with her during interviews when it is time to edit the story with national producers from outside outlets: "[Sara] was on the grind working with me on these stories. Being that she was doing that and experiencing that with me, she understood. . . . On top of that, we built a relationship, she had her job duty and personal interest, to advocate for the things I thought should be in the story or shouldn't be. . . . As opposed to 'That shouldn't be in the story because no one will understand that,' it's 'How can we make them understand?'" It bears emphasizing, however, that sometimes it can be equally powerful, even absolutely necessary, for a young person to go out alone. As we described in chapter 2, Sophie Simon-Ortiz was by herself when she interviewed an acquaintance who had married a U.S. Marine in exchange for a monthly cut of his paycheck and world-class health benefits. Although we will never know for sure, our sense is that the young woman would not have been nearly as willing to disclose her story had an adult producer been hovering over the conversation.[8]

On a recent reporting trip to New York, Karime Blanco covered a conference on juvenile justice reform. I (Lissa) was there as Karime's producer. When it came time for Karime to interview one of the panelists, a prison reform activist, I was torn about whether to accompany her on the interview or to let Karime do it herself. Karime said she was fine on her own, and when I listened back to the tape, it was clear that she understood the value of leaving the two of them alone. Karime's interviewee talked about her family, how she first got locked up, her analysis of the prison industrial complex, her ideas for reform. At one point she mentioned growing up Black, Italian, and Indian in a neighborhood that was predominantly Caribbean. People were always asking her "what" she "was." Several minutes later, just after she had argued that formerly incarcerated young people of color should be the ones reforming the system, not some "great white hope" from graduate school, Karime revisited an earlier theme:

KARIME: I agree. By the way, as far as people not knowing what you were, I feel you. They called me whitifa growing up.

INTERVIEWEE: What does that mean?

KARIME: Little white girl.

INTERVIEWEE: Oh, really, so you're, you're um . . .

KARIME: I'm Mexican.

INTERVIEWEE: Oh, really? Yeah, when I'm in Cali, I'm Mexican, too. Word.

KARIME: A different kind of Latino everywhere we go.

INTERVIEWEE: Yeah, exactly. Go uptown, I'd be Dominican. I'm like, "Okay." And then so many Latin women ask me, "You don't speak Spanish?" I'll be like, "No I don't." She'll say, "You just were neglected, I'll teach you." "Okay, but my grandmother didn't speak Spanish either, but okay." (laughing)

KARIME: See, and that's a trip, because the Latinos in the Bay, a lot of the parents don't want to teach their kids Spanish. Because they'll be like, I don't want to confuse them, I don't want them to grow up with this hardship or whatever, and I'm like—

INTERVIEWEE: And you're so setting them back. You know how many job descriptions I see come through that say "bilingual a plus"? Yeah, I wish I'd paid attention in Spanish classes when I was in school. . . .

KARIME: That's why they have Spanish bilingual programs in the white schools, for rich kids.

INTERVIEWEE: Yeah, French—all that.

KARIME: They grow up with Spanish, French and all that. You think you're gonna take my Latino jobs? I don't think so.

There's no way to know for sure how this conversation would have been different, or whether this portion of it would have happened at all, if I had gone along to check recording levels and make sure Karime was hitting all her key questions. Even if I had been there, the key issue wouldn't so much have been another person's presence, or an older person's presence, but a white person's presence in a conversation about race. It's certainly possible that Karime and the young woman she interviewed would have said the same things, or that the three of us together could have gotten into a different discussion about the politics of racialization and unwanted "passing." But on their own, the two of them were able to take the conversation in the direction they wanted it to go. It would be easy to dismiss this passage as tangential, even a distraction from the story topic. What did "whitifa" and French class have to do with juvenile justice reform (besides everything, to the extent that underlying these topics were critiques of inequality, but not in a form easily translated into a radio spot)? None of this bit of conversation made its way into the final interview Karime cut together. Yet the fact that the two connected this way may well have promoted a level of candor that made the whole exchange more honest. At the very least, Karime had to fend for herself, and that's a very different accomplishment and skill-development opportunity than managing an interview knowing that your producer is always there to fill in the blanks.

We tell students that the key to any interview is recognizing *themselves* as participants. They are not neutral interrogators, but engaged conversationalists, and moments of genuine connection between them and their interviewees translate into great radio.[9]

THE FEATURE

We began with the commentary: one voice. We moved to the interview: two or more voices. Now the feature: a multivocal story with scenes and endless options in terms of format and purpose. In the introduction to this volume, we used the phrase *acts and tracks,* radio producers' shorthand for a feature story at its most basic. *Acts* stand for "actualities," meaning characters' interview clips. *Tracks* refer to the reporter's narration. Listen to a bare-bones public radio news report, and you will likely hear an even rhythm shifting between acts and tracks. The reporter says a few sentences, then introduces another speaker, who says a few sentences; the reporter comes back and says a few sentences, then introduces another speaker, and so on until the reporter offers the final word and signs off. This description makes the format sound tedious, but with a strong reporter and compelling characters, even acts and tracks can rivet listeners. Still, the format undeniably lacks the very thing that distinguishes radio as a media art: sound. Sound includes ambience: an espresso machine spitting milk, children sneaker-squeaking across the floor of an elementary school gym, artillery blasts, protest chants. Sound also situates characters in scenes where something actually takes place that moves the story forward: a girl coming out to her mother, a teacher administering the SAT, a teenager visiting his childhood home. Ambience and scenes bring life, texture, and a sense of place to radio features.

Feature stories can be reports, like Sophie Simon-Ortiz's account of sham military marriages or Belia Mayeno Saavedra's piece exposing Marines' photo collections from the Iraq war. Reports uncover important, research-backed information related to news events. Features can also take shape as nonnarration audio documentaries, like *Oakland Scenes,* with its mix of spoken-word poetry and street corner conversations. Anyi Howell's feature on racial profiling shows just how creative a producer can get with the feature, mixing first-person writing with other voices, verses, and scenes.

Among the most pivotal moments in feature production is picking the best clips. After gathering and transcribing interviews, ambience, and scenes, producers sit down with all the logs and identify the strongest bits.

In this process, composition morphs into an editorial process. It requires imagination to envision the narrative arc and discipline to let go of elements that don't work for the story. Three criteria guide the process:

1. Moments you *must* include because of their direct relevance to the topic.

2. Moments you *really want* to include because they are so poignant, entertaining, honest, or unexpected, even if they have little to do with your story topic.

3. Moments you *wish* you could include because they contain vital information, but they just don't work (the sound is garbled, the speaker is incoherent, or an ambulance sirened by at just the wrong time).

The moments that meet the first criterion are perhaps the easiest to work with; these constitute the story's backbone. When Youth Radio's Brandon McFarland was working on a feature about his decision to stop sagging his pants, he knew he'd use a clip from his friend Pendarvis, describing how he first started sagging. Brandon knew he'd use his colleague Gerald's analysis linking sagging to code-switching in language. Elmer's adamant refusal to try pulling his pants up would definitely show up in the story. And Brandon knew his mom's recollection of the time her son tried to sag suit pants at church would for sure make the cut. Taken together, this collection of clips offered a range of perspectives on Brandon's topic and included some vibrant scenes of people revealing themselves in distinct and honest ways.

Moments that meet the second criterion pose more of a challenge. Take this clip from Brandon's conversation with his dad, when he asked his dad how he used to dress as a kid:

DAD: Men had platform shoes, big naturals, leather jackets, bellbottoms, Levi jeans.

BRANDON: So if you were going to the club what would you wear . . . back in the day?

DAD: Some bellbottoms, silk shirt, big collar, and a scarf around my neck.

BRANDON: Did you have a fro back in the day?

DAD: Yes.

BRANDON: This is radio but just for the record my dad has no more hair. It's all gone.

Brandon really wanted to use this clip in the story. It contained a nice visual image and a sweet interaction between father and son. But initially, I (Lissa) didn't see the connection to the story at hand. So Brandon had to fight for the clip, which is both a crucial learning experience and a production moment. He had to make a convincing case that his dad's statements would mean something to audiences who had no particular investment in Brandon or his familial dynamics. In his argument to keep the clip in the script, Brandon leveraged the power of history, which carries considerable weight, especially for a story at risk of being dismissed as a frivolous popular culture snapshot. Having the dad in the story revealed that the very same people who bemoan sagging today wore their own outrageous fashions when they were young. The broader lesson here is not to give up on brilliant clips too easily, even if initially they seem off-point. Some of the most transcendent moments on radio come when something unexpected happens. The story takes a turn listeners didn't expect. Perhaps a stuffy expert reveals something deeply personal, or the reporter himself or herself makes a discovery captured on tape. Even bad tape can turn into great tape if the reporter creates a reflexive moment in the script, when he or she actually stops the flow of the story and comments on something that went wrong in the production process. However, none of these unexpected moments work if they do not drive the story forward in some way. A producer needs to let go of clips that detract from the story's focus. The good news is that, if those moments are true radio gold, the producer probably has the kernel there for his or her next story.

The third criterion includes necessary elements that don't work in their present form. There are a few options when faced with these bits of tape. You can go back and rerecord if you absolutely must hear a specific piece of information directly from one of your interviewees. Or you can turn the actuality into a track by paraphrasing what someone else said in your own narration or describing a terrific scene that illuminates your story but somehow just didn't translate to tape. The third option is used very rarely at Youth Radio, but can be powerful. You can reenact a scene that you never could have captured because you didn't know you'd be working on a story when the incident took place.

That's what news and music producer Orlando Campbell did for his story about what it was like to come across rumors about his own death. His script starts like this:

(Music: "Get It, Get It")

ORLANDO: I'm Roach Gigz, I'm a rapper, and I'm very much alive. But recently I discovered that not everybody believes the third statement. I got a call from my producer when I first heard the news. The conversation went something like this.

(Sound: Ring Ring)

ORLANDO: Hello.

PRODUCER: Roach, you cool?

ORLANDO: Yeah bra', I'm good, Why?

PRODUCER: Man, somebody just told me that everybody been telling *them* you got shot and died.

ORLANDO: Died? Hell nah. Man, I'm at the Philly cheese steak shop on Divis.

(Music: "ET Fone Home")

ORLANDO: My brother from another mother, who himself survived a shooting, called me to inform me that rumors of my untimely demise had found its way to the internet.

(Sound: Keyboard clickety click)

ORLANDO: The online hip-hop heads were going back and forth on forums debating my alleged murder.

TM: *Aye, y'all . . . I was at ma patna house dis weekend n he told me that dat <BLEEP> Roach Gigz from the group B.I.G. got killed. Could somebody tell me if this is true or not?*

HDG: *Yes sir. . . . Nobody ain't heard this? Two <BLEEP>s from Vallejo and one <BLEEP> from Frisco told me that two weeks ago. I'm pretty sure about this.*

HDG: *Yeah he dead.*

SP925: *He's alive. He just posted a bulletin on MySpace.*

ORLANDO: This is a weird feeling. I had to pinch myself and make sure that I was really on earth and not looking down. With all the rumors about my death running laps in the streets and on the net, I started to think about my professional role models and the one thing that links them all together.

There are two clutch passages in this script Orlando had to bring to life: the first, when his producer tipped him off about the rumors of his death, and the second, a montage of lines from a series of blogs and forums. In both cases, Orlando lined up Youth Radio colleagues to record those passages, and the end product is clearly much more engaging than it would have been had he just reiterated or paraphrased those conversations in his own voice. That said, when using theatrical techniques like these it's crucial for the author to make it clear to the audience that they are hearing a reenactment or recitation, not words recorded by the original speaker in real time. Dramatization can be a beautiful thing, but not if listeners don't know that's what they're hearing.

Once the student producers have all their clips, the next step is to outline an order and sketch the narration by writing around them. The beauty of writing a radio feature is that there's no blank page. The writer's job is to service and shepherd the tape, to help it make sense. Students use the narration to tell the story the clips don't tell, describing scenes, introducing speakers, explaining confusing parts, filling in necessary information. Two techniques come in enormously handy, both of which have particular relevance for youth media literacy. If students are having trouble making a transition *into* a clip, we suggest they consider stealing their character's line. For example, during his interview for Brandon's story, Pendarvis said he started sagging to revolt against his grandfather, and then he described a typical scene in his household on a Saturday night. In the story script, Brandon is the one who says Pendarvis started sagging to revolt against his grandfather, and Pendarvis comes in only to describe the Saturday night scene. It's a smooth and seamless transition from narration to tape. A second technique applies to writing out of tape. Brandon's story includes a clip of his mom teasing him for trying to sag slacks: "You can't sag suit pants! But yeah, you tried." Brandon comes off the clip saying, "C'mon, Mom, you tried some ridiculous looks, too." He speaks directly back to his tape, addressing his mom in a way that sounds believable and creating the feeling of a conversation, thus avoiding the stilted, predictable rhythms of a radio story with abrupt shifts in tone between character and narrator.

Overall, to script a radio feature, young people must find and articulate a voice that frames other voices, scenes, and sounds to tell a compelling story. In this sense, the moment-to-moment demands of feature production challenge the conception of youth voice so often applied to media-making projects. As evident in the two techniques highlighted here, young people strategically invoke and appropriate multiple voices in their stories, even as they mix and blend their own voices with other people's utterances, by incorporating their lines and talking back to tape. These techniques challenge producers to complicate the singular authority attached to their own perspectives, even as the stories push listeners to hear young people in new ways.

THE FRAME

Surprisingly, some of the most heated editorial tensions we've faced at Youth Radio center not on the script itself, but on the *intro* and *back announce*. The intro is what the show host says as a lead-in to a reporter's story; a back announce is what the host says to transition out of that story. Editorial debates about intros and back announces grow especially fraught around two charged themes: framing and credit. The host's intro shapes how an audience hears the story. Youth Radio always comes up with a suggested intro before we ever pitch a story to an outlet, but the outlet editors get to decide precisely what they will say to frame the piece; that's *their* part of the script. In 2005 Youth Radio's Lauren Silverman produced a commentary about her struggle with anorexia, which started like this:

> Looking back in time, it's hard to unravel the mystery of my ongoing battle with Anorexia. When I was thirteen, the image of the perfect young woman began to form in my mind, and unfortunately, I looked and acted nothing like her. This raised the question, "How could I be special?" I wanted to escape my own body, ignore its basic necessities until I could ignore my emotions too.
> I started to focus on my menu instead of the problems in my life that were really making me depressed. I cut out junk foods, counted calories and excessively dieted (even though my regular size pants is 0), and

this led me on a downward spiral. Every day, I took one step further away from social situations . . . which left me alone with myself, obsessing, with no one there to distract me. I was performing a disappearing act, but at first, people didn't notice I was vanishing. I didn't want them to know . . . mostly because I had gotten so used to the friendship that anorexia provided me.

In shaping the introduction to Lauren's story, we labored over every word. The statistics on anorexia are contested and tough to state simply. Even the distinction between calling anorexia a *disease* and a *disorder* had implications for medical accuracy and Lauren's portrayal. But the intro was easy compared to the back announce. Youth Radio has a standard policy that the host credits both the young person and the organization on the air, as in "Lauren Silverman's story was produced by Youth Radio." Occasionally an outlet will want to add something else to a story's back announce, perhaps an update on the young person's situation or a line that connects the story that just ended with the one coming next. In the case of Lauren's story, at one point the editor suggested adding a line to her back announce about anorexia's bleak recovery rates: only half of those who suffer from this disorder fully recover. The suggestion set off intense discussion about what it would mean, for Lauren personally and the story, to end on that note. Just as intros frame the story from the top, back announces give the final message, and in the end Lauren and her Youth Radio editors did not feel comfortable with a last word that in her view undermined her point in telling the story, which centered on her recovery, not the risk of relapse.

One might easily dismiss these kinds of decisions, which center and sometimes obsess on single words, as excessively controlling, too much "wordsmithing." At a certain point, it's true that producers need to make a call about whether they're willing to jeopardize a story's broadcast for the sake of one turn of phrase. That said, the process and its consequences are never trivial, for the young person as well as the editorial and educational integrity of the environment where that emerging journalist works. Often a single word can raise questions that cut to the core of youth media, in particular how to balance youth development considerations with the collective desire and sense of urgency to get the story on the air. Nothing is more powerful than the final word.

REVERBERATIONS

But the final word of radio broadcast is rarely where the story ends.[10] Since its inception, radio has depended on listeners' willingness to complete audio stories by projecting their own images and individual meanings through a kind of "auditory voyeurism" (Douglas, 2004, p. 18). Public radio in particular aspires to extend civic life, free communication, and participatory democracy (Engelman, 1996), as evident in such conventions as call-in shows and playing listeners' responses on the air.[11]

That sense of audience engagement is rarely far from a producer's mind. Youth Radio's Cassandra Gonzalez had a feeling that her story, *Young Moms' Club*, would elicit a strong audience reaction. The feature focused on her group of friends who had had babies very young. To be good mothers, they found, it helped a lot to get out every now and then, to meet for a drink or listen to music, so they could still feel young, that they hadn't completely given up their former lives. But it wasn't easy to do so. At one point in the story, Cassandra described a scene in which she was headed out for a planned date with friends, when her grandmother brought her screaming baby to the door and yelled to the whole neighborhood, "What kind of mother are you?!" Cassandra pulled her car back into the driveway and stayed home. You then hear the grandmother herself, lamenting all the times she's left at home with her great-granddaughter late into the night. Still, Cassandra points out, "Even my psychotherapist says, 'You have to make time for yourself . . . or you might end up resenting your life and your child, and it might lead to depression.'"

Two days after this story aired nationally, the show host read letters from listeners, after saying that the mailbox had been filled with responses to the Youth Radio story. Many listeners seemed to feel that, although the commentator might be a good mother, she was an "inconsiderate granddaughter," the host said. One listener wrote in to say that the young mother "feels that she's entitled to go out with friends and have some 'me' time and still be young. . . . Wrong. The only person who has the right to be free from childcare worries is her grandmother."

Youth Radio typically receives lots of raves after stories air nationally, yet an email like this is rarely a huge surprise to young producers. With respect to her *Young Moms' Club* feature, Cassandra points out that listeners to national radio typically hear from "a scholar interested in teen pregnancy" rather than a young person speaking directly and at length from experience. Cassandra says the listeners who take offense at her stories are "the people I want to influence the most." She doesn't take the criticism personally, because if listeners are sufficiently engaged to form a critique, Cassandra has "helped them take a step towards framing the way *they* feel about the issue at hand." She knows that relinquishing some measure of control over her own voice, life, and experience comes with the territory of youth media production. One of the most important lessons young people learn in the process is how to work across various audiences, when to allow anticipated audience responses to influence a particular story, and how to draw insight and further inspiration when audiences talk back.

Stories like Cassandra's tend to elicit strong audience reaction on their own. In the old days, listeners who wanted a copy of a Youth Radio broadcast had to request a CD. Now they can find the story on our website, download it, link to it, repost it, comment on it, and take it in entirely new directions.[12] The appetite for youth media is especially strong among educators, who urgently seek materials that will enliven mandated curriculum and engage students. It was in response to this need that Youth Radio launched its "Teach Youth Radio" online curriculum resource in 2006, designed to help educators in a range of settings to integrate youth-produced content into their classrooms (see appendix). "News Breaks" based on Youth Radio stories offer standards-aligned lesson ideas, links to research and resources, and background information on the reporter and the production process. We have designed this chapter in the spirit of "Teach Youth Radio," hoping that the behind-the-scenes accounts and concrete practices detailed here support educators' efforts to integrate media production into their classrooms and community settings.

Educators who work directly with teens aren't the only ones for whom youth media holds promise for extended use. You're a university professor running a class on community health, and you want to teach your students to leverage the media and convincingly communicate research findings to public audiences. You're an ethnographic researcher eager to partner with a group of teenagers as co-investigators in your study, but you're not sure how to draw young people into the inquiry process. You're a veteran broadcast journalist or filmmaker wanting to appeal to youth audiences in ways that lend greater rigor, nuance, and edge to your stories. For these agendas, the youth media processes and practices outlined in this chapter, and across the book, have relevance.

In our own university teaching, both of us have drawn from youth media methods and archives to frame undergraduate and graduate courses. In Lissa's Urban Education course at the University of California, Berkeley, she opened many classes by playing a Youth Radio story, and she used interviews and radio commentaries to prepare students as ethnographic researchers and public intellectuals. For a course on Community Organizing in Public Health at San Francisco State University, Vivian assigned two commentaries integrating course themes connecting personal meaning to social action and violence prevention. Other professors from around the country use youth-generated content and methods in courses across a range of humanities and social science fields. The methods and genres elaborated in this chapter can be used to engage undergraduate and graduate students as producers rather than mere recipients of knowledge in the media, thus complementing and complicating assigned academic texts.

The methods used to produce even those academic texts are also transforming as a result of youth media possibilities. More and more researchers aim to partner with young people as study collaborators, while exploring uses of audio and video diaries and blogs as data sources. These developments in ethnographic and other qualitative and quantitative research methods raise new questions about ethics, transparency, and consent, as well as acceptable forms for presenting or even expressing fieldwork data and research findings. When a national organization called Listen Up! pulled together a 2007 online showcase of exemplary youth media projects, the line-up included products from Youth Radio and other established youth media organizations, along with a series called *Echoes of Brown*, developed by a university-based Participant Action Research collective that includes youth and adult investigators. This convergence of media arts and ethnographic research signals a coming together of previously separate realms of storytelling.

Storytellers in the media industry—reporters, producers, editors, commentators, and so on—increasingly find themselves surrounded by citizen journalists covering every newsroom beat, in some cases drawing a bigger buzz and getting more important scoops than established media professionals. Rather than dismiss these developments as amateur or regard them as a threat, journalists and media outlets are well served to connect with creative newcomers to the industry, including those who have followed various pathways to get there. Young people who have been trained to produce the genres outlined in this chapter are anything but amateur, but they do often bring their own distinct sensibilities to journalistic projects.

At the beginning of this chapter, we outlined the circles of production that no longer follow a lockstep path (if they ever did) from preproduction through production, postproduction, and distribution. Our intent is to launch emerging and veteran storytellers back into that cycle, to begin again producing *with* youth, telling new stories.

FIVE

Alumni Lives

Alumni lives means both the life that happens after Youth Radio and the lives that bring young people into the field of youth media. In many ways, this last chapter could have gone first. In previous chapters we dissected the ins and outs of literacy, pedagogy, and media justice. But just who are the young people who make up Youth Radio? Where do they come from? What attracted them to this particular afterschool media program? What's their story?

Six first-person essays from Youth Radio graduates ground our concluding chapter, including one from Vivian. A common theme you'll see among us is the desire to be heard. It was not Youth Radio that gave us voice. We showed up already having something to say and ways to say it. What we have in common is the desire for community, interdependence, and connection—something to belong to. What we share is the need to add meaning to our lives and transcend individual differences.

In this chapter we present personal narratives that suggest the complexity of *alumni lives*. You will also find scripts for stories produced by all the alumni featured in this chapter. In Vivian's case, you can look at the book itself as its own kind of script. Throughout the book, we regard the scripts not as raw data, but as multilayered analyses that tackle the key themes addressed within these pages. Because we couldn't include every graduate whose work is represented throughout *Drop That Knowledge,* we opted to highlight a range of writing based on Youth Radio's geographic, socioeconomic, gender, race, and ethnic diversity, as well as a diversity of topics: the war within the self and an ever-present, too long-lasting international war; community change and racial stereotyping; personal hunger and recovery; educational policy and inequality; lives and deaths in music, real and imagined; and discourses of hope in national politics.

Most people listen to stories to hear about other people. What did they do, and why? How did they react to this or that odd situation? How are they different from me, and how are we the same? Stories about people are certainly easier to tell than stories about ideas. Nonetheless we waited to share insights into where young people are now because our lede went directly to the issues behind young people's lived educational experiences. Furthermore there is a problem beginning and staying with personal stories (Wallack, Woodruff, Dorfman, & Diaz, 1999): stories that focus on individuals or isolated episodes do not always help audiences understand the issues and structures behind the personal. Coming at the end, our six storytellers personalize the issues explored throughout the book, as well as the theories and institutions that shape the circumstances around them.

So with this prelude we underscore the intersection of public politics and personal biography. We want to acknowledge the emotional level and humanity of this work and its ripple effects. Thus we start with Vivian's recollection, almost thirty years after the fact, of what youth media was like for her, back in the day.

VIVIAN CHÁVEZ

Hungry for learning and mad as hell, that was me, a junior at Berkeley High School, a woman of color, an immigrant with an accent, someone

with a nonconformist spirit growing up in one of the most progressive cities in the United States, rebelling against and experiencing racism. Teachers said strange things to me. One said he had never met a Latino who didn't have an accent. Then he asked me, in front of the whole class, "Why is that?" As if I knew. Everyone laughed. To this day I still don't know if they found humor in his words or in the stumped look on my face.

Being defiant was a necessary device, an antidote to guard against the adults in charge of my education, who were sometimes obstacles to it. Adults like my school counselor, who in an offensive, self-satisfied manner, recommended I take cooking class when I was inquiring about chemistry. Nothing wrong with cooking, but his tone and body language gave me the impression that to him, I was nothing more than a stereotype, someone not quite "college bound." Eager for opposition, I demanded to take chemistry and got out of his office as soon as I could.

The worst kind of put-downs came from home. Divorced twice from each other, my parents leaked a hate for each other that fed into my own anger. Bouncing between their places and sleeping over at friends' houses, I needed an outlet for the place of rage within me.

It was 1979, a new decade with space for innovation. Ellin O'Leary was working with Project Director Louis Freedberg at Youth News, the program out of which Youth Radio was established. They were recruiting teenagers to join a new afterschool program. I joined the crew and from the moment we met was challenged to speak my mind and be myself without ever getting in trouble for it. Curious about my life, putting aside their assumptions, they were open to hearing my personal experience. Genuinely interested in my opinions, they asked, "How do you know?" Followed by that harder question, "How do you know what you know?"

Youth News was the place where I learned how to investigate my community, including looking at my own home in a different way. As a journalist in training, I had a new power: the power to ask questions, to be creative and become civically engaged. It was a powerful time in my life, being a teenager and having the opportunity to frame a news story. As a first-generation Latina, I found it empowering to understand how people connect through their stories. Stories of struggle, stories of survival, stories of wanting something and not being able to get it, stories of failure and triumph over adversity.

My Spanish was not perfect, and English was my second language. Falling in love with language—speaking, writing, reading, listening—was the furthest thing from my mind, and yet here was an opportunity to switch the code. Prior to youth media training, I was outspoken, confident, and fearless, but my words were interpreted as confrontational and perceived as offensive. Through youth media training I gained effective communication skills and got the chance to amplify my voice. I discovered that "good English" was the language of power and the way I could make myself heard. The more I learned to play with language, the more profound my ideas became and the more open and persuasive I grew. Youth media teachers helped me write commentaries and radio features without trying to fix or change me. They helped me to tune into and unlearn some ideas that did not serve me, so that the media would carry my message through any self-doubt.

When the late great radio personality Roy Lee came in to teach us how to speak into the microphone, he saw me struggling with pronunciation. Looking for the "right way" to say things, I sounded

fake. Yet my goal was to speak "correctly" and to be considered credible. Respectfully disagreeing with my position, Roy insisted I speak
from the heart and not get rid of my accent, but instead use it to my
advantage. His words still echo as a sweet antidote to the climate of
prejudice around me. To this day, when someone comments, "You have
an accent," I don't get defensive. Nodding my head, I remember Roy's
advice. He influenced me to become comfortable with my accent and
the tonality of words. As my passion for speaking grew, I learned to
cultivate humility, realizing that my voice was not enough. My story
was important to the extent it represented the voices of others who have
not had a chance to speak and be heard.

For the first time in my education I was learning from teachers who
wanted to build knowledge with me. I gained technical skills, debated
the meaning of the word *community,* and faced the shyness that surfaced every time I heard myself on the air. The invitation to research a
news story made me an active participant in the creation of knowledge
and gave me a different way to look at the world. Reporting on a story
about a policy affecting education, I learned about the California
legislative process and even questioned elected officials. Writing a
feature on South Africa, I found personal meaning in the opposition to
apartheid and how students like me were protesting racial propaganda
in the official curriculum. With Pink Floyd's lyrics "We don't need no
education," I reported on how Bay Area high school students can relate
to injustice in Soweto.

When I graduated from high school I entered college ready to be
a Latino equivalent of Oprah. But fortune would have it differently.
Like many students at California's public universities, I found most of
my desired and required college classes were already full. To study
broadcast communication arts would have taken me years that I simply
couldn't afford. Luckily the tools gained at Youth News gave me the
critical thinking and social action readiness for any academic major.
I graduated from San Francisco State University with two bachelor's
degrees, in Spanish and La Raza studies (1985). Then I went to UC
Berkeley for my master's (1992) and doctorate degrees in public health
(1999). Currently I teach in my alma mater, putting into practice the
knowledge and skills gained through my experience with youth media.
My students anticipate that I will ask them, "How do you know?"
Followed up with the harder question, "How do you know what you
know?" My teaching philosophy mirrors the way I was taught: weav-
ing my own voice with historical documents, community members'
perspectives, and other forms of artistic and scientific data to produce
complex life stories.

BELIA MAYENO SAAVEDRA

If I had to identify a single sound that defined my childhood years, it would be the "Shhhhh!" (The exclamation point on the end is important, since I think it just might be the only quiet sound that feels to the listener like an emphatic shout.) In school, teachers constantly told me to stop talking. My mother told me my voice was way too loud, and my dad said I asked too many goddamn questions about grown folks' business. After a while, I carried around a feeling of wrongness inside myself. I was too loud, too nosy, I wanted too much.

As I got older, I started to recognize how this mixture of shame and enforced silence was used not only against me, but also against people who shared my gender identity, my ethnicity, and my class background. On the radio I heard politicians excoriating single teenage mothers like my mom, and TV news pundits decried all the "illegal" Mexicans who were supposedly descending on the United States to steal jobs from the rest of America. But just like when I was a little kid, I wasn't allowed to speak back.

I guess this is the point in the narrative where I could tie a nice little bow around my story. I could say that my frustration led me to Youth Radio, where I picked up a microphone and found empowerment and now I never have to be silent again. But if the stories in the book you hold in your hands have taught me anything, it's that simple clichés and happy endings are rarely true, and they definitely don't make for good journalism.

The truth is, I didn't come to Youth Radio to find my voice. My voice was never lost to begin with. I was not missing the ability or desire to speak. I was missing a community of people who let me know that they wanted to listen. Youth Radio gave me a very powerful gift. Coming into Youth Radio meant that I was coming to a place where adults and other young people reaffirmed that I was an expert on my own experience. Although I certainly loved the moments I got on air, ultimately it is this acknowledgment of the unshakable right of young people to tell our own stories that truly shaped who I am and the work I choose to do.

I spent time in New York City teaching creative writing workshops to homeless queer youth and incarcerated young women. These young people were not inclined to trust an outsider with a California accent, especially one who showed up at their facilities with a handful of tiny golf-score pencils (erasers aren't allowed inside), trying to get them to write poetry. But once they understood that I was there only to ask them questions and not speak for them, they opened up and wrote some of the most honest and brilliant poetry I've ever read. Whether I

was working with a twenty-one-year-old in a shelter in Manhattan or a fourteen-year-old in a group home in the Bronx, I took the approach that I had learned from my favorite mentors at Youth Radio. I respectfully asked question after question and truly listened to their answers.

These days I'm back at Youth Radio as a full-time staff person working with the students of the Community Action Project. These young people come to the program because they have been expelled or suspended from school for violence or are on parole or probation. They tell me they experience that same familiar feeling of being hushed and ignored by most of the people around them. I still can't promise any magical microphone. But I can show them how to wedge their mics into the cracks in the echo chambers of mass media, so that we make openings wide enough for our voices to ring through.

Map of My Mind

Belia Mayeno Saavedra
NPR/Day to Day

The war inside my brain began during my freshman year of high school. I remember the first time I really started to feel out of control.

I had a strong urge to translate the opening passage of a Raymond Chandler novel into Theban script and transcribe it all onto my closet door in multi-colored soap. I still remember the satisfaction I felt when I saw the rainbow of nonsensical characters zig-zagging all over my walls. But just like all the other times to come, like when I bought five identical dresses . . . or spent hours in a train station staring at the ground because it looked like the floor was *breathing* . . . when I tried to silence my mind by obeying its wild demands I didn't feel better for long. And even worse, all of my beautifully dreamed plans didn't even make sense to me a few days or weeks later. Amazingly, I didn't even know I had a problem. It never occurred to me that other people don't live like that.

But I recognized the dark mood that always came after my sprees wasn't right. When I was fifteen, I had terrible insomnia for months. I couldn't sleep, eat or concentrate. I filled my bed with kitchen knives to scare away the sadness, but it wasn't quite as comforting as I thought it would be. So I started mixing gin and pain-killers squirreled away from my parents' cabinets. It was the only way to rest and get a break from myself. I wasn't suicidal. I just wanted to go into a "mild" coma so that maybe one day I could just wake up and the tumult inside of me would be over.

In spite of all of this, it was hard to accept that anything was actually wrong with me. I believed if I tried hard enough, I could heal myself. It was like expecting someone with a broken leg to just "walk it off." My family wanted to believe that it was that simple too. I remember sitting with my mom, as she stroked my forehead just the way she did when I was a baby and she wanted me to take a nap. She asked me, with a hint of hope in her voice, "M'ija, are you *sure* it's not just PMS?"

When I finally made the decision to go on anti-depressants and mood stabilizers a few years ago, there was a part of me that was sad to say goodbye to those vivid highs and lows. Before, I could concentrate on drawing for ten hours straight and emerge with an amazing picture that didn't even look like it came from my hand. Everyone seemed to like me when I was on one of my highs. And when I was depressed, at least I wrote some good poetry. Just like anything else, when you live with pain, you get used to it. And those times when I felt intoxicated with energy or hid inside the dark cabinets in my head were retreats from the everyday life of clipping toenails and grocery shopping. When I first started the medication, I often felt like I was squinting in the sunlight, everything seemed too bright. Being awake was overwhelming because I couldn't escape back into my own mental wilderness.

Even now, it's still hard to trust myself. I might never know for sure if the war inside my brain is completely over. But I am enjoying the cease-fire.

Picturing War / Reflections on Return
Belia Mayeno Saavedra
NPR/Morning Edition

BELIA: A year ago, Former Marine reservist Ed [last name] returned from Iraq, after taking part in the U.S. invasion. Now he's back at University of California at Riverside, a twenty-six-year-old art student. Here's what he says about the stories of prison abuse coming out of Iraq. . . .

ED: *It's like Chris Rock said, I wouldn't do it, but I understand. I'm not saying I approve of it, but I understand the conditions that led up to them doing it.*

BELIA: Ed's buddy Luis [last name], a shy twenty-one-year-old, resumed his freshman year at Riverside when he returned from Iraq a year ago.

(Sound comes up . . . bit of quiet laughter, Luis: "Oh yeah, I remember that, but you know what happened . . . ")

BELIA: Luis was a field radio operator for a logistics unit in Iraq. . . . He says sometimes they had to round up Iraqis and detain them. And that when you see someone as your enemy, and you feel like they're going to kill you, you start to look at them with hate. At some point, Luis says, you're going to lose your judgment, even if it's just for a minute or two. And it's up to you to know how to manage it, he says. He tells this story.

LUIS: *I think we picked up prisoners, and put barbed wire around them. I recall one of the corporals offering me an opportunity to go in there and abuse some of them. I think it was Corporal—*

MARINE: *No, don't name him.*

LISSA: *No. Don't.*

MARINE: *Don't name him.*

LUIS: *He said, Hey, [last name], look, there's one of those Iraqi guys. Wanna go in there and kick em? I thought about it for a split second, but then I guess my judgment came into play, and I said, that's not the right thing to do. Just go back to my five-ton, and if I'm called upon to do something, gotta do my job.*

BELIA: When you ask him about what happened at Abu Ghraib, Luis says the soldiers responsible should be treated harshly, possibly including higher-ups. But like his buddy Ed, Luis says the abuses don't really surprise him.

LUIS: *People see it on TV, they're not living it, so they find it surprising, "oh, this is obscene." But then, you tell me one thing that happens during war that is not obscene.*

(Bring up computer sound . . .)

BELIA: And as we've seen over the past weeks, the graphic images of war are not only televised, they're digitized. After Ed [last name] was called to Iraq, one of the first things he did was stock up on camera supplies.

ED: *We spent a lot of time patrolling, driving around, so I'd whip out the camera, real quick, take a picture. I mean, we wouldn't be taking out the camera when we were doing anything mission-critical or important. But I mean, half the time we spent on the road, we got to see a lot of Iraq. . . . But I just took the pictures as a record of my travels, I guess. Because me going to Iraq, going to war and back, was the only real adventure I'll ever have. (laugh)*

BELIA: These reservists say, when they come home from Iraq, it's normal for them to scan their pictures onto a computer, email them around, or burn them onto a CD. It's a digital yearbook of a military unit's shared experience in Iraq. Ed put *his* photos on the web.

(Bring up sound . . . Ed, "Here's—okay, we're gonna go in, and it says—and here's a link to it . . . ")

BELIA: Some of the pictures are just pretty shots of the desert and the ruins in Babylon. But many of them are graphic shots of charred dead bodies, or truncated torsos lying in the sand. The photos show us *what* he saw, and the captions he added tell us *how* he saw it. Ed and his fellow Marines nicknamed one burnt corpse "Mr. Crispy."

ED: *When I first saw dead bodies, I was like, I've never seen dead bodies like that before, so out of curiosity, I whipped out the camera and stuff. I was in the car, we were still driving the whole time, I didn't get out and say, oh, Kodak moment. Just gave it to my driver, my guy on top, the gunner, take pictures, basically what it was, you find your photo ops when you can. . . .*

BELIA: Ed points to another shot, one of Americans in camouflage giving candy to Iraqi children, and his caption reads "Hey kids, here's some candy. Now make sure you don't sneak up on me tonight or I'll have to shoot you."

(Bring up sound: Ed, "So here's a picture of blown up tanks, big old statue of AK 47s on an Iraqi flag, that's pretty good . . . ")

BELIA: Ed's grisly photos and captions are disturbing. And what may have started as a personal travelogue is now part of a growing stream of images soldiers are bringing home, changing the way the world sees this war.

ANYI HOWELL

I've always been funny, outspoken, and ready to give my two cents. That didn't come from Youth Radio. It's the blend of my originality with journalism's etiquette that took my words and ways of presenting them to another level. I am from the Bay; originally came to Youth Radio when I was twenty years old and collecting unemployment. A friend of mine's girlfriend said I should train to be on the radio. Came to find out, at the end of the training was money—and skills. Once I came into the program, my teachers, Mike and Chuy, introduced me to the term *agent of change*. That term resonated with me. It actually described who I am, and for the first time, I felt like running my mouth could actually make a difference.

After a commentary I did about the passing of Ronald Reagan, I was introduced to the newsroom. My first story was a personal one about my grandmother, Frankie Mae Howell, who decorated her home every month with a holiday theme. One Halloween, vandals tore up her place, which made her want to cancel her big Christmas decorations. I know what those meant to the neighborhood of East Oakland, and they brought back so many wonderful memories for me when I was a child, so I couldn't NOT share this story. What was funny about this story was a trend I set by naming the document *Holidon't* as a working title. Lissa Soep loved the working title so much that it became the actual title of the piece. That happened so often that it became a constant. My working title would become the actual title, the *DNA of the Black Experience* being another example of my play with words.

In the beginning, writing in my own voice had me bump heads in the newsroom. I was supposed to formulate my thoughts and organize them from a space that was different than my usual knee-jerk reaction. I had to write the words and collaborate with others to massage my message and represent my thoughts. I had to think about reaching the listener, not only focus on my ability to speak out and name life as I see. The end product is worth it. I get to speak out loud in a recording studio, send the end product to an outlet and hear my voice on the radio. It is not just about my voice, or finding humor in the pain or the play with words, it is that I am actually heard, and that others can relate. That's why I developed my own radio show. Not just because I have the skills to make it happen, but to use it as my platform to perform, to tell jokes about political events, share insights on music, musicians, life . . . basically, find the rhythm to say it how I see it.

Youth Radio made me more aware of how to approach situations

with professionalism and confidence, not only in myself, but also in any goal I am setting out to accomplish. I've charmed my way through and around countless barriers trying to get interviews with subjects and access to press booths. Having an audience has created tremendous opportunities for me; for instance, I opened for the inauguration address of Oakland mayor Ron Dellums. I told my jokes; I spoke my mind and touched people. Currently, I am a comedian working in Los Angeles and continue to work as a correspondent with Youth Radio's newsroom. I can find humor even in the ugliest of things.

Holidon't

King Anyi Howell
KQED fm

As far back as I can remember, my grandmother, a retired Oakland High cafeteria manager, has gone all out during the holidays to decorate her home in East Oakland. Sometimes I helped, but for the most part I just watched in amazement. Santa's sleigh and his reindeer were on the roof, along with carolers. Inside, a miniature Christmas town, complete with an ice skating rink, sat in the front window for the neighborhood to see.

Together, my grandparents put days into the details, placement, and positioning of the Christmas statues, lights, and decorations. When they plugged everything in, thousands of lights would illuminate the scene—leaving me in awe. To this day, I've never seen more dancing Santas anywhere.

The most amazing sight, however, was the families that came by the house with their children. They wanted to witness the Christmas scene that magically transformed an otherwise glum and grimy neighborhood. My grandmother's street is magically transformed. People would say, "That's YOUR grandmother? Yeah, I know that house—I always bring my kids by there." Nothing could make me more proud.

But this year, for the first time in my life, there will be no decorations. My Grandmother decided to quit because spineless chumps from the neighborhood steal her displays right off the front lawn and damage her crafts. Because of its reputation for violence and homicide, some proudly call my grandmother's neighborhood the Murder Dubs. The vandalism has taken a toll on her spirit.

As a young black man, I know life is hard out here. Some of us are hungry and poor, and we face aggressive racism on a regular basis. I understand the anger in the hearts of my people, but why take it out on my grandmother? She only wants to celebrate Christmas and improve the quality of life in the Dubs. Their anger is completely misplaced.

My Grandmother and her community are routinely disrespected by the "get stupids" and "go dummies" who park their cars on people's lawns during sideshows. It's time for them to "get smart" and "go intelligent." What these youngstas don't realize is that the folks they're hurting are the same ones who understand them and what they're going through best. When the police go upside the heads of one of these young brothas, it's these seniors and long-time homeowners with fresh tire marks on their grass who organize and attend rallies to support these fellas.

There was a time when a common sense of respect and consideration existed among all of us, even hustlers and street criminals. Today it's gone—either because it is no longer given, or it is no longer demanded. When this mutual honor and respect is restored, the Christmas spirit will return to the Dubs. And Santa will dance again in my grand-mother's yard.

DNA of the Black Experience
King Anyi Howell (with Dahlak Brathwaite, poet)
KPFA

ANYI: The first time I fit the description of a suspect, I was ten. A cop wanted to know if I had been with my uncle all day. The kid he was looking for was twelve, but I was his size, according to the officer, who drove off—but not before repeating, "Are you sure he's been with you all day?"

My uncle told me, "You're going to fit a lot more descriptions when you get older." And the more I was stopped for conversations with police, the more I began to make adjustments in my life. I had to learn not to stand outside the house with nondescript cups, or ride four deep to the club. Some of my friends like to keep all the regis-tration papers in their glove box ultra updated. Others get nervous about how many people in their backseats are wearing ballcaps.

For as long as the term *racial profiling* has been around, fools have been denying the phenomenon exists. But I contend every black man in America at some point will be racially profiled or harassed by the police. It's a part of the DNA of our experience in the United States.

(Poetry on tape)

Red, white and blue lights blaze the sky like it's the fourth day of July
but it's not the 4th day of July it's a Friday night in the winter
f*ck firecrackers, these crackers fire at n****s
born black and your birth right is the fear of what the boys in black and blue do
you ain't even got to know what happened in the past to know what might
*   happen to you*

ANYI: One morning last spring, while I was parking my car at the BART train station, a police officer looked at me and ran my license plate. He entered a false number, and my Oldsmobile Royale Brougham 88 came back as a stolen Honda. So now, I'm a car thief. My friend Elmer and I weren't prepared for what happened next. . . .

ELMER: *Our conversation was interrupted very rudely and abruptly. In the distant background, I hear a voice of a police officer saying everybody move aside and I turned around to see the barrel of this officer's handgun staring me down face to face and he tells me to step back and stand on the concrete.*

(Poetry on tape)

Innately inserted into the black subconscious are three kings
You got Martin King, Don King and Rodney King
One spoke of the American dream, one lived the American dream and the
   other got put to sleep and thus had the American nightmare

ELMER: *He said, "Brothers like you, I know how y'all get down. Ya'll be in the*
   streets, ya'll steal cars." He's not talking to us like citizens, you know, he's
   talking to us like we're convicted criminals that he's delivering to Massa-
   chusetts for multiple murders.

ANYI: The BART Police Officer realized his mistake on the triple check,
   and after embarrassing himself, he let us go. That wasn't the first
   time a police officer came at me sideways. But I was floored by the
   reality that an officer's simple mistake was enough for him to
   approach me at gunpoint.

(Poetry on tape)

And out of the night, sirens blare, lights flare up, I'm scared
But doubly terrified since realizing not everybody is as scared as I
Some people's fears are a whole lot more subtle
"Oh my god, my parents are going to KILL me!"
Forget that—I'm worrying about this cop saving my parents that trouble

ANYI: I talked to my dad about the situation at BART. Officers I've
   spoken to claim all their decisions are based on the descriptions
   they get, whether vague or extremely detailed. But that doesn't
   explain away my experiences, like a cop saying I was stopped
   because I was in a "high crime area." I'm not buying it, and neither
   is my father.

DAD: *It's not right. There's other ways to handle what they do without making*
   it appear like they're going after one segment of society.

ANYI: The situation is so bad, I know brothas who are putting magnets
   and stickers on their cars that read, "Support Our Troops" because
   they think displays of patriotism will stop them from getting profiled. That strategy would only work if you could slap a "caucasian"
   bumper sticker on your black self. But please believe when I got my
   new car, I went to the auto parts store and bought a case of oil, transmission fluid, and a couple of American flags. You know, just to keep
   my car running.

(Poetry on tape)

Those lights flash and the blinding shine the flashlights gimme flashback of
blacks bashed in the midst of a black night by black knight stripping blacks
right out of their damn rights feeling the nightsticks I measure the worth

of a black life and I aint just talkin' about no Rodney King Keep it real,
Diallo's story was as real to me as Radio Raheem's

ANYI: I remember in elementary school one Christmas season, a police officer visited a group of us kids dressed up as Santa Claus. We were taught police are people you can go to when you have a problem or when you see something wrong. But my experiences have taught me to classify the "friendly neighborhood police officer" with other mythical figures like the Tooth Fairy and Jolly Old St. Nick.

(Poetry on tape)

I don't wanna dishonor them all
because there are good ones I shouldn't blame
but I cant help but view cops the same way some cops view blacks
and therefore, them fools all look the same
I can't tell the difference
Good cop, bad cop, that one, this one
All I think is black man trying to hit up the club
Police man trying to hit me with one

ANYI: When you go from being a black boy to a black man, you start to understand police will use deadly force on you. I could sneeze and get shot to death. I feel like I'm living in a bottle—constantly under pressure. While I understand that this is a dangerous world, where the most scandalous things take place, I wouldn't call the police if I got robbed and beat. I don't trust them. They don't serve me and I know they won't protect me. In fact, I'm the one to be protected from.

I've been handcuffed and let go several times. And the next time police harassment happens to me, I'm demanding a certificate of release. That means work for the officer—he's got to document my detention and release. It means that I have a piece of paper in my hand proving what happened. More than just another story to add to my experiences with out-of-pocket police.

LAUREN SILVERMAN

Everyone used to say I had a voice "meant for the radio." They also used to say that I asked too many questions. Today I see these remarks as great compliments.

Ever since I learned to hold a crayon I loved to write—but I also loved to share my thoughts. I was one of those kids who covered walls and furniture with words. Then I got a journal. In middle school I explored haikus and short stories. I had a passion for playing with

words, for making them rhyme and dance and fall in unusual patterns, but I didn't just want to see my thoughts lying flat on the page, I wanted them to be heard. That's when I enrolled in Youth Radio.

One of the first assignments I remember having at Youth Radio was to go out and get "vox." This meant asking strangers random questions and trying to convince them to take seriously a group of teenagers who had never held a minidisk recorder before. This simple activity taught me an important lesson: as a young person in an adult-dominated media industry, it can be difficult to get the respect, and especially the air time, you deserve. It was *this* challenge, of getting more "voices of the future" talking about issues like racial profiling, teen religion, and increasing high school dropout rates, that kept me plugging away at the computer and in the recording studio day after day after day.

Being a reporter allowed me to speak my mind and ask questions about topics ranging from the war in Iraq and elections to sexually transmitted diseases and credit card debt. Being a reporter also changed the way I interacted with the world and the people around me. Every interesting event became a potential story, and every person a prospective interviewee. One of my favorite sets of interviews was with a group of college students at UC Berkeley. I had been working on a story exploring college and allowance when I was offered the opportunity to go to a party my friend's older brother was having with his UC Berkeley roommates. I had never been to a "college" party before, and I don't think standing in the packed living room clutching a sweaty microphone instead of an ice-cold beer helped me blend in *at all.* But I was determined to get my story. Somehow I was able to convince all of the roommates to step aside for personal interviews. One of the roommates said that the difference in financial assistance each room-mate received from his parents definitely affected his relationships with his housemates. Sitting on the grimy used couch in his bedroom, he commented, "We have a royal rumble way of working things out. My roommates have taken to counting slices of bread and marking milk jugs. Just the other day, Matt definitely put a threat up on the board for anybody who was taking sips out of his milk carton." It's moments like these, when I hear a line that is so perfect for the radio, so visual and expressive, that I forget about the drama of daily life and think only of the story I want to help share.

As a reporter I learned to be willing to let myself stand out, to take risks, and even get turned down. When I'm lucky, I take chances, approaching people in awkward situations, and hear fascinating stories. For example, a few years ago I had a conversation with a manicurist about her face mask—while she was filing a friend's toenails. And just recently, I spoke with a mother about disastrous parenting techniques while recording her screaming baby in the background.

As a reporter, I confronted pressing issues in my community of Oakland, California, on public radio. Today, as a student and activist, I further my commitment to tackling issues such as environmental justice and civic engagement off-air. Since I first picked up the newspa-per one afternoon at Youth Radio, I have become fascinated by politics and public policy. As an intern in Washington, D.C., I used my writing and researching skills to help create policies that addressed the very issues I used to report on. While it is a bit scary to be venturing off into the world of politics, I'm comforted by the fact that my computer and a recording studio will always be nearby.

Hunger's Diary
Lauren Silverman
NPR/Morning Edition

When I was thirteen, the image of the perfect young woman began to form in my mind, and unfortunately, I looked nothing like her. This raised the question, "How could I be special?"

It's not like I woke up one morning and decided the answer was to stop eating. My diet just kept getting more restrictive—like a half-cup of cottage cheese for dinner.

I was performing a disappearing act. And for a while, no one noticed I was vanishing. By the time they did, I had gotten used to the friendship anorexia provided me: it promised to make me feel unique. In a matter of months, I went from 95 pounds to 60 and was losing my ability to think straight.

On a Wednesday morning in March of 2003, when I should have been in school, my parents took me to a nutritionist and then to a doctor, who said my pulse and heart rate were dangerously low. Without a change in my behavior, I would have to go to the hospital.

I had tried to get better on my own, but it didn't work. So I just surrendered.

That night, I was admitted to the hospital.

March 21, 2003
Around 2:30 am, I was lying in bed, shivering and alone. Since my heart was weak, when I finally fell asleep, it slowed down . . . too much. So I woke to the sound of the heart rate monitor alarm going off. The nurse rushed into my room, clutching a heat blanket in one hand, and a nasty high calorie milkshake in the other. I thought I was going to die, right then and there.

April 4, 2003
I waited for the nurse to come and draw my blood like he had every day for two weeks. I wore only a paper gown and tugged at the uncomfortable scratchy edges with my bony fingers. The nurse made me stand up to take my blood pressure, and I got dizzy. I lost my balance in front of my friends who were visiting. It was so embarrassing.

The memories of my three weeks in the hospital are really vivid . . . but now I can't even imagine that person was me.

April 11, 2003
My parents began to watch me at home like the nurses did in the hospital. So there I was, at the dining room table for one of my endless meals. I watched the clock flip its numbers like a deck of cards. Watched the food on my plate, looked down at it, as if it were the problem. Watched my parents stare hopefully at me, dicing and rearranging my carrots, steak, turkey sandwich with extra cheese, slice of butter and toast on my oversized plate. I glanced back at the clock. Back at the plate. Took one bite. Just one small bite, then another, and another. Then I laughed. For the first time in over a month. Mouth curved into a wide-open smile, as I realized what I had done. I had begun to defeat anorexia, begun to conquer my old companion.

NZINGA MOORE

It was the summer of my junior year of high school. I had taken two part-time jobs and was on my way to my second job when I passed a sign that struck me as odd. It said "Youth Radio." That's all, nothing on the door. So I tried to peer through the glass but couldn't see past the closed blinds. I thought, "What could that be?" The next day, I passed the sign again on my way to my second job and again the following day. Finally after a week of wondering what this sign could mean and not having any satisfactory theories, I decided to take the plunge and find out what Youth Radio was all about. I never expected things to turn out the way they did.

Nervously, I opened the door and was immediately greeted by one of the friendliest faces I had ever seen. Her name was Beverly Mire. She immediately set me at ease. So much so, that I was confident I had seen her before and eventually referenced her similarities to my grand-mother. "So what is Youth Radio?" I finally asked. She walked over to the receptionist's desk to grab an application, and after we talked a bit about the program, I left. At home, I pondered the questions on the application as if I were taking a personality test that would determine whether or not I'd be offered a job I desperately wanted.

I felt it was the first time in my life I had been given a real shot at a long-lasting opportunity—and a chance to see if radio was something I actually liked and might pursue after high school. Once I started the program, Youth Radio motivated me to dream big. So after high school I went on to obtain a Bachelor of Arts degree in radio and television from San Francisco State. I continued working at Youth Radio all four years of my college career and thereafter.

I remember how nervous and excited I was the first time I got to read my own news spots on KPFA. I prepared myself by reading and rereading my thirty-second bites over and over again, highlighting any important words. When the microphone was hot and the "On Air" sign glowed bright red, I cautiously began to read my copy over the air-waves, live. And when the red light went black after I finished my last words, "For Youth Radio, I'm Nzinga Moore," I was hooked.

I began following news stories and working on my pronunciation. I became obsessed with getting it right. I practiced my reading and my writing skills so that every Friday night when the light went red I was more prepared than before. I found myself dreaming of being one of the top reporters in the San Francisco Bay Area. After finishing the training program, I went on to hosting shows, writing commentaries, producing and reporting, and even teaching other students. My train-ing never stopped, and my desire to be the best only grew stronger. I began writing about my life and reading my stories on NPR, KPFA, and

KQED. I drew from my own life experiences and from those close to me. I felt very empowered to share my stories with the world, because it was rare that stories about youth of color were discussed in mainstream media from their point of view. And I was glad to have the opportunity to contribute on such a high level.

I loved coming up with story ideas that were commonplace in my world but not for NPR's listening audience. For instance, I broke a story of child identity theft, a phenomenon that was known among my peers and often joked about, and yet no one was reporting on it in the national news.

So I discussed my idea with the head of the newsroom and we realized we had a big scoop. I immediately went to work finding youth in the area who had had their identity stolen. In most cases the victims were victims of their own parents, who had easy access to their personal information. Parents had opened cable and phone bills in their child's name. The most extreme case of this was a young boy who, when applying for college loan money, was denied due to bad credit. He had never even opened a credit card in his name. Apparently his estranged father had several delinquent accounts open in his son's name.

My most memorable piece aired on NPR during my summer internship there in Washington, D.C. My report was on scratch deejays. Again, this topic had never been reported on National Public Radio. I mean, hip-hop had been mentioned from time to time, but never before had this specific type of deejaying been thoroughly explored on their airwaves. I had such a great time sharing an art form I had grown up with, danced to, and experienced for the better part of my life. Researching was great as well. I got to sit down with the person who invented scratching, Grand Wizard Theodore, who explained how he accidentally happened upon it. It was the first piece I pitched, researched, reported, and sold. I was eighteen, and this experience would not have been possible without the experience Youth Radio had provided years earlier.

I recently finished one year of graduate school at Columbia University's School of the Arts in acting. I plan to continue to pursue acting and eventually move to Los Angeles.

Testing: Students Opting Out
Nzinga Moore
NPR/All Things Considered

NZINGA: Paloma Salazar skipped this year's California statewide SAT 9 exam. But she didn't skip homework on test days.

(Zipper undoing, paper sounds)

PALOMA: *The only homework I have to do today is math. . . . It's too quiet, I need the radio on. . . .*

(Radio on, flipping through stations . . . Madonna song—"MUSIC, come together" . . .)

NZINGA: Paloma is NOT a slacker looking for excuses to skip school. But she believes the SAT 9—which doesn't count towards her grades or graduation—has nothing to do with her education. She went to school every testing day, in May, and sat in the same classroom with her test-taking friends. While they answered questions with number 2 pencils, Paloma put on her headphones, spread out her books and papers, and caught up on some extra homework. . . .

PALOMA: *And I'm listening to my music while I'm doing my work, so they're like "Oh, I wish I could be doing that," it looks by their expression, they're thinking, "Oh, maybe I should have waived out."*

NZINGA: To waive out, or skip the test, all Paloma had to do was get a signature from her mother—an option schools don't advertise. That's because a school needs 90 percent of its students to take the test if they want any of the almost 700 million dollars in state testing money. A school that shows the greatest improvement can receive payments as high as 25 thousand dollars per teacher. There ARE students who are tired of bad teaching and old textbooks who think the test might help. When Antonia Afamasaga heard that one of her classmates was getting a parental waiver, she tried to convince him to take the test.

ANTONIA: *It's okay to have your own opinion, but you have to think about the outcome—what will benefit you most—taking the test, or not going to school at all. . . . A school is a place for you. If they make more money, your school is in better shape, the library will have more books, you're gonna have better computers. That gives you a better environment to learn in.*

(Fade in hallway sound, "Where you guys going, okay, let's go, hello . . . come on you guys, let's get the hallway cleared out." Cross fade.)

NZINGA: It's test day at Balboa High School.

LISA: *Right now, in my classroom right now taking this test are about 70 percent of the students who are supposed to be here. And that's been pretty consistent each day. And I'm actually really proud of them they've been hanging on and doing really well. . . .*

NZINGA: In Lisa Moorehouse's classroom, most students worked through the entire period. But a couple stared out the window or put their heads down on their desks. Last year only 67 percent of the students at Balboa took the test, and the school ranked last on the state index. This year Vice Principal Ted Barone needs to show improvement to qualify for state money. He raffled off prizes to students who completed each section of the test. But that didn't always work.

VP: *This young man who is a tenth grader, was brought to me because he was refusing to take the test. So I laid out to him the three reasons why he should take the test. Learn about yourself, helps us help you so we can adjust our curriculum, and then thirdly you help the school. And then finally I said, if none of those work, you need to go to another school, because you're not welcome here at Balboa. So he says, okay I'll take the test. And he's been here every day taking the test.*

NZINGA: Ed Haertel, a professor at Stanford University, thinks tests can help struggling students. But he says placing so much emphasis on tests can create other problems.

ED: *I was at a conference a few years ago, and one of the most telling things I've ever heard a teacher say in a long time was about the high stakes testing. She said the worst thing about it was that it caused the teachers to resent the students who couldn't get good scores, and that so undermines the relationship that we want between teachers and students.*

NZINGA: It's hard to convince every student to suffer through a test that doesn't even count for their grades or graduation. But in a couple of years, all seniors in California will have to pass a high school exit exam to get their diplomas. Ditching that test means ditching high school. In the meantime, adults and administrators who believe these tests will benefit ALL students—even low performers—have a long way to go to prove it.

ORLANDO CAMPBELL

My rap career started in a closet with a Radio Shack microphone
and bootlegged beats I downloaded from the Internet. Soon after my
mix-tape songs gained a little popularity, I came up with a concept for
my own song and beat while high in class, obviously not paying any
attention to whatever science we were doing. I had plenty of ideas, but
the only bad part was I had no tangible outlet to turn my idea into a
reality. I was looking for a studio to record in, which began to seem
impossible, and a producer to make the beat for this song I had come
up with. Failed attempt after failed attempt led me to call one of the
few people who had given me a chance before, Jason Valerio at Youth
Radio. He said I could come by before classes started and work on
whatever it was I had to. About four trips later, with a little help here
and there, I had finally completed the perfect beat, and it was ready to
record with my group-mate Lil' 4 Tay. After we recorded the song titled
"Git It," things began to happen very fast. The song got the attention
of Bay Area rapper Mistah Fab, who got it played on Wild 94.9 on the
Yellow Bus Radio show, and eventually the Hood Hop mixes. My life as
Roach Gigz the rapper was officially on its way!

Rewind just a little to when I first heard about Youth Radio. I was
attending high school in San Francisco and a girl in my class was
involved in this afterschool program. She convinced me to try it out.
I was hesitant at first because it was all the way in the East Bay and nor-
mally I didn't ever leave San Francisco. Forget an afterschool program,
I would usually just go to the Fillmore neighborhood and hang out,
losing brain cells, and getting nothing accomplished. But faithfully I
hopped on BART at Balboa Station in San Francisco and traveled the
crowded train all the way to Berkeley every week. The hands-on video,
beat, and radio production classes opened my mind and eyes, keeping
me more informed and knowledgeable about opportunities that were
within my reach—things I previously might have wanted but would
not have given myself the chance to obtain. The trips also took me away
from a lot of the negative aspects of life I was dealing with back home
in the city. At this point in my life, my friends and I were into a lot of
drugs and robbing. In my own conscience, I knew that was not the life
I wanted to be a part of, but now I had an excuse to get away. After the
Core class ended I was invited back to take the Bridge course, which I
accepted. At some points along the way, I admit it was the push of my
mother that kept me going to the program, instead of following the
pack and putting this opportunity on the back burner.

Now, for an eighteen-year-old on the radio, doing shows, and living

on my own, life could get kind of wild, which it did. I had a job here and there, but it was definitely not my focus. After a while I realized it is much more difficult to become a successful rapper than I expected. Fast-forward about a year, and I was still struggling trying to find a steady job, go to school, and maintain my status as a known Bay Area rap artist on my way to national success. No regular job would hire me for anything more than a midnight shift, which did not work out with my busy schedule. That's when I contacted Jason again and boom, after a simple application process, I was back at Youth Radio as an intern. Not only that, but they had moved to this huge building in downtown Oakland, which was much nicer and easier to get to. When I came to orientation and found out I was assigned to work in the newsroom, my first thought was, damn, this is going to be hella boring. I came in

thinking I was going to be teaching the new students music or something, and now I'm stuck doing news.

With the help of Nishat Kurwa and Reina Gonzales, my abilities as
a writer were able to shine through, and I started creating commentaries and features about issues that were real and important to me and
my close friends. It was basically taking issues that might come up in
my raps and delivering them in a way that a middle-class white public
broadcasting audience could understand. Before I knew it, my voice
was on local and national radio stations, and I was getting positive
feedback everywhere I went. The staff in the newsroom were so nice
and understanding, something I wasn't really used to. On top of that I
learned the digital editing program Protools almost in and out, which
lets me mix my own radio pieces, and the skills transferred over to my
music as well. When there were situations in my home life that affected
my time at work, instead of getting fired, I got to take a little time off
(as long as I called in advance) and then come back and write about it.
It was kind of like the perfect situation for someone like me.

Roach Gigz Ain't Dead
Orlando Campbell
KALW

(Music: "Get It Get It")

ORLANDO: I'm Roach Gigz, I'm a rapper, and I'm very much alive. But
recently I discovered that not everybody believes the third statement.
I got a call from my producer when I first heard the news. The
conversation went something like this.

(Sound: Ring Ring)

ORLANDO: Hello.

PRODUCER: Roach, you cool?

ORLANDO: Yeah, bra, I'm good, Why?

PRODUCER: Man, somebody just told me that everybody been telling them
you got shot and died.

ORLANDO: Died? Hell na. Man, I'm at the Philly cheese steak shop on Divis.

(Music: ET Fone Home)

ORLANDO: My brother from another mother, who himself survived a
shooting, called me to inform me that rumors of my untimely
demise had found its way to the Internet.

(Bring up typing sounds)

ORLANDO: The online hip-hop heads were going back and forth on forums debating my alleged murder.

TM: *Aye, y'all . . . I was at ma patna house dis weekend n he told me that dat <BLEEP> Roach Gigz from the group B.I.G. got killed. Could somebody tell me if this is true or not?*

HDG: *Yes sir . . . Nobody ain't heard this? Two <BLEEP>s from Vallejo and one <BLEEP> from Frisco told me that two weeks ago. I'm pretty sure about this.*

HDG: *Yeah he dead.*

SP925: *He's alive. He just posted a bulletin on MySpace.*

ORLANDO: This is a weird feeling. I had to pinch myself and make sure that I was really on earth and not looking down. With all the rumors about my death running laps in the streets and on the net, I started to think about my professional role models and the one thing that links them all together.

(Music: Mac Dre's Get Stupid)

ORLANDO: My biggest musical influence is Mac Dre, who was shot and killed on Nov. 1, 2004. Dre was already respected as the "King" of Bay Area rap. But it wasn't until after his violent death that he became a legend. All of a sudden, local commercial radio started playing his music all the time, and R.I.P. Mac Dre shirts popped up everywhere from liquor stores to eBay.

(Music: Tupac's Only God Can Judge Me)

ORLANDO: Tupac was an internationally known rap artist who started his career in the Bay Area. He grew from a respected actor, artist, and activist to a Jesus-like figure in the hip-hop community after he was rattled with bullets for the second and last time in 1996.

The two people I most respected and looked up to as an aspiring rapper were both from where I was from, and they both were murdered. And now, here I am Google searching my name and finding out that I too am dead. I was flattered that I made enough of an impact to get people on the Internet writing blogs and forums about me. And if I really had been killed, it looks like my funeral would have a good turnout. But on a more serious note, I have had my own real-life brushes with the angel of death.

Bullets have traveled in my direction more than once; I was blessed to safely make it out of those situations. Other people close to me have not been as fortunate. And because of that, I know the unexplainable feeling one gets in their stomach as they pass by and say their last goodbyes to stiff bodies of friends and family. I don't want anybody who I hold close to me to get that gut-wrenching feeling while looking down at my own lifeless body.

More painful for me than my own narrow escapes are the nightmares my mom's told me about. She's dreamt of police knocking on her door and delivering the dreadful news that no mother wants to hear. The most I can do as a son is reassure her I'll be fine, and pray that it is true.

I'm pursuing a dream, and the people who have done it before me have tragically met a fate that is all too common in this world. But this is the reality of the life I fell in love with. Rap starts in the streets and unfortunately, regardless of a person's status, fans, or income, can have a bloody ending in those same streets. I'm going to do what I can in my own life to keep rumors like those about my death just rumors.

Hope out of the Box
Orlando Campbell
NPR/Morning Edition

ORLANDO: Ancient Greece gave us the myth of Pandora's Box. Forbidden to be opened, but opened anyway, the box spewed out a torrent of plagues to torture people forever. Pandora slammed the lid back down trying to trap the worst of it, but only one thing remained there at the bottom—hope.

(Montage: I think it's hope just to live because I mean it's hope just to think that the next second is even going to happen. . . . You believe something can happen and you have to have a positive attitude about what you believe. . . . Hope is kind of exactly like faith to me. I think human beings need it to just be able to keep going.)

ORLANDO: That's Caitlin Grey, Raven-Simone Atkins, and Quincy Mosby adding their voices to a thousand-year debate about whether hope was the best thing Pandora's box had to offer . . . or the worst. Now Barack Obama promises hope and we're wondering the same thing.

It's young people like me who are promised hope the most. Our teachers, they tell us we can go to the best schools, and our parents tell us that we can be whatever we want. Most of my peers say yeh, it's their moms who fill them with the most hope. For eighteen-year-old Rynesha Snowden, it was her great-grandmother. . . .

RYNESHA SNOWDEN: *She was kind of my hope. She had rules and she was strict and but you know she showed that love and she showed how much she cared about people. and I always was like, ooh I'm going to start cry-ing . . . (crying) . . . but she was strong and I want to be like her.*

ORLANDO: Strong hopeful leaders can be huge inspirations and help us improve our lives. But the hope that adults push onto us isn't always realistic. Like when people have told me and my friends that getting a job would keep us out of trouble, we believed in the hope that someone somewhere would hire us. When some of us got turned down time after time, application after application, we lost hope in the possibility of getting a legal job and in the people who preached to us it was possible. Quincy Mosby is twenty-two years old and his mom used to fill him with hope.

QUINCY MOSBY: *I remember when, when I was very young you know. We just were in a bad spot you know, barely could keep the lights on, my dad wasn't around anymore, and ahh, I think she gave me hope, but it was strange cause I think she believed in me more than she believed in herself. Like she would tell me to go put my hand on the refrigerator and pray for food to come But the older I got, the harder it became to believe in that type of stuff.*

DR. SPIEGEL: *If hope gets too far off the mark then it becomes fantasy and it's more likely to hurt you than help you.*

ORLANDO: That's Dr. David Spiegel, a Stanford psychiatrist who researches cancer patients and the role of the mind when it comes to healing the body.

DR. SPIEGEL: *If you have too much concrete belief that your hope is going to change everything, then when things don't go the way you hope, who do you have to blame, you blame yourself. One of my cancer patients started to cry and her husband said don't cry you'll make the cancer spread. It's not that you have bad cancer, it's that you didn't hope enough or you didn't hope right. I think what makes hope work is when it's realistic. Or when the person who's promising you something is genuine about trying to deliver it.*

ORLANDO: Barack Obama inspired me, and for the first time ever I voted, with a belief that our country and my life could change. His promise sits like a weight on his shoulders, but the most challenging thing for all voters and young people like me to remember, is that it sits just as heavy on our own.

(Tape: (Barack Obama from Iowa Caucus Victory Speech) Hope is that thing inside us that insists, despite all the evidence to the contrary, that something better awaits us if we have the courage to reach for it and to work for it and to fight for it. Fade out.)

Epilogue

BY ELLIN O'LEARY

Lissa Soep has asked me to write about how Youth Radio got started, and also to reflect on aspects of our organization and other youth media groups that hold some keys to the future of journalism and the new "public" media.

I'll start at Castlemont High School in Oakland, California, in the early 1990s. I went to this extremely underresourced school as a radio reporter to cover urban violence. At the school I met many amazing young people who didn't match any of the media stories being told about them. They were doing well academically, trying to get to college, and trying to stay safe in spite of the surrounding violence. I did stories about the violence, and also about other topics of interest to teens, such as flirting and music. Soon I started working at other high schools with Youth News and Pacific News Service and then producing youth commentaries for KQED FM.

These essays were fascinating chronicles of their time, but the young people told me, "This is kind of boring." They wanted to write, but they also wanted to be deejays and engineers. The problem was, after a brief stint at KECG at El Cerrito High School, we had nowhere to work.

That's when KPFA, Berkeley's community-supported radio station, was building a high-end broadcast facility. The chief engineer on the project, Tim McGovern, was looking for a solution for us when he identified an extra closet drawn on the plans; then, with great enthusiasm, KPFA's Pat Scott and David Salniker agreed to turn the closet into a small studio for their repeater signal, KPFB. Thus the core of our program was started, with the support of a community station that handed over a studio closet and a repeater signal for two hours a week on Friday nights. The Friday night show became the entry point for our students, and it remains the heart of Youth Radio's program to this day. The KPFA management also shared some staff time with fund-raising expert Greg Lassonde, and an empty space they owned next door became our "headquarters."

The room had no heat and barely enough space for our broken-down couch, but with ten young people we started covering news, movie reviews, sports, community events, and music. The start-up money ran out at the end of the first summer at KPFA, and I was sure the young people would move on, but they didn't. "We have to keep this going." That's what one of Youth Radio's original students, Deverol Ross, always said. Long before I did, Dev had a vision for how the program could become an organization, something that would last. Without cash, we couldn't pay instructors, and to my surprise Dev, Chano Soccarras, Ayoka Medlock, Noah Nelson, and Jacinda Abcarian all volunteered to teach the next class of students. That's how Youth Radio's peer teaching model got started. Throughout this book, you've read about how peer teaching works, how powerful it can be. And it all started because the young people created it. They saw a gap and stepped up and created the solution themselves in order to keep this brand new community program going. This phenomenon, young people giving back a thousandfold once you show you care, is perhaps the most powerful learning I've experienced working at the grassroots level as part of a community.

As more and more students joined Youth Radio and stayed, advisors started telling me, "You really need youth development and some pathway for matriculation here." I didn't know where to begin, but it was clear that the problems young people faced far outstripped the goodwill of even the most hard-working journalists and community members. Our students needed additional expertise, reaching beyond media and technology, and we needed new ways to frame our work; Beverly Mire opened the door to Lissa Soep. Lissa started volunteering at Youth Radio while she was finishing her dissertation, and in short order she developed the core educational framework for Youth Radio and the blueprint for other programs that followed.

I remember spotting her sitting with a student and commenting, "I thought Lissa was observing. Why is she working directly with a student? If she's a Stanford University doctoral student in education, what's the connection to Youth Radio?" We hadn't yet made the connection that Youth Radio's program *is* education, community-based education. At a moment when public high schools were failing a majority of our students, like so many other post-Columbine afterschool groups around the country, Youth Radio was providing new options for students who previously had had no alternatives. As time went on, young people kept opting into rather than out of our programs, so Youth Radio needed to develop and document a curriculum that could take students from their entry into the program at age fourteen or fifteen all the way through until age twenty-four.

As the media staff grappled with this (good) problem, we were elated when Lissa Soep said, "I can develop curriculum." From that day on, Lissa has led the design of myriad curricula at Youth Radio, always working in her unique and dynamic model of collaboration with outside experts, staff, and students. Lissa was committed to leading Youth Radio into the education world, and she brought the education world to our door. She did this by connecting Youth Radio's teaching and media production process to her documentation and evaluation as well as lectures that included Youth Radio students and teaching at Harvard, Stanford, San Francisco State, and UC Berkeley and countless journal articles. More recently Lissa joined with Jacinda Abcarian, Ahmad Mansur, and Rick Ayers to achieve accreditation, so that our students receive high school and college credit for Youth Radio classes.

Youth Radio's first transition was growing from a project into an organization, and that would not have been possible except for our very first board member, Teri Yeager, who continues to help us strategize a solution for every major problem Youth Radio faces. I'd say a second key transition was transforming from an organization into a community institution—what Youth Radio Board member Arnold Perkins calls "growing from the storefront to the forefront." Key to that shift was having a strong, visionary, and committed board of directors. By 2002, ten years after Youth Radio officially started as a nonprofit organization, the programs had outgrown the storefront rental property in Berkeley and started exploring options for more space. Our board advised that it might be more cost-effective to buy.

To justify all of the investment from the community and hard work that move would require, board member Lori Kaplan said, "We need a bold vision." As executive director of the Latin American Youth Center in Washington, D.C., Lori has developed a dozen or more buildings. Her experience was like a map we could always turn to. Beyond filling the need for additional space, the impetus for developing a new facility was to offer a unique and sustainable media and technology education to the youth of the Bay Area region, expand services to young people growing up in poverty, and explore the role a youth media organization could play in community economic development. These criteria eventually led us to Oakland. I recall touring two different buildings that involved sharing space with attorneys' offices. "The kids would have to come in through the back door," the realtor said. Our own attorney, Bill Sokol, who has fiercely protected the organization throughout, and the leader of our capital campaign, Julie Jensen, would have none of that. "Are you kidding? No way." At that point the board resolved that Youth Radio's new location would be a top-of-the-line building with only the best equipment and facilities, a home for diverse youth working together creatively with media and technology professionals. Over the next three years our capital campaign director, Erin Callahan, and other staff visited dozens of spaces. After a handful of deals that didn't work out, we toured 1701 Broadway, and there was a consensus: this is it!

At the corner of Seventeenth and Broadway, 1701 Broadway is in the heart of downtown Oakland. It has glass windows all the way to the street, so the students can be on the air and visible to passersby, just like Radio Arte in Chicago, which we admire so much. It's near public transportation. And it is audacious.

Youth Radio had four months to come up with 2.9 million dollars to purchase the building. That figure was a fortune to us, but we were told it was a depressed price because of all the pot clubs in the neighborhood. Rather than Youth Radio's betting on Oakland coming back, we bet on the need that we could fill and the assets that young people bring to a community.

Youth Radio was eligible for a loan from the Northern California Community Loan Fund because board members had earlier started donating to a Youth Radio building fund. Our board's Gary Rydstrom of Pixar was the first to give and the first to believe we could own a building. When a purchase first came up as a serious idea, Gary said, "The board has to give, and we can do this." The purchase of 1701 Broadway would not have been possible except for crucial gifts from Julie Jensen and from her family. Without Julie's support, in spite of the gifts and loans we had assembled, 1701 Broadway would have been one more "dream deferred" for our community. Instead, Youth Radio had the money for a down payment in August 2005 and took ownership of 1701 Broadway on January 11, 2006. The next challenge was raising more money to remodel and equip the facility. Tim McGovern stepped in with his signature genius for technical design and installation. Mark Bauman provided a vision for the digital future. Maria Martin and Kevin Guillory did the same for public media. And Colin Lacon provided guidance navigating the world of philanthropy. The community members who formed the committee that made the move to downtown Oakland possible were David Salniker, Pat Scott, Wally Haas, Carolyn Johnson, Martin Paley, Frank Martin, Jayme Burke, Keith Carson, Rodney Brooks, and Erin Callahan.

Youth Radio is blessed with a senior staff with diverse expertise and talents who raised the money and prepared for the transition, and a parallel team of young staff who essentially kept the program running and the students learning while we focused on the move. The young people never gave up. Even when it became so much harder than we could ever have imagined, they told me, "We always knew it was going to happen."

Actually, there were many times throughout the process when I couldn't see how Youth Radio would complete the purchase and the build-out, but because the students and the board members had faith in us, the staff just kept moving, also trying to believe. The members of the Senior Team became codevelopers of 1701. Individually and together they came to me on some of the most challenging days and said, "You can't do this alone. The Youth Radio Senior team that made the move happen was Jacinda Abcarian, Nishat Kurwa, Rebecca Martin, McCrae Parker, and Lissa Soep.

This institution is constructed by community wealth, which was created by youth talent. After Youth Radio developed 1701 Broadway, a five-million-dollar project, including purchase, a student turned to me the week it opened and said, "I've never even been in a place this beautiful." And that was just the beginning.

Inside 1701 Broadway and beyond, through our bureaus and correspondents across the nation and globally, we now frame our work as a full-service community-based organization and a youth-driven production company, Youth Media International. Youth Radio graduate Jacinda Abcarian has assumed the role of executive director and she is bringing new excitement and vision to Youth Radio services, including academic credit, a health department, an expanded college-bound division and workforce, and social messaging as both service and revenue for Youth Radio. Jacinda brings a fresh brand of leadership to our organization; at the same time, her attention to the importance of detail, finances, and staff integration keeps the organization on solid ground. Our joint leadership, with my new role as chief content officer and president, is an exciting shift.

On the media production side, journalism and hands-on technology remain at the center of everything we do, but what that means is in a state of dramatic change. Until recently both commercial and public broadcast media had become a huge funnel. You'd be lucky to get in at all, and disenfranchised young people were shut out more than anyone else. Even many of the stories in this book were produced at a time when adult media professionals held the key to being heard by large audiences. Now that's reversed, and our young people know how to get the coveted online audience of their peers. Many mainstream media companies are scrambling to figure a way into the world of social media and youth-generated content. With millions of dollars now invested in our online content, Youth Radio's challenge is to create excellence within this new space for media creation and distribution. Our mandate is to prepare young people to maintain and reinvent journalism's best principles, so they can deploy today's new tools and platforms to speak truth to power, to cultivate credible sources, to tell the story no one else is telling, and to create art and report on emerging trends and cultures.

Sometimes that story is happening far away—in Appalachia, Gaza, New Orleans, Iraq—and Youth Media International is set up to cover those events with young people on the ground and online. At other times the story hits right here at home. That's what happened on New Year's Eve 2009, when a twenty-two-year-old Oakland resident, Oscar Grant, was shot and killed while held face-down on a subway platform by a transit police officer. Passengers captured the shooting on their cell phone cameras, and soon anyone with an Internet connection could watch the shooting on YouTube. Our young reporters were covering this story from all angles: news, music mixes, and interviews for web, video, radio, and newspaper outlets. Days after the shooting, I stood with Youth Radio graduate Anita Johnson as she interrogated Oakland's Mayor Dellums in the middle of a protest, surrounded by crowds of young people facing police in riot gear. In two weeks the first African American president of the United States would take office, and yet thousands, if not millions, of people had witnessed a young black man shot in the back, and the protesters—not the officer—were the ones getting locked up. Barack Obama's victory had no currency on that day, or at least no visibility on the streets of Oakland.

And yet I believe that young people trained in youth media will continue to bring about change—by revealing both the connections and the gaps between what happens in Oakland and what happens in Washington, and places in between and beyond. Youth Radio's roots are in public media, and the question we face today, given the shifting technological, cultural, and political landscape, is: What is the new public for media and democracy? What today's young people are building does not and will not look like the media that preceded it because they are the pivotal group that spans the hip-hop generation to the Obama generation. They've experienced the best and the worst this country has to offer and now have witnessed, if not participated in, electing a president by harnessing the media in a way that's never been done before. If educators, parents, community organizers, health providers, journalists, and engineers stay engaged with young people and support them in their quest to reinvent public media, once again they will give back a thousandfold.

APPENDIX Teach Youth Radio

Teach Youth Radio is an online curriculum resource designed to encourage educators in a range of settings to use youth-generated content. The model and curriculum were a co-creation of Dawn Williams (lead author) and Lissa Soep. Stories featured in the Teach Youth Radio series have aired on some of the nation's most influential public media outlets, taking up social and cultural issues from the perspectives of young people. Veteran educators and youth producers have worked together to develop companion lesson ideas to go along with these stories. One inspiration for launching Teach Youth Radio came from the calls Youth Radio regularly received from classroom teachers, university professors, and community advocates after hearing an especially powerful or provocative Youth Radio story on the air. Callers didn't always agree with the story, but they wanted to use it in their own work with young people. Teach Youth Radio answers that call by framing youth-produced media as a point of departure to inspire student discussions, develop new literacies, introduce digital tools, and initiate further inquiry.

You can find the full Teach Youth Radio archive, three years' worth of monthly curriculum materials, on Youth Radio's website, www.youthradio .org. Here we've selected five examples, including scripts and lesson ideas, to exemplify ways to integrate youth narratives into your own practice.

1. GUERRA EVERYWHERE, BY EVELYN MARTINEZ

In this commentary, Youth Radio LA's Evelyn Martinez explores how her mother's memories of guerrillas in El Salvador intersect with her own reality of nighttime gunshots, helicopters, and sirens at home in East Los Angeles.

My mom tells me that she fled that war only to find herself in between feuding gangs and police shooting at each other in our Los Angeles neighborhood of Boyle Heights.

During the 1980s and 1990s, over one million Salvadorans fled the civil war in their country and settled in the United States. Over 50 percent of those who arrived in the United States decided to make Los Angeles their home. Evelyn is a product of this history. Her story provides a powerful way for educators to explore several themes, including transnational identity, the relationship between storytelling and healing, the notion of history unfolding in the present, and the ripple effects of violence for individuals, communities, and nations.

Script

EVELYN: My mom says she hated the night sky growing up. It was a place of danger.
    The thing is, my experience in East Los Angeles is no different. It's 2:30 am and I'm tired, sleepy, trying to rest, because in a couple of hours I have to go to school. The gunshots echoing in the street are scaring the hell out of me. I imagine guerrillas and soldiers climbing up the staircase of my apartment building—visions I have inherited from my mother. You see, a long time ago, before I was born, was a big civil war going on in my mom's homeland in Sensuntepeque Cabanas, El Salvador.

MOM: *Una noche un 5 de Marzo pasaron por mi casa y se llevaron a mi hermano mayor se lo amarraron se lo llevaron y nunca mas supimos nada de el.*

EVELYN: She tells me that on the night of March the 5th, 1984, soldiers came into her house and took her brother. They just tied him up and took him with them.

MOM: *Yo tenía mucho miedo. Pues yo venia huyendo de unos balazos y resulta que enfrente de donde viviamos pasaban los cholos y los policias.*

EVELYN: My mom tells me that she fled that war only to find herself in between feuding gangs and police shooting at each other in our Los Angeles neighborhood of Boyle Heights. I remember this one time when I was just about four and a half. My sister and I were playing when this guy bangs on our door, shot in the stomach and bleeding. My mom cracked open the door and he pushed it open. He begged my mom for help.

MOM: *Me dijo, ¿Señora, me ayuda por favor? ¿ Me deja entrar a su casa? Y yo le dije que no.*

EVELYN: I'm sorry but I have kids, she said.

MOM: *Yo queria ayudarlo pero . . . los soldados—estos los policias..*

EVELYN: She says she saw soldiers behind the man. . . . She means police. It's held over from El Salvador. It was the first time I witnessed my mother's trauma in action.

After that day, my mom would often talk about her memories of war in her home country. She taught us about the dangers of the world, and how to deal with them.

ASHLEY: *She overreacts sometimes because it's not like if anytime the guerilleros and the soldiers are going to come over here, y'know?*

EVELYN: That's my sister Ashley. Age fourteen. We both struggle with how strict my mom can be. Do you rebel? 'Cause I know like when my mom used to tell me oh you're not gonna go—like I'd find a way to go outside anyways.

ASHLEY: *Usually for me 'cause I clean everything in the house, I'm her baby, so she lets me go outside. So like for example I wash the dishes for her or sweep the house or mop it or go water the plants . . . that's my ticket for freedom.*

BRIAN: *If she lets us do whatever we want, we'll die—faster.*

EVELYN: My brother Brian is just eleven. He sees things differently. He chooses to play it safe over going out and having fun.

BRIAN: *If we go to a party, and they start shooting, who would they shoot? Us? Yes, they'll shoot us. So many bad things can happen. But if she raises us strict we can learn.*

EVELYN: Even though we do live around violence, we do have choices. We can either stay paralyzed about it or find a way to overcome the trauma that has been passed from generation to generation in my community. If my elders who went through the civil war could talk about it like my mom has, maybe they could begin their process of healing, and I could know enough about my history to not be afraid for the future.

Lesson Ideas: English and Composition

Opening Scenes: Evelyn's story starts with a striking visual image: "My mom says she hated the night sky growing up. It was a place of danger." Have students brainstorm a series of nighttime images, and write them up on the board. Then hold a five-minute free-write that starts with this sentence: "I always hated (nighttime image—fill in the blank). It was a place of danger." Have students share their writing. Then have students write off this line: "I always loved (nighttime image—fill in the blank). It was a place of safety." Next, mix it up, and ask students to talk about instances when they hated safety or were drawn to danger. To close, have students reflect on how writers imbue everyday images with deeper meanings. This exercise lends itself to fiction and nonfiction writing.

Caregiver Interviews: Evelyn's story comes to life through her conversation with her mom, which reveals how her mother's past in El Salvador affects the way she's raising her family in the United States. Have students create a list of questions to interview their own parents, guardians, or caregivers about the challenges they faced growing up. See if your students can learn something about how their family members' personal histories affect the choices they make as parents today. Notice the memory Evelyn shares of the time the man showed up at their home bleeding, begging for help (more on this below). Make sure your students get their interviewees to share at least one specific memory, a story that illustrates something important about how they were raised or how they are now raising their children. Encourage students to share that moment with the class.

Moral Dilemma: Evelyn recalls a situation from her childhood: "I remember this one time when I was just about four and a half. My sister and I were playing when this guy bangs on our door, shot in the stomach and bleeding. My mom cracked open the door and he pushed it open. He begged my mom for help." If this happened to your family, how do you think your family members would respond? Do your students understand why Evelyn's mother responded the way she did? How did Evelyn build a story that helped this scene make sense? Have students break into three groups, each writing the moment Evelyn describes through one of the following points of view: the mom, the young girl, the injured man. Have them describe in detail what they imagine going on right before the incident at the door, and then add the interior thoughts of the character they've been assigned.

Lesson Ideas: Health and Wellness

PTSD: Students can go back to two past Teach Youth Radio curricula where we've touched on the topic of posttraumatic stress disorder. One, called *PTSD,* centered on a young man who came back from the war in Iraq; the other, *Blacksburg to the Bay Area,* explored the legacy of violence in the United States. Using concrete textual examples from all three stories and their own experiences, have students explore how even faraway, long-ago violence has ripple effects on individuals and communities. You might have students review recent research that links urban violence to posttraumatic stress disorder in children and other studies suggesting that violence should be seen and treated as a virus. How useful is it to frame violence and its effects as disease?

Making Choices: At the end of her story Evelyn says, "Even though we do live around violence, we do have choices. We can either stay paralyzed about it or find a way to overcome the trauma that has been passed from generation to generation in my community." Have students write and reflect on their long-term goals. What are some of the choices that students have to make on a daily basis? Have them write these choices on big pieces of paper and give them category titles. What kinds of choices are they: life or death, success or failure, individuality or community? Have students discuss their choices and how they want to live to achieve their goals.

The Process of Healing: Evelyn says, "If my elders who went through the civil war could talk about it like my mom has, maybe they could begin their process of healing, and I could know enough about my history to not be afraid for the future." How does talking help to heal? Whom do students talk to? How often do they have intergenerational dialogues? What resources are in their community to support young people who need someone to talk to?

Lesson Ideas: Social and Cultural Studies

War in El Salvador: Evelyn's mother gives a personal account of her experiences during wartime. Students can check out public broadcasting sources (e.g., PBS) to learn more about the Salvadoran Civil War. What are the causes and effects? Who has been affected? Have students find a second source of information on the war and compare all three (including Evelyn's) to notice themes and possible contradictions.

Gangs in Los Angeles: Evelyn's story draws a connection between war and violence in El Salvador and in the United States. Have students explore other youth media resources for information on the history of gang violence, starting with Homies Unidos, a transnational gang prevention and intervention initiative founded by gang-involved young people. Your students can put together a resource curating the strongest examples of youth-generated storytelling about gang prevention and intervention from across the United States.

Lesson Ideas: Media Literacy

The Human Face of War: Evelyn's mother gives a personal account of war and its unexpected next-generation effects. Have students find stories of Iraqi people, particularly youth their age, who are living in a war-torn environment. What stories do they find? What perspectives are not available? How do different news sources (mainstream press vs. alternative press; U.S.-based media vs. media from other countries; television vs. print, etc.) compare in their coverage?

2. SEXUALITY: UNACCEPTABLE, BY ANNE SANTOS

In this story, Youth Radio LA's Anne Santos reflects on the life and death of middle school student Lawrence "Larry" King, who was killed by a fellow student who had tormented King for being openly gay.

> *The reason I want to talk about this after what happened to Lawrence King is that it didn't just happen to him. The killing happened to everyone who cares about him.*

Anne connects the hatred King experienced to her own life and shares a personal account of a violent attack that she endured. Anne talks about a huge personal choice that she has had to make in her life in the name of safety.

Script

ANNE: One night last week, I was talking to my mom on the phone, and I broke the news about what happened to fifteen-year-old Lawrence King, the openly gay boy shot by a classmate in Oxnard, California. The tone in her voice changed, and I knew what was coming. She asked me to come back home. For me, that's asking a lot.
   See, last May, two guys verbally harassed me, followed me to my car, and then physically attacked me for being gay. It all happened on Mother's Day. I had just gotten off of work when two guys started

yelling homophobic insults at me. I drove to the cemetery where my father is buried . . . and the men followed me there. I guess I didn't lock my door, and suddenly someone was grabbing me and pulling me out really hard, then slamming me against my truck. Well, they kicked my ass pretty bad. They ripped my shirt. They were just laughing the whole time. Calling me names, saying I deserved this. And I was just quiet. Finally after I don't know how long, it felt like a long time, the guy standing in the back said "let's just go, let's just go."

My right eye was swollen shut. I don't remember if there was blood. My left eye was kind of shut, and that's the eye I was looking through when I was driving to the hospital. My shirt was ripped; I think my pants were ripped. I looked like crap. I didn't want anybody to see that. Except for my mom and sister. Here's how my sister Iza remembers that day.

IZA: *You called me on my cell phone and I thought you just needed me to get something from your car. And I opened the door and I saw your shirt ripped. And you weren't moving. I tried talking to you but you weren't talking. Then I started getting mad because you weren't answering me. You got hurt. You could tell you got hurt.*

ANNE: *What about mom? Do you remember how mom was reacting?*

IZA: *Mom said I don't care what happens to me if I see them again, one of them is going to be dead . . . and she doesn't care if it's her.*

ANNE: The reason I want to talk about this after what happened to Lawrence King is that it didn't just happen to him. The killing happened to everyone who cares about him.

MOM: *. . . My whole being was in rage, because they hurt you. Because I never never lay a hand on you, and you know that — you and your sister. Y'know when those people hurt you, I just don't want to hurt them — I want to kill them for what they did to you.*

ANNE: I was in the hospital for a couple hours before the cops came and started asking me questions and taking pictures of me. One officer was telling my family to "roll up her shirt" so they could take pictures of the bruises. "Roll up her pant leg" so they could take pictures of my ankles. "Let me take pictures of her face." It made me feel like I was one of the victims on TV, like on CSI when you see police taking crime scene pictures. And so I felt violated and I got pissed off.

The next day my whole family showed support for my mom, sister and me. They came with food and with helping hands. But that day when I took a nap, the nightmares started. My mom said I'd be yelling for her, and I'd have my hands over my face like I was blocking someone. Then I started swinging my arms around and I'd start moving around. And she said I'd yell, "No! No! Don't touch me!" They got worse to the point where I'd wake up and I'd have a black eye. And it was because I was hitting myself. I felt them hitting me, but it was me hitting myself. And my mom had a hard time with that. What my mom and I decided was that I should move to L.A. to live with my aunt, Tita Bebot.

MOM: *It breaks my heart when I say okay you can go live in L.A. It's a never ending responsibility of thinking about you guys' welfare. It's hard but I have to—I have to show the strength that I have. Because I know if you see me crying here and there, you will change your mind. And I don't want to hold you up because you might have a better opportunity in L.A. than here.*

ANNE: Moving to Los Angeles was definitely the right decision. I feel that people are more accepting here of who I am. My family will always protect my heart in Sacramento, but I'm grateful to be somewhere I can feel physically safe. At least, that's how I felt until I called my mom up to tell her about what happened in Oxnard. I had no idea where Oxnard was, but my mom did, and the simple fact that it was closer to me than to her, scared her.

I reminded her of everything I went through back home. Here in L.A., I haven't experienced anything negative, nothing near what I went through every day in Sacramento. And I think that's because diversity is more visible in places like L.A. People are more willing to accept those who are different.

True, there are safe spaces in my hometown—and I'm sure there are some in Oxnard too. But those small safe spaces do not extend overall safety in the community for gay and lesbian people.

Back home, in Sacramento, we all knew about the little Rainbow Triangle in Downtown. As soon as I turned 18, that was the first place I went to. Finally seeing other gay people, just hanging out, having a good time, made me feel safer and it made me feel accepted even if it was only on one block. But then I started to see that even there I wasn't safe. Gay bashers would walk by and bang on the windows, yelling slurs, and they even went as far as to break into a bunch of cars parked at a gay club. In my opinion, Lawrence was a brave kid. He wasn't afraid to be who he was, even though he was being teased for it AND without having a visible gay community and lots of safe spaces.

Lesson Ideas: English and Composition

A Tale of Two Cities: Anne says even her safe zone back in Sacramento, the Rainbow Triangle, was not safe: "Gay bashers would walk by and bang on the windows, yelling slurs, and they even went as far as to break into a bunch of cars parked at a gay club." She further explains, "Moving to Los Angeles was definitely the right decision. I feel that people are more accepting here of who I am." This acceptance translates into a feeling of safety. How accepted do your students feel in your town, and in other places where they've traveled? What are some of the indicators that a town, or even a neighborhood or a block within it, is accepting or not accepting, safe or unsafe, for different groups of people? What are the signs that your students look for to indicate that they are safe? What are the kinds of things that make them feel unsafe? In other words, how do they read the various social and cultural geographies they pass through over the course of their daily lives?

Family Voices: Anne's mom's response to the attack was "I want to kill them for what they did to you." Her sister's response was "I tried talking to you but you weren't talking. Then I started getting mad because you weren't answering me." Anne's response to the police examination was "I felt violated and I got pissed off." Students can reflect on an experience that deeply affected their lives. Have them interview parents or guardians, siblings, and friends, just as Anne did. What perspectives do they hear? How and why do those perspectives differ from their own personal interpretation of the event they're exploring?

Lesson Ideas: Health and Wellness

No Fear: Anne describes Larry King as a young man who "wasn't afraid to be who he was." Have students read the article in the *New York Times* to learn more about King, his community, and the circumstances of his death (search his name). The article quotes one of King's classmates making an observation similar to Anne's: "They teased him because he was different . . . but he wasn't afraid to show himself." What is the fear that many youth face in wanting to conform? Audre Lorde, a black feminist lesbian writer, wrote in *Transformation of Silence*, "That visibility which makes us most vulnerable is also the source of our greatest strength." What does this quote mean to students? How can conformity mean subscribing to values that one does not necessarily agree with? Can conforming keep one safe? Can conforming be dangerous?

Retaliation: Anne's mother says she responded to her daughter's violent experience with a feeling of wanting to kill the people who hurt her. Have students been in similar situations, wanting to retaliate? What are strategies one can use to de-escalate violence? Have your students research resources in their community to deal with violence after it has occurred and to prevent cycles of violence involving young people.

Personal Accounts of Violence: Anne describes her encounter with the police in the hospital: "One officer was telling my family to 'roll up her shirt' so they could take pictures of the bruises. 'Roll up her pant leg' so they could take pictures of my ankles. 'Let me take pictures of her face.' It made me feel like I was one of the victims on TV, like on CSI when you see police taking crime scene pictures. And so I felt violated and I got pissed off." What does using the pronoun "her" do to give an impersonal feel to police dialogue? How would your students rescript the dialogue in ways that would be more humanizing for those who have survived a violent event?

Lesson Ideas: Social and Cultural Studies

Homophobia and Gay Rights: Often violence is enacted out of fear, ignorance, and a desire for control. Have your students do some research on the history of homophobia and the gay rights movement in the United States. What is the history of the pink triangle? Where did the rainbow flag originate? Anne's commentary shines a light on various social geographies. Have your students research key places in gay rights history, including the Stonewall uprising in New York City and San Francisco's Castro district. What conditions were in place at key historic moments that supported the formation of a social movement supporting gay rights? What role did young people play then, and what role do they play now in LGBTQ politics in the United States?

Lesson Ideas: Media Literacy

In the News: Anne was inspired to share her story when she heard the news about Lawrence King. Have students search for a news article on a topic of interest and write about how it relates to them, using Anne's commentary as a model. Have them start with an adaptation of Anne's line: *"The reason I want to talk about this after what happened to BLANK is that it didn't just happen to BLANK. It happened to everyone who cares about BLANK."*

3. KILLING OFF CANCER? BY ALANA GERMANY

The new HPV (human papillomavirus) vaccine can prevent cervical cancer and is being recommended for girls ages nine to twenty-six. In 2007 states around the country were considering mandating it. Skeptics of the vaccine were speaking up from different sides of the political spectrum. Some claimed the vaccine would encourage early sexual activity; others raised questions about how the vaccine's manufacturer might be profiting from its mandatory use. Meanwhile young women and their parents were trying to sort through all the information to decide whether or not they should get the vaccine. Youth Radio's Alana Germany was one of those young women:

> *I learned about cervical cancer in health class, but it never seemed like that big of a deal. Now I see these commercials, and the statistics about how many people will be affected by HPV and how it can lead to cervical cancer and . . . well . . . it's all shocking. I'm wondering—should I get the vaccine?*

Script

ALANA: The past few weeks, every time I take a seat to relax and watch a little TV, I see that new Gardasil commercial: One Less. I learned about cervical cancer in health class, but it never seemed like that big of a deal. Now I see these commercials, and the statistics about how many people will be affected by HPV and how it can lead to cervical cancer and . . . well . . . it's all shocking. I'm wondering—should I get the vaccine?

> When I want to find out anything, my first instinct is to go to the net. You can find anything on Google right?

(Typing sounds)

ALANA: I'm going to Planned Parenthood to see what I can find. "It's best for the vaccine to be administered before the onset of sexual activity, but young women who are sexually active should still be vaccinated." Okay . . . (more typing). So here I am on TeenWire— this is a sister site for Planned Parenthood. It says that, "The vaccine should be given to girls and boys before sexual activity with partners begins."

> Okay, so that's confusing. And that's from the source a lot of my friends turn to with questions about sex and sexually transmitted diseases. Even though I might check the Internet, a lot of girls, like 18-year old Sarah Beth McKay in Atlanta, are going to their parents. Sarah's mom has breast cancer.

SARAH: *Do you think I should get the vaccine?*

SARAH'S MOM: *If it keeps you from getting a cancer, it's worth thinking about because cancer is a road nobody wants to travel. My question back to you is that—do you think when you're talking to your buddies at school that getting this vaccination offers you some freedom to have sex, where you might be a little more reluctant thinking about STD's?*

ALANA: Here's a controversy. A lot of parents are worried that administering the vaccine promotes sexual promiscuity, since HPV, the virus that can cause cancer, is a sexually transmitted disease.

SARAH'S MOM: *It's tough to think that my daughter would be interested in or prepared for frequent sexual partners.*

SARAH: *Well I'm going to be married one day and what happens if my husband is carrying the HPV virus?*

SARAH'S MOM: *But I don't think it's [the vaccine] a bad idea, but you shouldn't use the vaccination as a freedom to do whatever you want.*

ALANA: It's up for debate whether or not getting the vaccine affects girls' decision to have sex. But Gina Mootrey, a medical officer from the Centers for Disease Control and Prevention in Atlanta, says the CDC is recommending that girls get the vaccine as soon as possible, starting as young as nine.

GINA MOOTREY: *The effect of this vaccine will have both individual and population effects. The current information we have is that it's been nearly 100 percent effective in preventing precursors to cancer and the development of cervical cancer.*

CURRY ANDREWS: *I got the HPV vaccine three weeks ago.*

ALANA: That's eighteen-year-old Curry Andrews.

CURRY: *I'll tell you how the shot was—when they put it in your arm, it burns. Different from other shots—hurts more. But then you weigh that against the side effects of cancer, and I think it's bearable.*

ALANA: Curry is more afraid of cancer than the HPV vaccine, which is why she got vaccinated right away. Eighteen-year-old Taylor Flanagan in Austin, Texas, is more skeptical. She has never been vaccinated, even as a baby.

TAYLOR FLANAGAN: *And so I've always been raised in a household that talked very openly about problems that can arise from very well accepted medical practices.*

ALANA: Taylor is worried about side effects that might show up later. I worry about the same things . . . especially as states like Texas and my state—California—consider mandating the vaccine. Personally, this isn't a decision I want to make right away. I'm seventeen, and the vaccine is recommended for girls up to age twenty-six. And since I'm not sexually active right now, I'm not at risk for HPV. Plus, the vaccine is still in the early stages of actually being used by the public. Who knows what negative side effects we might see ten or twenty years from now? I'll feel a lot more comfortable getting the vaccine after I have more information about its effectiveness over time.

ANNOUNCER: This story was produced with help from Sarah Beth McKay, Emma Din and Rebecca Gittelson in Atlanta, and the students from Youth Spin in Austin, Texas.

Lesson Ideas: English and Composition

Diverse Perspectives: Alana draws on a range of sources in this story to develop her understanding of the HPV vaccine. Have students map the perspectives offered in the piece, an exercise that will sharpen their ability to identify and then question various points of view. List these characters on the board or in a handout: Alana, the TeenWire website, Sarah's mom, the Centers for Disease Control, Curry, and Taylor. Pose these questions: What is each character's position with respect to the HPV vaccine? On the basis of what evidence do you know each character's position? What perspectives aren't represented? What more do you want to know?

New Voices: Building on the previous exercise, have students identify one source they'd like to hear from to learn more about the HPV vaccine (e.g., the agency that produced the "One Less" PSA campaign, a conservative group concerned about teen sexual activity, a doctor who administers the vaccine, a medical insurance company about whether the vaccine is covered). Working in small groups, have students do research to find a new source, develop a series of questions related to the story, and interview that source.

Collaborative Storytelling: The back announce to Alana's piece says, "This story was produced with help from Sarah Beth McKay, Emma Din and Rebecca Gittelson in Atlanta, and the students from Youth Spin in Austin, Texas." Three different organizations across the country collaborated in producing this story. It's an interesting model for students to consider as they undertake projects in which individual students contribute to a single narrative. One of the biggest challenges with this kind of work is integrating young people's various "elements" into a coherent story. Have students identify a topic in their community that's kicking up controversy. Working in teams, have them come up with a task list (interviews and research) and then distribute the responsibilities across the group. Once they've completed their fieldwork have them present it to the class as a collaborative demonstration of what they learned.

Lesson Ideas: Health and Science

Virus and Cancer: Something surprising in Alana's report is the connection she reveals between a virus girls can contract at a young age and the development of cervical cancer many years later. This connection is a powerful way to help students understand what a virus is and how it operates, what cancer is and how it develops and runs a course, and the relationship between viruses and cancer.

Health and Gender: This Youth Radio story draws attention to a link between cancer and a virus transmitted through sex. Some STDs affect men and women differently. HPV affects more women than men. Students can form research groups to find images and articles about different STDs and present their findings to the class.

Vaccination Time: When thinking about the side effects and the relatively short period of time that Gardasil has been tested, Alana expresses ambivalence about getting the vaccine. Have students look into the history of medical testing, including the landmark Tuskegee syphilis study and other experiments on humans that have gone bad or grossly violated ethics, as well as testing that has led to health breakthroughs. What do students consider the key criteria defining ethical medical testing? How does that list compare with U.S. government policy and law in this area?

Health Care for All: Alana talks about the issue of health care not being available to everyone. Students can research and compare different proposals for universal health care and find out which countries currently implement this system.

Lesson Ideas: Economics

Business of Health: Have students research Merck (see, for example, *New York Times* coverage from 2007). How much does the HPV vaccine cost? Who pays? Who profits from making the vaccine mandatory, defining profit in terms of health benefits and financial benefits? Who is placed at risk, again defining risk in terms of health and money? Why did Merck decide to stop pushing for the vaccine to be mandatory? How did money factor into this decision?

Lesson Ideas: Media Literacy

Media Search: In the opening lines of her story, Alana says, "You can find anything on Google right?" What search terms would students use to find out about the HPV vaccine? Working with the entire class, brainstorm a list of possible terms, making sure to include words that will reveal various sides of the vaccine's controversy (e.g., "HPV and sexual activity"). If you've got access to computers in your classroom or library, break into small groups and assign different search term clusters to each team. Come back to the full group and compare what students found in the first three listings under each Google search they performed. So, what can you find on Google? Use this exercise to explore search engine optimization, the process that determines which sites show up at the top of a Google search. What is a *sponsored link?* What is an *organic* result? What determines the order of organic search result lists that show up through Google?

Public Service Announcements: Students are bombarded with television commercials, some designed to sell products, and others, like the Gardasil advertisements, doing that and conveying a health message. Have students analyze the "One Less" campaign. What message does the campaign convey? Who appears in the ads? How effective is it in branding the vaccine and clarifying its use? What would make it better? What story is not being told? Compare the "One Less" campaign with other social messaging ads students see on television. Which stand out? Who are the target audiences? Ask students to research the effectiveness of various campaigns. How would they design a campaign at their school to spread a pro-social message?

Big Companies, Big Profits: Merck is the company that distributes Gardasil. Students can research the companies that produce the drugs they find in their own medicine cabinets. How unusual is the controversy Merck is experiencing right now? What other big pharmaceutical companies have generated products that have incited public debate? How have these controversies compared to the one surrounding the HPV vaccine? Drawing from this comparison, have students identify the hot-button issues likely to heat up debates around industry, drugs, and public health in the media.

4. THAT SICKENING SMELL, BY SOPHIE SIMON-ORTIZ

Youth Radio's Sophie Simon-Ortiz grew up in West Berkeley, near a steel manufacturing plant, and still has vivid memories of the smell that poured regularly from its smoke stacks and permeated the neighborhood. Her friend Katri remembers how much the smell used to bother her dad:

> *We would go for walks every now and then around the neighborhood and every now and then he would start complaining about the smell in the air and be really grossed out by it and I didn't really know what that meant. . . . I think I thought that was just what the neighborhood smelled like, like what are we gonna do?*

The smell is still there. So Sophie decided to find out why, after so many years and complaints from nearby residents, not much seems to have changed at all.

Script

SOPHIE: During World War Two, West Berkeley became a center of industry in the Bay Area, and if you walk along the train tracks that still run through the western edge of my childhood neighborhood, you'll still pass dozens of warehouses and rusted smokestacks. The sound of the train whistle is so much a part of my childhood memories, that when I hear it now, it's still comforting to me. There's something else that reminds me of that time. The best way to describe it is the smell of a burning pot handle that's been left on the stovetop too long.

KATRI: *I don't remember what it smelled like as much as I remember my dad and me being outside. . . .*

SOPHIE: That's one of my oldest friends, Katri Foster, who also grew up in West Berkeley.

KATRI: *We would go for walks every now and then around the neighborhood and every now and then he would start complaining about the smell in the air and be really grossed out by it and I didn't really know what that meant. . . . I think I thought that was just what the neighborhood smelled like, like what are we gonna do?*

SOPHIE: Katri's house is only a few blocks from one of the few remaining factories in West Berkeley—Pacific Steel Casting. Now that we're in our twenties, Katri and I talk about the pollution in the neighborhood. Her little brother Joe is ten. He developed asthma as a baby, and had to go to the hospital often. The asthma got better for a while, until last October, when he started having headaches.

KATRI: *. . . And he wasn't eating a lot and he had been throwing up and they found out he had a brain tumor and for a ten-year-old that's just not obviously very common and it was really I mean there's no history of this in the family.*

SOPHIE: Katri says the first thing that popped into her head to explain her brother's condition was the pollution.

KATRI: *I mean of course there's always a possibility that it was a coincidence and there's so many things that could cause this to happen but it just seemed really weird and given that he developed asthma so young I don't think it's that far off to think it's a possibility.*

SOPHIE: Katri's family is convinced of the connection, although they don't have any direct proof that pollution is what caused Joe's health problems. But there are some frightening statistics about our zip code. The most recent city of Berkeley health reports show that the West Berkeley zip code has the highest asthma hospitalization rates in the city.

BEATRIZ: *What I have seen is an increase in children with asthma.*

SOPHIE: That's Beatriz Leyva-Cutler. She's the director at the childcare center I attended before kindergarten.

BEATRIZ: *Whereas before one child out of sixty-two, now two to three children in any one classroom showing asthmatic symptoms. Coughing, wheezing . . .*

SOPHIE: The center is right up the street from the steel plant, and not far from the freeway and the city's bus yard. While her observations make it seem like Katri's family has legitimate concerns, to be fair, there are two sides to every story. So I went to the plant—the source of the distinct smell in my neighborhood—to get their perspective. Even though I lived just a few blocks from Pacific Steel Casting, I had never been inside until now. The PR people at the plant don't deny the smell. Elizabeth Jewel is a consultant for the company and says the odor is a product of the manufacturing process. She also says production has increased in recent years making the situation worse.

ELIZABETH JEWEL: *And so the neighbors have been upset about the smell, understandably so, and the company has responded to them by coming up together with a proposal to install a two million dollar filter that the company is confident will address all of if not the majority of the odor problems.*

SOPHIE: As the neighbors see it, getting rid of the smell doesn't necessarily take care of the toxins in the air. They want the plant to stop using toxic products in the first place. But the company isn't planning on stopping their business. And Elizabeth Jewel points out that the neighborhood was industrial before it was residential.

ELIZABETH JEWEL: *It's an age old problem where you have industry, freeways . . . and housing. You know housing has grown up around Pacific Steel and so we have understandable conflicts where you have people living next to an industrial site.*

SOPHIE: What complicates the situation is that many of the employees for Pacific Steel live in the neighborhood and it's one of the biggest employers in Berkeley, with union wages. And for many people who depend on those paychecks, it's more of a health risk to be unemployed than exposed to bad air. But David Schroeder at the West Berkeley Alliance for Clean Air and Safe Jobs says everyone is entitled to clean air.

DAVID: *We've done a bit of research . . . on what's in the air and there's all sorts of stuff you wouldn't want to be anywhere near if you had the choice about it.*

SOPHIE: David points to a test his organization conducted of levels of formaldehyde, a known carcinogen.

DAVID: *. . . And there the levels of formaldehyde were about twenty-four times the threshold for EPA region 6 . . . and so that's kind of scary to us.*

SOPHIE: And those fears are real for neighborhood people like my friend Katri. For now, it looks like her brother is going to be okay when he finishes chemotherapy and her family plans to stay in West Berkeley. Meanwhile, the conversations between community groups and Pacific Steel continue, and people keep moving into the area. Now there's a new generation of children falling asleep to the sound of the trains passing. And I'm sure they'll grow up to love this neighborhood like I do, because it's rich in a strong working class history, shared among many different kinds of people. My hope is that they don't have to hold their breath when they go outside like I had to.

Lesson Ideas: English and Composition

Community Asset Mapping: At the beginning of Sophie's story, she focuses on the industrial aspects of the neighborhood where she grew up—the warehouses, the smoke stacks, the railroad—and her story explores some of the risks associated with living in that environment. But she also mentions other parts of her neighborhood: a preschool, a strong working-class history, and diversity. Have students tour their neighborhoods and map what they see. Discuss how their perceptions of their neighborhoods differ from other representations (e.g., those in the local press), and have them consider what factors determine whether a neighborhood is known for its assets or its problems. To draw public support to address neighborhood problems, you need to be able to tell the story in a powerful and convincing way. Based on their community maps, how would your students persuasively present a story about their neighborhood in such a way that inspires others to join community improvement efforts?

Voices in Dialogue: Sophie speaks with a friend, a spokesperson for Pacific Steel Casting, a representative from a nonprofit organization, and her former preschool director. How does this story compare with other literary works or journalistic reports that offer several different perspectives on an issue? How does Sophie rely on these different characters to bolster her story and build her argument? How does she establish each character's specific credibility? What perspectives, if any, are missing?

Lesson Ideas: Health and Science

Environmental Inquiry: In her story Sophie explores the relationship between environmental conditions and public health. She's careful to draw on a range of sources. Have your students identify an environmental problem that affects their own community. Have them research both the scientific issues and social debates circulating around the problem, and ask them to conduct at least two interviews: one with a scientist and one with a community member directly affected by the problem. Have students compare what they learn from these two perspectives and discuss the relationship between the *scientific* and the *anecdotal*. Then ask your students to identify what additional research they would need to do to tell the whole story, and what innovative solutions they'd propose.

Health Risks: In preparing this story, Sophie did some research suggesting that in the late 1990s, out of all Bay Area facilities subject to Toxic Release Inventory reporting, Pacific Steel Casting ranked number two for carcinogenic risk. Additionally she found a recent study that concluded that asthma hospitalization rates for all Berkeley children are 2.5 times higher than for all California children, and that asthma hospitalization rates in her childhood zip code are highest in all of Berkeley. What are some of the ways that these health risks affect the human body? Why are children more susceptible than adults? How do scientists determine carcinogenic risk, and what is the Toxic Release Inventory?

Lesson Ideas: Economics

Profits and Health: Although the PSC representative Sophie quotes doesn't deny that a noxious smell permeates the neighborhood, Sophie says the company is one of Berkeley's largest employers, brings in tax dollars for the city, donates to city organizations, and participates in the Spare the Air program. Students can research corporations that generate environmental pollutants yet support positive programs. What cost-benefit analysis is the corporation undertaking in making these decisions? And what cost-benefit analysis do local people make in determining how hard to push for reforms?

Ethical Dilemmas: In Sophie's words, "What complicates the situation is that many of the employees for Pacific Steel live in the neighborhood and it's one of the biggest employers in Berkeley, with union wages. And for many people who depend on those paychecks, it's more of a health risk to be unemployed than exposed to bad air." In groups of three to four, students can come up with an issue that poses a moral dilemma for a company or for environmental advocates. Each group can give their issue to another group to brainstorm how they will handle the situation, taking various perspectives, and present back to the whole class.

Good Business: Have students find companies that are socially and environmentally responsible. What are the philosophies of these companies? Are the products of these businesses offered at reasonable prices? What are some of the trade-offs for being a responsible business? What incentives do your students believe would be effective in encouraging companies to create and maintain environmentally responsible practices?

Lesson Ideas: Media Literacy

Environmental Justice: Sophie reports that the neighborhood primarily affected was working class and diverse. Have your students carry out research to find out the socioeconomic and ethnic makeup of areas in their regions of the country that are more and less affected by pollution.

Youth Battles for Social Justice: Reflecting on growing up in a neighborhood filled with chemical odors, Sophie's friend Katri says, "I think I thought that was just what the neighborhood smelled like, like what are we gonna do?" Students can do research on social justice actions in their local vicinities that young people have organized. What are some strategies these groups can use to draw media attention to their campaigns?

PRspeak: Elizabeth Jewel, the spokesperson for PSC, responded to community concerns about the foul smell by bringing up the company's "proposal to install a two million dollar filter that the company is confident will address all of if not the majority of the odor problems." She doesn't, in this statement, draw a connection between the proposed filter and toxic emissions or health problems. Students can use newspaper articles to find other statements made by spokespeople. What is the role of a spokesperson at a company or organization? What training does a spokesperson receive? What are some investigative reporting strategies journalists can use to get real answers from spokespeople or to get access to others from within a given company or organization who might bring different perspectives?

5. UNDERGROUND MARKET FOR ADD DRUGS, BY MICHELLE JARBOE

Michelle Jarboe introduces a growing phenomenon on U.S. college campuses: students misusing stimulants prescribed for attention deficit disorder (ADD). Although medications such as Ritalin and Adderall are intended for kids with doctors' diagnoses, more and more students are taking these drugs without ever seeing a doctor, just to help them concentrate, churn out papers overnight, and cram for exams. Some are selling the drugs around campus for a profit. Michelle shares her firsthand experience:

> *The few times I took Ritalin, I got the pills from a boyfriend whose parents were psychiatrists. He didn't have Attention Deficit Disorder (ADD), but mom and dad were willing to write him a prescription so he could stay up nights to cram for exams. I was 17, and figured if someone's highly educated and expert parents would casually hand him a drug, then it had to be safe.*

Michelle likens the misuse of ADD drugs to underage drinking, and she says that because the medications are legal, students aren't too afraid of getting in trouble for experimenting with them. The story raises some provocative questions about the lengths students will go to in high-pressure academic settings to perform well. She also uncovers the microeconomies that have sprouted up around these drugs. Michelle's story is likely to inspire lively discussion about the kinds of things policymakers, educators, and students themselves should do to curtail the underground market for Ritalin and other stimulants.

Script

MICHELLE: The few times I took Ritalin, I got the pills from a boyfriend whose parents were psychiatrists. He didn't have Attention Deficit Disorder (ADD), but mom and dad were willing to write him a prescription so he could stay up nights to cram for exams. I was 17, and figured if someone's highly educated and expert parents would casually hand him a drug, then it had to be safe.

The first time I tried Adderall wasn't much different—this time, the source was a friend who got the drug from a roommate with a prescription. Look, I wasn't a habitual drug user. But I was driven to do well in school, and couldn't see my way through all the papers, tests and projects on two or three hours of sleep a night. That is, until I encountered my friends' little pills.

Sometimes they were free, and sometimes a single pill could cost as much as seven or eight dollars. Whatever the cost, the returns were amazing.

JESSE: *The whole time you're on it, you just feel like that's the way things are supposed to be. You feel like it's gotten you normal.*

MICHELLE: That's Jesse Anderson, a friend of mine who used Adderall for the first time in a college study group. Someone gave it to him, and he thought, "Sure, why not."

JESSE: *I remember everyone sitting around and thinking, "You know, maybe we all have ADD, because this stuff makes me feel great, like I don't feel weird. I feel like I want to do my work."*

MICHELLE: You can pop a pill at midnight, he says, write a 10-page paper in a few hours and still have time to clean your room and catch breakfast before your 8 a.m. class. And though transactions in these stimulants aren't always in the open, they don't carry the same stigma as many recreational drugs. Jesse knows a lot of people who won't touch marijuana—but it doesn't take much for them to chow down Adderall without a prescription.

JESSE: *Because it's made by a company, it comes in a nice pre-packaged way. They're not going to sell anything to millions of kids that's going to kill them. It seems relatively safe.*

HAMRICK: *When a student brings up the fact that stimulant use actually makes them perform better, I can't deny that.*

MICHELLE: That's Psychiatrist Allen Hamrick. He says it's tough to fight abuse because the little pills work so well.

HAMRICK: *The stimulant itself would lead any of us to feel more attentive and probably do better on a test. But so would crack cocaine.*

MICHELLE: Hamrick is one of the higher-ups with UNC's Counseling and Psychological Services. He's seen students taking 500 milligrams of Ritalin a day, a huge jump from the 10 milligrams a day typical for a new ADD patient. Hamrick's office has stopped prescribing stimulants to students without a full battery of psychological tests. He says counselors worried they were contributing to the black market for Attention Deficit drugs.

Tobias Butts, a recent UNC graduate, says the docs are right. He saw lots of students make a killing off selling pills during his time in college.

TOBIAS: *So, you've got roughly 90 pills, and then you sell each one of those for $5. Do the math. That's $450 for a $30 investment. If that's not highway robbery, then I don't know what is.*

PSYCH MAJOR: *I have to stockpile that stuff during exams and midterms.*

MICHELLE: That's a psychology major who asked to remain anonymous, since he freely shares Adderall with his friends. Using his knowledge of ADD symptoms, and a little bit of help from the field's diagnostic manual, he faked the learning disorder to get a prescription. He takes a small percentage of his pills each month and gives away the rest.

PSYCH MAJOR: *I never have a surplus, but I have to take into consideration that demand fluctuates depending on what kind of university-wide pressures are placed on the student body.*

MICHELLE: Those pressures also hit students trying to protect their medications. Melinda Manning, an assistant dean of students at UNC, talks to students every week who say they're being pestered for their Adderall supply. She graduated from UNC a decade ago, and says this kind of stimulant abuse didn't exist when she was an undergrad.

MELINDA: *The most my friends were taking were No-Doz and other caffeine. I don't remember hearing of anyone who took anything like Ritalin or Adderall. But, honestly, I didn't know any friends who were prescribed Ritalin or Adderall for ADD. So I don't think there was any access to it at that point.*

MICHELLE: Times have changed. Myself? I didn't consider what might happen if I got caught taking someone else's prescription medication. Sure, my friends and I knew sharing regulated stimulants was illegal, but it didn't seem that different from underage drinking. Kids in every college town do it, and most of them don't get caught. My stint taking the pills was brief. It ended after I realized that I'd rather fail a paper than risk dependency on a drug in order to achieve my goals. But I still hear a lot about stimulant abuse at UNC, and, more and more, it's not just academic. Plenty of people pop an Adderall with a beer before heading to a party, making the night last longer . . . and expanding the market for these drugs.

Lesson Ideas: English and Composition

First-Person Reporting: In school writing we often make a distinction between objective reports and personal narratives. The same is true in journalism, and yet in this story, as in many Youth Radio pieces, Michelle Jarboe combines investigation and first-person commentary. How does Michelle use the "I" pronoun in her story? How does she present hard data? How does her own experience experimenting with ADD drugs affect her credibility as a reporter, and your interest in her story? When do you use the "I" in your own writing, and when do you leave out your own personal experience?

Balance: Michelle includes several perspectives in her story, each representing various positions with respect to the market for ADD drugs on college campuses. What perspectives can you identify? How balanced is her report? Does she take a strong side in the debate about the seriousness of the phenomenon she describes or what should be done about it? What implications do you draw from her report? Are any perspectives missing, in your view?

No reporter can include every perspective in any given story. What other voices would you want to hear?

Context: Usually when we hear stories about teenage drug use, the focus is on illegal substances such as marijuana and cocaine. Very often those stories criminalize youth and sound alarms about the effects of these substances on young people, their families, and their communities. Michelle's story draws attention to an illegal practice surrounding *legal* drugs, and most kids misuse ADD meds not to get high, but to perform well in school. How is Michelle's story different from the typical report on drug use among youth, not only in terms of the kinds of drugs she's talking about, but also in terms of the way she presents her narrative?

Lesson Ideas: Health and Science

Side Effects: Students can talk about common drugs that they are exposed to or have heard of, such as marijuana, ecstasy, heroin, cocaine, crack, tobacco, and alcohol. What's the difference, in their view, between experimenting with illegal drugs and the misuse of stimulants as described in the Youth Radio story? In groups they can choose a drug to research along with its history, slang terminology, side effects, and uses (medicinal, recreational, etc.). Have students create posters and share with the rest of the class.

Stress Effects: Michelle describes a pressure-filled academic environment on college campuses: "I was driven to do well in school, and couldn't see my way through all the papers, tests and projects on two or three hours of sleep a night. That is, until I encountered my friends' little pills." What is the academic environment like at your school? What are some ways students can advocate to reduce stress levels in their schools and create a healthier environment? Who are the stakeholders students would have to influence? What arguments would convince those key players?

Survey Says: Students can create a survey in which they can ask other students anonymously about their experiences with off-label use of drugs and make graphs and charts to show their findings. What was or was not surprising about the results?

Lesson Ideas: Social Studies and Economics

Microeconomies: What are some of the economic principles driving the market for ADD drugs? What defines a microeconomy? What about a cottage industry? To what extent do these terms apply to the market described in Michelle's story? What role do economic factors play in creating incentives for students to buy and sell these stimulants for uses other than those for which they are prescribed? To what extent should the pharmaceutical industry be held accountable for abuses of ADD drugs on college campuses? Who profits from the use of these drugs? Who pays the cost?

Lesson Ideas: Media Literacy

Ads That Subtract: How does the media market drugs to youth? Students can find song lyrics that mention drugs and alcohol, movies that promote drug usage, and examples of government-approved pharmaceutical industries advertising drugs in commercials. Have students research guidelines drug advertisers must conform to in their television campaigns. Are there special rules regulating marketing campaigns targeting children and teens?

Race and Class Analysis: Ask students to research the demographics of young people using Ritalin and Adderall drugs, with and without doctors' prescriptions, as well as the demographics of young people using other drugs. How accurate are mainstream media portrayals? What consequences do students who misuse ADD drugs typically face? Are young people ever incarcerated for using or selling these drugs illegally? How do those incarceration rates compare with punishments faced by uses and abuses of other drugs by teens?

· Notes

INTRODUCTION.

1. For more on dialogic and reflexive methods, see Tedlock & Mannheim, 1995; Clifford & Marcus, 1986; Behar & Gordon, 1995.

2. For more on autoethnography, see Ellis & Bochner, 2000; Reed-Danahay, 1997; Trinh, 1992.

3. For more on community-based participatory research, see Minkler & Wallerstein, 2003; Torre & Fine, 2006.

4. See, for example, García-Canclini, 2001; Ginsburg, Abu-Lughod, & Larkin, 2002; Jenkins, 1992; Kinder, 1999; Sefton-Green & Soep, 2007; Willis, 1990.

5. Buckingham, Burn, & Willett, 2005; Campbell, Hoey, & Perlman, 2001; Goldfarb, 2002; Goodman, 2003; Hull & Katz, 2002; Ito, forthcoming; Kinkade & Macy, 2003; Kirwan, Learmonth, Sayer, & Williams, 2003; Sefton-Green & Soep, 2006; Tyner, 2003.

6. This figure comes from market research published in 2006; see www .commonsensemedia.org/resources/general_research.php?id=68.

7. See, for example, Burgin, 2000; Fisher, 2003; Gee, 2003; Ito, Okabe, & Matsuda, 2005; Kearney, 2003.

8. In the early stages of framing this project, we had structured conversations with leaders from nine youth media organizations representing a range of media forms, geographic locations, organizational histories, and methodologies for engaging youth, communities, and audiences. These perspectives richly informed our thinking about the field and the story we wanted to tell here, as you'll see in references to these conversations throughout the remainder of the introduction and through echoes of these themes throughout the book.

9. Ken Ikeda, personal communication.

10. William Ayers, personal communication, 2006.

CHAPTER ONE

1. Both of us have been involved directly with Youth Speaks over the years, Lissa as a board member and Vivian as a participant on the Education Committee. This discussion of Ise Lyfe's poem builds on an analysis originally presented in Soep (2006b).

2. See Soep, 2005a, for discussion of the aesthetic elements of this story and the assessment process it set off among youth producers.

3. When this story aired on National Public Radio, it drew strong listener reactions, and the piece was recognized with several media awards, including honors from the National Association of Black Journalists and the Third Coast International Audio Festival.

4. He flipped to a drawing of an Iraqi man with tape of the American flag across his mouth, and an image of an Iraqi child sucking on a baby bottle shaped like a rocket marked with the Israeli flag.

5. This discussion builds on a conversation among Lissa, Belia Mayeno Saavedra, and News Director Nishat Kurwa, presented in our chapter (Soep, Saavedra, & Kurwa, 2008) for a handbook on social justice and education.

6. Youth media producers working on stories like this one often highlight their "authenticity," as if what young people say were somehow pure, uninterrupted, unmediated, a direct expression (Fleetwood, 2005). The desire to celebrate youth voice in this way can obscure adult interventions and institutional constraints that shape what young people express and what audiences hear.

7. We had worked with a young soldier who wanted to broadcast passages from his journal during the early stages of the war, but when the outlet stipulated that he'd need to reveal his real name, he decided to seek permission from his chain of command, and they flatly refused—with no obligation to offer an explanation. Military public affairs officers can very easily kill stories. Free

speech rights do not function under the Uniform Code of Military Justice the way they do under civilian law.

8. Ed says it was a matter of course, when packing up for war, to grab a digital camera. The Marines took pictures of historically significant places such as Babylon, personally meaningful sites such as soccer fields, dramatic vistas and horizons, and lots and lots of photos of themselves with their buddies, dirty and grinning, weighed down with gear and nearly unrecognizable compared to their civilian selves, now thinner and softer, lugging backpacks around campus instead of firearms through the desert. But the spectacle of death, captured with snapshots like the one the Marines call Mr. Crispy, seemed to show up in their photo collections with special frequency, providing something to bond over. Ed told us his unit accumulated two CDs' worth of digital photographs, at least five hundred pictures, and Mr. Crispy appeared again and again. So did shots of charred and truncated corpses, heads dangling lifeless from the cabs of trucks, flattened bodies.

CHAPTER TWO

1. The survey report can be found at www.kff.org/kaiserpolls/pomr0129040 th.cfm.

2. We first presented and developed the concept of collegial pedagogy, drawing on some of the stories discussed here, in Chávez & Soep, 2005; see also Chávez, Turalba, & Malik, 2006.

3. James Ewert, California media law expert and legal counsel, personal communication, 2001.

4. For a more fine-grained linguistic look at this story and sequence of interactions as "crowded talk," see Soep, 2007b.

5. We make this observation knowing that it can be problematic, ethnographically speaking, to highlight what a person in any given context does not do, but the point seems worth making nevertheless, given the frequency with which adults, unlike this principal, dismiss young people's legitimate involvement with serious work.

6. BET is Black Entertainment Television, MTV is Music Television, and PYTs means "pretty young things."

CHAPTER THREE

1. Despite their next-generation mystique that inspires envy and spending.

2. This is true whether they're moving through a traditional media produc-

tion process presided over by an official editorial board or strategizing about how to shape their content in ways to maximize its likelihood to rise through the ranks of user-curated or social media sites to achieve traction with audiences.

CHAPTER FOUR

1. In the planning meeting before this event, the group reviewed how the drama would unfold, everyone urging Jennifer that she better not laugh. Jason emphasized that all authority figures who weren't peer teachers needed to look busy behind cubicle walls, because if it were obvious that they could see what was happening, the students would know they'd intervene, and that would give it all away.

2. Fan fic is fiction produced by readers who integrate existing characters— those first created by other, often highly established authors—into new stories. See, for example, Jenkins, 1992.

3. What we do not cover here is technical training: how to record clean audio, edit using ProTools, or compose beats using Reason. Specific applications and industry standards change rapidly, and training on these systems requires step-by-step operations not well suited to a chapter like this one. We also do not go into detail here on music production, only because that process is sufficiently different from digital storytelling to warrant its own treatment (and book!).

4. We are grateful to Sara Harris for this insight.

5. The proliferation of digital distribution channels means we no longer have to abide by any one outlet's policies in order to reach an audience, but national outlets guarantee an audience of millions of listeners compared to the unpredictability of peer-to-peer outlets.

6. See the introduction to Robin Kelley's (1998) *Yo Mama's DysFUNKtional* for an inspired example of a scathing critique of social science that contains kernels for a great radio story.

7. As young people prepare for production to begin, none of these skills matters if the equipment doesn't work, or if users don't know how to troubleshoot when they hit "record" and nothing happens. Young people should have ample opportunity to get out there and use the equipment long before they're on deadline for a high-stakes story. Youth Radio packs kits with everything a reporter will need to gather sound: a minidisk, DAT, or flash recorder; microphone and mic cord; headphones and cord; a cheat sheet with basic recording instructions; blank disks; extra batteries; and a cell phone number for a producer who can help troubleshoot in case of malfunction or confusion. After an instructor demonstrates how a given piece of equipment works, students should run through every step: getting it out of the box or bag, attaching all the wires, rolling tape, checking levels, and playing back. Microphone techniques should be reviewed,

and students should practice micing someone close (just a fist's distance away from the mouth, with the mic held at an angle), at medium distance, and from several feet away (making sure to emphasize that tape recorded from a distance will *not* be usable as anything but ambience, as elaborated below). The best place for gathering tape is quiet, preferably with soft surfaces so the sound isn't "boomy" (e.g., a living room with a couch is better than a kitchen with running appliances). Windows should be closed. Before starting the interview, students need to roll one full minute of "room tone" (no talking, just the sound of the room) so they can lay this sound underneath cuts in and out of clips from the interview to smooth the transitions. We tell our students to write down a room tone reminder at the top and bottom of their interview sheet. It's the single most common thing to forget.

8. For the process to be ethical and legal, Sophie needed to be sure that her interviewee knew she was being recorded, and that her remarks could end up on the radio.

9. Like any inquiry process, media production is at turns fabulously creative and mind-numbingly tedious. The interview is often among the most engaging processes. One of the dreariest, which soon follows, is logging tape. A log is essentially a transcription marked with time codes every minute or so. One way to save time on logging is to scribble down notes on a pad while you're gathering tape, identifying time codes for the strongest moments. If you can't write as you go (say it's dark, or you've got your hands full with the equipment), jot notes as soon as you stop recording and leave the scene. No matter how hard you try to convince yourself that you'll remember all the juicy stuff the next day, that you're tired and you want to be done, force yourself to write the notes. It's never as fresh even one day later. The notes save you serious log time. But even with these best moments marked, very often you've got to log much more than you'll actually use. Rarely can you know in advance precisely what your story will need.

10. In chapter 3 we talk at length about the process and politics of story distribution, and so we will not go into detail here about that. What we do want to emphasize in this chapter has to do with what can happen after a story airs, in terms of both listener response and extended use.

11. For further discussion of this topic and Cassandra Gonzalez's Youth Radio story, please see Soep, 2007b.

12. It is beyond the scope of this book to take on the subject of comment sections in online publications as a site for audience engagement. Suffice it to say here that Youth Radio values comments as indicators that stories have struck a chord and is actively developing new guidelines for engaging or not with comments that can be deeply troubling and yet indelible.

Bibliography

Alim, H.S. (2005). Critical language awareness in the United States: Revisiting issues and revising pedagogies in a resegregated society. *Educational Researcher, 35,* 24–31.

Behar, R. & Gordon, D. (1995). (Eds.). *Women writing culture.* Berkeley: University of California Press.

Bennett, W. L. (2007). *Changing citizenship in a digital age.* Paper prepared for the OECD/INDIRE Conference on Millennial Learners. Florence, Italy. Retrieved Jan. 15, 2008, from www.oecd.org/dataoecd/0/8/38360794.pdf.

boyd, d. (Forthcoming). Why youth (heart) social network sites: The role of networked publics in teenage social life. In D. Buckingham (Ed.), *MacArthur Foundation Series on Digital Learning: Youth, identity, and digital media volume.* Cambridge, MA: MIT Press.

boyd, d. (2007). Friends, friendsters, and top 8: Writing community into being on social networking sites. *First Monday.* Retrieved Jan. 15, 2008, from www .firstmonday.org/issues/issue11_12/boyd/.

Buckingham, D. (2003). *Media education: Literacy, learning and contemporary culture.* Cambridge, UK: Polity Press.

Buckingham, D., Burn, A. & Willett, R. (2005). *The media literacy of children and young people.* London: Centre for the Study of Children, Youth and Media.

Burgin, V. (2000). Jenni's room: Exhibitionism and solitude. *Critical Inquiry,* 27(1), 228–235.

Campbell, P., Hoey, L. & Perlman L. (2001). Sticking with my dreams: Defining and refining youth media in the 21st Century. Campbell-Kibler Associates, Inc. Retrieved Jan. 18, 2008, from www.campbell-kibler.com/youth_media .html.

Chaiklin, S. & Lave, J. (1996). *Understanding practice: Perspectives on activity and context.* Cambridge: Cambridge University Press.

Charmaz, K. & Mitchell, R. (1996). The myth of silent authorship: Self, substance and style in ethnographic writing. *Symbolic Interaction, 19*(4), 285–302.

Chávez, V., Duran, B., Baker, Q. E., Avila, M. M. & Wallerstein, N. (2003). The dance of race and privilege in community-based participatory research. In M. Minkler & N. Wallerstein (Eds.), *Community-based participatory research for health* (pp. 81–97). San Francisco: Jossey-Bass.

Chávez, V. & Soep, E. (2005). Youth Radio and the pedagogy of collegiality. *Harvard Educational Review, 75*(4), 409–434.

Chávez, V., Turalba R.-A. N. & Malik, S. (2006). Teaching public health through a pedagogy of collegiality. *American Journal of Public Health, 96,* 1175–1180.

Clifford, J. & Marcus, G. (1986). (Eds.). *Writing culture: The poetics and politics of ethnography.* Berkeley: University of California Press.

Cope, B. & Kalantzis, M. (2000). *Multiliteracies: Literacy learning and the design of social futures.* London: Routledge.

Darder, A. (2002). *Reinventing Paulo Freire.* Boulder, CO: Westview Press.

Darder, A., Baltodano, M. & Torres, R. (2003). *The critical pedagogy reader.* New York: Routledge Falmer.

DeBell, M. & Chapman, C. (2006). *Computer and Internet use by students in 2003* (NCES 2006–065). Washington, DC: National Center for Education Statistics.

Douglas, S. (2004). *Listening in: Radio and American imagination.* Minneapolis: University of Minnesota Press.

Duncan-Andrade, J. (2007). Urban youth, media literacy, and increased critical civic participation. In S. Ginwright, P. Noguera, & J. Cammarota (Eds.), *Beyond resistance! Youth activism and community change* (149–170). New York: Routledge.

Ellis, C. & Bochner, A. (2006). Analyzing analytic autoethnography: An autopsy. *Journal of Contemporary Ethnography, 35*(4), 429–449.

Ellis, C. & Bochner, A. (2000) Autoethnography, personal narrative, reflexivity: Researcher as subject. In N. Denzin & Y. Lincoln (Eds.), *The handbook of qualitative research* (2nd ed., pp. 733–768). Newbury Park, CA: Sage.

Ellsworth, E. (1992). Why doesn't this feel empowering? Working through the repressive myths of critical pedagogy. In C. Luke & J. Gore (Eds.), *Feminisms and critical pedagogy* (pp. 90–119). New York: Routledge.

Engelman, R. (1996). *Public radio and television in America: A political history.* Thousand Oaks, CA: Sage.

Finders, M. (1997). *Just girls: Hidden literacies and life in junior high.* New York: Teachers College Press.

Fisher, M. (2003). Open mics and open minds: Spoken word poetry in African diaspora participatory literacy communities. *Harvard Educational Review, 73*(3), 362–389.

Fleetwood, N. (2005). Authenticating practices: Producing realness, performing youth. In S. Maira & E. Soep (Eds.), *Youthscapes: The popular, the national, the global* (pp. 155–172). Philadelphia: University of Pennsylvania Press.

García-Canclini, N. (2001). *Consumers and citizens: Globalization and multicultural conflicts.* Minneapolis: University of Minnesota Press.

Gee, J. (2003). *What video games have to teach us about literacy and learning.* New York: Palgrave Macmillan.

Gee, J. (2000). The new literacy studies: From "socially situated" to the work of the social. In D. Barton & M. Hamilton (Eds.), *Situated literacies* (pp. 180–196). London: Routledge.

Geertz, C. (1973). *The interpretation of cultures.* New York: Basic Books.

Ginsburg, F., Abu-Lughod, L. & Larkin, B. (2002). (Eds.). *Media worlds: Anthropology on new terrain.* Berkeley: University of California Press.

Ginwright, S. & Cammarota, J. (2002). New terrain in youth development: The promise of a social justice approach. *Social Justice, 29*(4), online.

Giroux, H. A. (1992). *Border crossings.* New York: Routledge.

Goldfarb, B. (2002). *Visual pedagogy: Media cultures in and beyond the classroom.* Durham, NC: Duke University Press.

Goodman, S. (2003). *Teaching youth media: A critical guide to literacy, video production, and social change.* New York: Teachers College Press.

Goodwin, M. H. (1990). *He said she said: Talk as social organization among black children.* Bloomington: Indiana University Press.

Heath, S. B. (1986). What no bedtime story means: Narrative skills at home and school. In B. Schieffelin & E. Ochs (Eds.), *Language socialization across cultures* (pp. 97–124). New York: Cambridge University Press.

Heath, S. B. (1983). *Ways with words: Language, life, and work in communities and classrooms.* New York: Cambridge University Press.

Henry, N. (2007). *American carnival: Journalism under siege in an age of new media.* Berkeley: University of California Press.

hooks, b. (2000). *All about love: New visions.* New York: Perennial.

hooks, b. (1994). *Teaching to transgress.* New York: Routledge.

Hull, G. (2003). Youth culture and digital media: New literacies for new times. *Research in the Teaching of English, 38*(2), 229–233.

Hull, G. & Katz, M. (2002). *Learning to tell a digital story: New literate spaces for crafting self.* Paper presented at the meeting of the American Anthropological Association, New Orleans.

Ito, M. (Forthcoming). Technologies of the childhood imagination: Yugioh, media mixes, and everyday cultural production. In J. Karaganis & N. Jeremijenko (Eds.), *Structures of participation in digital culture.* Durham, NC: Duke University Press.

Ito, M., Okabe, D. & Matsuda, M. (Eds.). (2005). *Personal, portable, pedestrian: Mobile phones in Japanese life.* Cambridge, MA: MIT Press.

Jenkins, H. (2006a). *Confronting the challenges of participatory culture: Media education for the 21st century.* Chicago: MacArthur Foundation.

Jenkins, H. (2006b). *Convergence culture: Where old and new media collide.* New York: New York University Press.

Jenkins, H. (1992). *Textual poachers: Television fans and participatory culture.* New York: Routledge.

Kearney, M. C. (2003). Girls make movies. In K. Mallan & S. Pearce (Eds.), *Youth cultures: Images and identities* (pp. 17–34). Westport, CT: Praeger.

Kelley, R. D. G. (1998). *Yo' mama's disFUNKtional: Fighting the culture wars in urban America.* Boston: Beacon Press.

Kinder, M. (Ed.). (1999). *Kids' media culture.* Durham, NC: Duke University Press.

Kinkade, S. & Macy, C. (2003). What works in youth media: Case studies from around the world. International Youth Foundation. Retrieved Jan. 17, 2008, from www.iyfnet.org/uploads/WW%20-Youth%20Led%20Media.pdf.

Kirwan, T., Learmonth, J., Sayer, M. & Williams, R. (2003). Mapping media literacy. London: British Film Institute, Broadcasting Standards Commission, Independent Television Commission. Retrieved Jan. 17, 2007, from www .ofcom.org.uk/static/archive/itc/uploads/Mapping_media_literacy1.pdf.

Klinenberg, E. (2007). *Fighting for air: The battle to control America's media.* New York: Metropolitan Press.

Kress, G. (2003). *Literacy in the new media age.* New York: Routledge.

Lave, J. & Wenger, E. (1991). *Situated learning: Legitimate peripheral participation.* Cambridge: Cambridge University Press.

Lipsitz, G. (2001). *American studies at a moment of danger.* Minneapolis: University of Minnesota Press.

Lorde, A. (1984). Poetry is not a luxury. In *Sister outsider: Essays and speeches.* Berkeley: Crossing Press.

Mahiri, J. (2003). *What they don't learn in school: Literacy in the lives of urban youth.* New York: Peter Lang.

Maira, S. & Soep, E. (2005). (Eds.). *Youthscapes: The popular, the national, the global*. Philadelphia: University of Pennsylvania Press.

Mariscal, J. (2005). Homeland security, militarism, and the future of Latinos and Latinas in the United States. *Radical History Review, 93*, 39–52.

McChesney, R., Newman, R. & Scott, B. (2005). (Eds.). *The future of media*. New York: Seven Stories Press.

McLaren, P. (2002). *Life in schools: An introduction to critical pedagogy in the foundations of education*. New York: Pearson Allyn & Bacon.

McLaren, P. (1989). *Life in schools: An introduction to critical pedagogy in the foundations of education*. New York: Longman.

McMurria, J. (2006). The YouTube community. *Flow TV*. Retrieved July 26, 2009, from http://flowtv.org/?p=48.

Minkler, M. & Wallerstein, N. (2003). *Community-based participatory research for health*. San Francisco: Jossey-Bass.

Morrell, E. & Duncan-Andrade, J. (2002). Toward a critical classroom discourse: Promoting academic literacy through engaging hip-hop culture with urban youth. *English Journal, 91*(6), 88–94.

Ochs, E. & Capps, L. (2001). *Living narrative: Creating lives in everyday storytelling*. Cambridge, MA: Harvard University Press.

Ong, A. (1999). *Flexible citizenship: The cultural logics of transnationality*. Durham, NC: Duke University Press.

O'Reilly, T. (2005). What is Web 2.0? Retrieved Jan. 15, 2008, from www.oreilly net.com/pub/a/oreilly/tim/news/2005/09/30/what-is-web-20.html.

Orner, M. (1992). Interrupting the calls for student voice in "liberatory" education: A feminist poststructuralist perspective. In C. Luke & J. Gore (Eds.), *Feminisms and critical pedagogy* (pp. 74–89). New York: Routledge.

Prensky, M. (2006). Listen to the natives. *Educational Leadership, 63*(4), 8–13.

Prensky, M. (2001). Digital natives, digital immigrants. *On the Horizon, 9*(5), 1–6.

Puar, J. (2005). On torture: Abu Ghraib. *Radical History Review, 93*, 13–38.

Reed-Danahay, D. E. (1997). *Auto/ethnography: Rewriting the self and the social*. Oxford: Berg.

Sefton-Green, J. (1999). (Ed.). *Young people, creativity, and new technologies*. London: Routledge.

Sefton-Green, J. & Soep, E. (2007). Creative media cultures: Making and learning beyond school. In L. Bresler (Ed.), *International handbook of research on arts education* (pp. 835–856). New York: Springer.

Shor, I. & Freire, P. (1986). *A pedagogy for liberation*. South Hadley, MA: Bergin & Garvey.

Sinker, R. (2000). Making multimedia: Evaluating young people's creative multimedia production. In J. Sefton-Green & R. Sinker (Eds.), *Evaluating creativity: Making and learning by young people* (pp. 187–215). London: Routledge.

Soep, E. (2007a). Jumping for joy, wracking our brains, searching our souls: Youth media and its digital contradictions. *Youth Media Reporter,* 102–109.

Soep, E. (2007b). Working the crowd: Youth media interactivity. In S. B. Heath & D. Lapp (Eds.), *Handbook of literacy research: Visual, communicative and performative arts* (pp. 271–278). Mahwah, NJ: Lawrence Erlbaum.

Soep, E. (2006a). Beyond literacy and voice in youth media production. *McGill Journal of Education, 41*(3), 197–213.

Soep, E. (2006b). Critique: Assessment and the production of learning. *Teachers College Record, 108*(14), 748–777.

Soep, E. (2005a). Critique: Where art meets assessment. *Phi Delta Kappan, 87,* 38–40, 58–63.

Soep, E. (2005b). Making hardcore masculinity: Teenage boys playing house. In S. Maira & E. Soep (Eds.), *Youthscapes: The popular, the national, the global* (pp. 173–191). Philadelphia: University of Pennsylvania Press.

Soep, E., Mayeno Saavedra, B. & Kurwa, N. (2008). Social justice youth media. In W. Ayers, T. Quinn, & D. Stovall (Eds.), *Handbook of social justice in education* (pp. 477–484). Mahwah, NJ: Lawrence Erlbaum.

Sontag, S. (2004). Regarding the torture of others. *New York Times Magazine.* Retrieved July 26, 2009, from www.nytimes.com/2004/05/23/magazine123 PRISONS.html.

Spittler, G. (2001). Teilnehmende Beobachtung als Dichte Teilnahme. *Zeitschrift für Ethnologie, 126,* 1–25.

Street, B. (1984). *Literacy in theory and practice.* Cambridge: Cambridge University Press.

Surowiecki, J. (2004). *Wisdom of crowds: Why the many are smarter than the few and how collective wisdom shapes business, economies, societies and nations.* New York: Doubleday.

Tannock, S. (2004). Response to "Learning to serve." In J. Mahiri (Ed.), *What they don't learn in school* (pp. 163–168). New York: Peter Lang.

Tedlock, D. & Mannheim, B. (1995). (Eds.). *The dialogic emergence of culture.* Urbana: University of Illinois Press.

Torre, M. & Fine, M. (2006). Researching and resisting: Democratic policy research by and for youth. In S. Ginwright, P. Noguera, & J. Cammarota (Eds.), *Beyond resistance! Youth activism and community change* (pp. 269–286). New York: Routledge.

Trinh, T. M. (1992) *Framer framed.* New York: Routledge.

Trinh, T. M. (1991). *When the moon waxes red: Representation, gender, and cultural politics.* New York: Routledge.

Tyner, K. (2003). Beyond boxes and wires: Literacy in transition. *Television and New Media, 4*(4), 371–388.

Tyner, K. (1998). *Literacy in a digital world: Teaching and learning in the age of infor-mation*. Mahwah, NJ: Lawrence Erlbaum.

Wallack, L., Woodruff, K., Dorfman, L. & Diaz, I. (1999). *News for a change: An advocates' guide to working with the media*. Thousand Oaks, CA: Sage.

Willis, P. (1990). *Common culture: Symbolic work at play in the everyday cultures of the young*. Boulder, CO: Westview Press.

Index

Note: Page numbers in italics indicate a photograph. Page numbers with a t indicate a table.

Text:	Palatino
Display:	Univers Condensed Light 47 and Bauer Bodoni
Compositor:	BookMatters, Berkeley
Indexer:	Naomi Linzer
Printer & binder:	Sheridan Books, Inc.